FORGIVENESS
IS A CHOICE

FORGIVENESS IS A CHOICE

A Step-by-Step Process for Resolving Anger and Restoring Hope

ROBERT D. ENRIGHT, PhD

APA
LifeTools

AMERICAN PSYCHOLOGICAL ASSOCIATION
Washington, DC

First printing May 2001   Fourth printing November 2003
Second printing November 2001   Fifth printing April 2005
Third printing March 2002   Sixth printing October 2005

Published by
APA LifeTools
American Psychological Association
750 First Street, NE
Washington, DC 20002
www.apa.org

To order   Tel: (800) 374-2721, Direct: (202) 336-5510
APA Order Department   Fax: (202) 336-5502, TDD/TTY: (202) 336-6123
P.O. Box 92984   Online: www.apa.org/books/
Washington, DC 20090-2984   Email: order@apa.org

In the U.K., Europe, Africa, and the Middle East, copies may be ordered from
American Psychological Association
3 Henrietta Street
Covent Garden, London
WC2E 8LU England

Typeset in Sabon by EPS Group Inc., Easton, MD

Printer: United Book Press, Inc., Baltimore, MD
Dust jacket designer: Naylor Design, Washington, DC
Technical/Production Editor: Catherine Hudson

The opinions and statements published are the responsibility of the authors, and such opinions and statements do not necessarily represent the policies of the American Psychological Association.

Library of Congress Cataloging-in-Publication Data
Enright, Robert D.
     Forgiveness is a choice / Robert D. Enright.—1st ed.
       p. cm.
     Includes bibliographical references (p.) and index.
     ISBN 1-55798-757-2 (acid-free paper)
       1. Forgiveness. I. Title.

BF637.F67 E57 2001
155.9'2—dc21

                                      00-048493

British Library Cataloguing-in-Publication Data
A CIP record is available from the British Library.

Printed in the United States of America

For Nancy, with whom I have discovered the secret to a long and happy marriage.

CONTENTS

ACKNOWLEDGMENTS

Thank you, James McManus of Beachside Capital Partners for the generous funding that made this book possible.

I am indebted to Margaret and Nancy Enright for their careful reading of various drafts of the manuscript and to Dale O'Leary for helping me shape the words and set the right tone for the book. Thank you, Mary Lynn Skutley of APA Books, who saw the importance of forgiveness within psychology before it became popular in the field, and to Marilyn Abraham, whose editorial skills transformed the book. To Barb Lienau of the Department of Educational Psychology at the University of Wisconsin–Madison, thank you for all of the help in making the manuscript look far more professional than my homespun word-processing efforts could accomplish. I am indebted to Dan Lapsley and Darcia Narvaez for help with the galley proofs; thanks Dan and Darcia.

Finally, I am indebted to my family, Nancy, Shawn, and Kevin, for the loving support and encouragement that always seem to accompany a forgiving family.

Part I

FORGIVENESS IS A CHOICE

CHAPTER I

FORGIVENESS: A PATH TO FREEDOM

Mary Ann, a 38-year-old mother of three children who suffered a turbulent marriage, sat in a tiny office staring across the desk at the unsmiling counselor. Dr. Malaki had come highly recommended—"one of the best counselors in the community." She had waited a month for this appointment and driven over an hour to the office hidden in the woods of western Connecticut to ask his advice. She wanted to vent her frustrations about her mother. At the same time, she was trying to save her marriage, protect her children, and drag herself out of a hole of despondency. She had expected comfort and consolation, which she received, but Mary Ann was not ready for this question near the session's end: "Have you considered the possibility of forgiving your mother?"

That was impossible. She went through it all again: how night after night her mother had made her endure hours of biting criticism and punished her if she answered back or even had a "sassy look on her face"; how every birthday and every holiday had culminated in a knock-down-drag-out fight; how even after she had married and moved away every visit had ended in a shouting match; and how finally her mother and her husband Brendan had gotten into a drunken brawl while she was in the hospital having her third baby.

Dr. Malaki listened and said sympathetically, "It may seem like too much right now, but I would like you to consider the various options open to you regarding your mother. Forgiveness may be one of those options."

Mary Ann had not come to Dr. Malaki to hear that. The bout between her husband and mother had severed their relationship and, frankly, she was relieved, wasn't she? Yet, recently she had been feeling guilty. Will she ever have a relationship with her mother again? She hoped that the counselor would assure her that severing the relationship was a good idea. She definitely had not expected to consider forgiveness.

Waves of anger and fear swept over her. How could she possibly forgive?

Dr. Malaki ended with, "It's your decision. Let's meet again next week."

Four weeks and four sessions followed, with Mary Ann alternating among anger, ambivalence, and confusion at the idea of forgiveness. In the fifth session, without feeling or conviction, through clenched teeth, and as a simple act of the will, she said to the counselor, "I forgive my mother."

With that she began a journey into freedom.

Mary Ann had no idea what to expect; she didn't have any guideposts. She stumbled along with the help of the therapist, discovering that forgiveness was far deeper, far richer than she had imagined. Looking back, she realizes that her statement "I forgive my mother" was merely the first step, in many ways no more than an intention to begin the process of forgiveness. It would take time before that process was complete, and for Mary Ann, as for most of us, the work of forgiveness is ongoing. What Mary Ann did not know at the time was how much her decision to forgive would change her life for the better.

When Mary Ann went to Dr. Malaki, the problem she brought to the table was only the tip of the iceberg. Although she didn't realize it, Mary Ann was suffering from depression. Her husband Brendan had a serious drinking problem. After work, he would stop at the local tavern, rarely making it home before midnight. She was left alone with three small children. She spent her days escaping into fantasy or watching TV, her nights in rage watching the clock. Hopelessness and anger drained her energy. She neglected the children and then turned on them with harsh words when they misbehaved. When she begged her husband to come home earlier or to help with the children, he accused her of being a bad wife and mother. Their fights were in many ways replays of the confrontations between Mary Ann and her mother.

Mary Ann was being pulled down into a whirlpool of resentment and self-pity from which there seemed no escape. Some nights she sat for hours on the staircase, looking out the window down the road leading to town, watching for Brendan's car and thinking, "Why is he doing this to me?" She would alternate between rage at Brendan and self-recrimination. "Tomorrow I'll change, tomorrow I'll pull myself together." But then her anger would return, and she'd remember the times when she had cleaned the house and cooked a beautiful dinner and Brendan hadn't come home. Eventually, Brendan would arrive, too drunk to stand up, and Mary Ann would swallow her anger and put him to bed. In the morning he would be too hung over to endure conversation, and she would be too exhausted to cope with three recalcitrant children. She would leave them to their own devices and then scream at them because they had made a mess or had gotten into a fight.

And so it went. Occasionally, Mary Ann blew up. She and Brendan would have a real fight, and he would walk out. Mary Ann, terrified, would back down and apologize. Not only was Mary Ann's life a disaster, but also she was afraid that if things proceeded on this track, the pattern would be repeated in the next generation.

Forgiveness Is a Choice is a self-help book for people like Mary Ann who are caught in a vortex of anger, resentment, and seemingly endless destructive patterns and who are looking for a way out. In 1985, the Human Development Study Group at the University of Wisconsin–Madison began an intensive investigation into forgiveness. I was part of that group, and this book is a product of our investigation. Our work was so fruitful that in 1994 we expanded our group and founded the International Forgiveness Institute, a nonprofit organization that helps people understand forgiveness so they can make their own decisions about the topic.[1]

In the following pages you will be introduced to a scientifically tested program for forgiveness. Its purpose is to benefit you, the forgiver. If you are willing to use the forgiveness process, I believe that you may be able to find freedom from anger, resentment, bitterness, and the self-destructive behavior patterns that accompany them. You may have inherited a family tradition of anger and bitterness, but you don't have to pass it on to your children and grandchildren.

I can't, of course, promise that the forgiveness process will work for every person and every problem. Such a claim would be absurd. There are no panaceas, but I have seen amazing changes in people's lives.

Martha had not seen her grandchildren in years because of a rift with her daughter-in-law Agnes. Finally, Martha swallowed her pride, picked up the telephone, forgave Agnes, and reconciled with her. She was then able to resume a joyous relationship with her grandchildren. Gary's constant travel in his job led to a separation from his wife Barbara, until they both realized that bitterness had destroyed the family. Forgiveness and the building of trust restored the relationship and the family. Alexandra was pursuing a college degree until she had a serious argument with an instructor over a grade. She was so aggravated at the teacher that she dropped out of school. Only upon struggling to forgive was she able to return to school and pursue her dreams, instead of pursuing her rage.

Our research group has conducted scientific tests using forgiveness as a form of therapy and education. We have researched the world's great religious traditions, read works of philosophy, and held discussions with therapists and counselors. Our work is by no means completed but, after 15 years of research, I feel that we have found sufficient evidence of the power of forgiveness so that I can offer our knowledge to those who want to be free from the bondage of anger and resentment.

If the prospect of forgiving those who have injured you is as terrifying to you as it was to Mary Ann, this book will serve as a guide to light your way through that fear to a place of peace and relief. I will try to answer your questions and help you through the phases of the forgiveness process.

One of the questions I am most frequently asked is "How did you begin studying forgiveness in the first place?" I am almost embarrassed to say that my interest was not the result of some incredible childhood trauma or a tragic relationship in adulthood but instead grew out of my deep curiosity about the "wisdom of the ages." People almost expect that if you dedicate your life to the study of forgiveness, then, of course, you were probably chained to a basement wall for a while during those formative years or at least you married the world's most insensitive partner. I am happy to say that none of this is true in my own case, people's expectations notwithstanding.

I came to study, write about, and speak about forgiveness because I grew enormously dissatisfied with my own area of research—moral development. Those in university settings asking the questions about morals were not exciting the general public, as far as I could see, and they were not asking the kinds of questions that might change people's lives. I thought that forgiveness, as one aspect of moral development, just might change people's lives for the good. My many years exploring how people forgive, and the results obtained after people forgave, have not disappointed me. In fact, I am more impressed today with the power of forgiveness than when I first began.

It is a bit ironic that, since beginning the scientific study of forgiveness, I've had to practice the art of forgiveness far more than before. Many of my colleagues in the social sciences, quite frankly, thought that I had lost my mind studying such a "soft" or "inappropriate" topic as forgiveness. "Leave the examination of forgiveness to the clergy," I was told. "You'll never get a job working in academia if you stick with Enright," my graduate students were counseled. "This topic has nothing to do with social science," I heard whispered more than once. I've battled through misunderstanding, indifference, and anger from others as I've tried to bring some perspective and depth to the questions What is forgiveness? How do people go about forgiving? What happens when people forgive? Yes, those who've criticized me and what I study at times have made me angry. Encountering a growing anger led me to the need to forgive. I also know from experience that forgiving is not for wimps but is instead hard work. Yet, as you stick with it, forgiveness offers untold rewards.

ARE YOU ANGRY?

Had they been asked, Mary Ann's acquaintances probably would not have picked the word "angry" to describe her. Most people saw her as vaguely "out-of-it" or eccentric. Her anger at her mother manifested itself by a rebellion against every social convention. Her rage at her husband Brendan was concealed with rationalizations about his poor health and business obligations. Her verbal attacks on her children never took place in public. She never mentioned Brendan's excessive drinking, and because their social friends were *his* friends, drinking to excess as he did, no one ever suggested that Brendan was an alcoholic.

Occasionally, Mary Ann would pour out her pain to a friend, and she had, on several occasions, sought counseling, but nothing had come of it. Everyone agreed that she had been mistreated, but none of the good advice she had received had really addressed her problem. The black clouds of long-standing resentments could not be dispelled by a decision to "Cheer up," or "Just don't think about it," or even by the insight that what happened to her was unfair. There must be more.

The first step in forgiving is recognizing that you are angry and, surprisingly, for some people this may be the hardest step. Mary Ann knew that she was angry at her mother. She believed that her anger was completely justified. On the other hand, she felt guilty for being angry at her husband and vacillated between blaming herself and blaming him. She refused to admit that she was angry with her children, because she rightly believed that being angry at small children was irrational.

Mary Ann would eventually have to face the full extent of her anger.

ARE YOU LOOKING FOR CONDITIONAL FORGIVENESS?

Some people are willing to forgive only if they can be assured that the people they forgive will change. Mary Ann would have been happy to forgive mother, husband, children, everyone, if only they would come to her on bended knee begging for her forgiveness and promising to never hurt her again. She did not think that she wanted revenge; she just wanted everyone to change.

She would learn that the first person that forgiveness changes is the person doing the forgiving.

Very often those trapped in an abusive situation are afraid to forgive, especially if they have given the abuser forgiveness in the past, only to have the abuser respond with more abuse. Mary Ann feared that forgiving her mother would require her to allow her mother's continued abuse. She would learn that forgiving gives her the freedom to deal with her mother without internalizing her mother's anger.

Many people confuse forgiveness with trust. They are not the same. In the following chapters we will see how going through the forgiveness process does not require accepting continued abuse and, in fact, helps people learn how to remove themselves from abusive situations.

Forgiveness is not a bargain or negotiation. Forgiveness is not a magic trick that allows us to control other people. A wife cannot say "I will forgive my husband and then he must change." Forgiveness is a risk, because we don't always know what the results of our forgiveness will be.

Sometimes the person we forgive is transformed; sometimes there is no change. Sometimes the forgiver is changed and discovers that the offenses that seemed so terrible are easily tolerated. Other times, forgiveness gives forgivers the courage to extricate themselves from a destructive relationship. For those of you who are in a codependent relationship, forgiveness is often an essential step in the process of healing.

Mary Ann had cut her mother out of her life, but anger toward her mother still controlled her. Resentments and anger don't just disappear. An angry woman can divorce her husband. She can take the children, withdraw every penny of the joint assets, leave town, marry again, and start a new life, but if she doesn't forgive she may suffer recurring resentment-related problems, and her children may be infected by recurring resentments, which will affect their future relationships and emotional life for decades. I have seen men and women in their 80s who are still angry over injustices they endured as children. Although their childhood tormentors are long dead, they still see themselves as "victims."

The therapist Judith Wallerstein interviewed family members decades after divorce and found that they were still suffering from the emotional pain related to the divorce.

> Incredibly one-half of the women and one-third of the men are still intensely angry at their former spouses, despite the passage of ten or more years. Because their feelings have not changed, anger has become an ongoing, and sometimes dominant, presence in their children's lives as well.[2]

FORGIVENESS IS A PROCESS

Professor of theology, Lewis Smedes, long an observer of the forgiveness process, puts a few qualifiers on the benefits I discuss here. He cautions that forgiveness is for imperfect people, those of us who are not necessarily the saints of the world. We less-than-saintly types sometimes find that the release from resentment is less than complete months or even years after we forgave. Sometimes we awaken with a sense of anger that surprises, especially when we thought that our bitterness was on a speeding train south. Sometimes we get discouraged about the injustices that we experienced in our distant past.[3]

Forgiveness is a process. Our research group discovered that simply saying "I forgive you" is usually not enough. Although the words are said, the angry feelings often return. People need to go through a process to understand their feelings. They also need to take concrete action.

Sometimes forgiveness involves facing not a single incident but a long series of hurts. Sometimes we forgive one person only to discover that there are others whom we need to forgive. Mary Ann began by forgiving her mother but later realized that she also had to forgive her father. She recognized her need to forgive her husband but found it difficult to face her anger toward her children, certainly not for the times they acted up when she was neglecting them, but for the times when they truly were unruly. Indeed, as she worked through the process of forgiveness, she discovered that the list of people against whom she held resentment was long, and it was easy to add new names to the list.

Many people have shared their stories with us. Except in cases where the story has already been published, we have changed the names and the details because each has a right to privacy.

Those who have walked its path are the best witnesses of the benefits of forgiveness. They admit that forgiveness does not remove all the pain, but that after forgiveness, the remaining pain is bearable. After forgiving, they realized that anger and bitterness had made bad situations worse.

Through anecdotal evidence and scientific studies on forgiveness, by comparing groups who were instructed in forgiveness with groups who were not, we believe that we have found substantial and credible evidence that forgiveness produces benefits for those who forgive. We are not alone in our assessment of the benefits to forgiveness. Consider a few observations by therapists who work with people on forgiving others.

THERAPISTS OBSERVE THE BENEFITS OF CHOOSING TO FORGIVE

Therapists are in an excellent position to observe the forgiveness process. Their reports provide documentary evidence of the benefits of forgiveness and how the process works. When working with a client who wishes to forgive, the therapist is able to track the process and observe the effects. The therapist can observe changes in the client's mood, physical well-being, basic outlook on life, relationships, and work habits.

Not everyone who is experiencing anger and resentment seeks the help of a therapist or even needs to. Anger doesn't necessarily drive you to utter distraction, but it can cause psychological problems and exacerbate existing ones. Some very angry people are able to lead reasonably normal lives. Some are able to compartmentalize their anger or push their feelings out of sight. American society allows people to manifest a substantial amount of anger. Not forgiving is socially acceptable. Talk shows are full of people exhibiting pathological levels of anger who are treated as though their rages were completely normal and acceptable. On the other hand, some people with serious psychological and emotional problems are extremely angry and resentful. Their problems provoke mistreatment, their psychological condition causes them to misinterpret the motives and actions of others, and their mental condition robs them of the ability to deal with their anger. Their anger needs to be taken seriously. Although forgiving won't cure psychosis, many therapists report that even clients with serious psychological problems often benefit from forgiving.

R. C. Hunter, a Canadian psychiatrist, was one of the first therapists to report on the benefits of forgiveness. He reported that people who have a wide variety of psychological symptoms can experience healing through forgiving. He found that those who are anxious can experience an increased inner peace through forgiveness. Those who are depressed, intensely angry, or even paranoid have shown a significant reduction in their symptoms.

Dr. Hunter observed significant improvement in clients who forgave. Their feelings of bitterness and resentment toward people who had hurt them were reduced. He reported on a 25-year-old woman—let's call her Harriet—with acute emotional distress who was excessively demanding and tended to lash out at others when she was angry. She seemed to create barriers between herself and others, which trapped her in a kind of agitated loneliness. She had few friends and still lived at home, and her relationship with her parents was quite strained.

In therapy, Harriet learned that her mother was a captive of her own anger, condemning her daughter for the slightest deviation from her unreasonable standards. Growing up with condemnation, Harriet learned to condemn. Her anger toward her own mother turned Harriet into a highly critical, caustic person with symptoms of anxiety and depression. Having been on the receiving end of unjust criticism, she learned how to dish out unjust criticism and was now giving better than she had been given.

By examining her mother's background, Harriet was able to see that her mother, like everyone else, is "inevitably caught up in the effects of their experiences and possessed both good and bad qualities."[4] She was able to see that she, too, was a product, at least in part, of family upbringing and that she was capable, like everyone else, of both positive and negative behavior. With Dr. Hunter's help, Harriet came to understand how she had reacted to her own victimization by victimizing others. When she was ready to forgive both parents for their failings, she did so, according to the psychiatrist, "with tenderness and some ruefulness."[5]

Forgiving allowed Harriet to see that she was responsible for her own behavior. She didn't have to criticize and belittle others. Once she had forgiven her parents, she experienced greater self-acceptance and was able to establish meaningful friendships. She learned how to express and receive love. Shortly after her therapy ended, she married.

Harriet's transformation required two important steps: first, a readiness to forgive and second, an openness to love.[6]

Morton Kaufman, an Israeli psychiatrist, found that genuine acts of forgiveness lead to an overall improvement in a person's emotional maturity. Dr. Kaufman believes that as one forgives, one grows as a person capable of courage, nurturance of others, and love. In one of Dr. Kaufman's case studies, Uri, an army officer in his 40s, came to therapy because of his inability to establish positive relationships with women. Through therapy, Uri realized how much he hated his father, who died when he was young, and his mother, whom he blamed for the family's subsequent poverty. His anger was the cause of his intense anxiety and poor relationships with women. Uri had grown older, but he had not grown up. He frequently indulged in immature behaviors more appropriate to a rebellious adolescent than a 40-something army officer.

Forgiving his father for dying allowed Uri symbolically to bury his father. Forgiving his mother for not providing a higher standard of living allowed Uri to leave behind the debilitating anxiety that had plagued him since childhood. As a result, Uri grew in courage and was able to accept adult responsibility. He married and was also able to love and provide for his mother, eventually mourning her death.[7]

You may be surprised that someone can be angry at a person for dying, but it is common. On an intellectual level, Uri knew that his anger was irrational, but on an emotional level he experienced the death as a betrayal. Not only are some children angry at their parents for dying, but also widows and widowers can be furious at their spouses for leaving them.

Richard Fitzgibbons, a Pennsylvania psychiatrist, has done pioneering work in the use of forgiveness in therapy. He observed that when a person forgives, fear is reduced. He traces this reduction in fear to a reduction of guilt. Many people who are angry at a loved one who hurt them feel guilty for their unconscious violent impulses. Forgiveness puts a stop to the impulses. Dr. Fitzgibbons finds that as a client forgives, he or she begins to express anger in more appropriate ways. This conclusion is consistent with Dr. Kaufman's theory that a forgiver gains in emotional maturity. Dr. Fitzgibbons speculates that anger may cause physical symptoms, and forgiving may improve health and perhaps even lower blood pressure. This speculation is backed up by several studies that have found that hypertension may be affected by anger. Of course, most cases of hypertension are not caused by unforgiveness, but there is evidence that even in cases where the hypertension has a physical cause, anger can make it worse.[8]

SCIENTISTS EVALUATE THE EFFECTS OF CHOOSING TO FORGIVE

We could fill volumes with case histories and first-person accounts of how forgiveness has set people free. One of our goals at the University of Wisconsin–Madison was to scientifically test the effects of forgiveness. Therapists provide detailed case histories, but their observations can be influenced by their commitment to the therapeutic process. They are not conducting controlled research.

The scientist's observations differ from the therapist's in this way: The scientist collects data in such a way that his or her own impressions in forming conclusions are minimized. In contrast, the therapist's impressions are part of the therapeutic process and cannot be put aside for the sake of objectivity.

To test a thesis scientifically researchers have to set up a controlled situation. We set up tests in which we recruited people experiencing specific kinds of anger and divided them into two groups. We educated only one group on forgiveness and encouraged them to forgive. We tested these groups before and after the study and compared the results. Then to confirm the findings we educated the control group on forgiveness and tested them again.

Our results were strong. We were able to demonstrate that those who take the time to go through the forgiveness process become psychologically healthier. Our scientific tests support what we saw in the case histories and first-person accounts: Forgiveness works. Consider two examples from our research.

Forgiveness and Incest Survivors

Suzanne Freedman and I studied 12 women ages 24 to 54 who were incest survivors. Three were married, four were divorced, and five were single. Four of them had full-time careers, one worked part-time, two were full-time college students, and the rest combined schooling and a career. All were anxious, depressed, and suffering from low self-esteem when they entered our program. None had forgiven the perpetrator. Dr. Freedman randomly assigned six of the women to a group where for over one year they worked on forgiving the perpetrator, and she assigned the other six to a group that received no instruction on forgiveness.

The forgiveness group was led by an educator trained in the forgiveness process. Each participant received a manual that described the process involved in forgiving and met individually and weekly with the educator. All 12 participants were given a battery of psychological tests before and after the program. Those in the forgiveness group improved significantly. Before therapy they had been, on average, moderately psychologically depressed. After forgiveness therapy they were, on average, not depressed at all. Their anxiety decreased, and their sense of hopefulness toward their own futures increased. All six were able to forgive the perpetrator. One visited her father's grave for the first time. Another visited her father in the hospital and helped with his care. When he died, she grieved, and she was convinced that she would have been devastated if he had died before she had been able to forgive him.

During the first year, the control group showed no measurable psychological improvement. To further test the benefits of forgiveness, we introduced this group to the forgiveness process. Following 14 months of one-to-one forgiveness instruction, these women also showed evidence of major improvements in their psychological health. When we reassessed the original forgiveness group one year after they stopped the program, they had retained good psychological health. All 12 women showed substantial psychological improvements. No other treatment program for incest survivors has, to our knowledge, produced such positive results.[9]

Forgiveness and Men and Abortion

The Freedman study dealt only with women. We wondered if men would also benefit from forgiveness therapy. Cathy Coyle, now a lecturer in psychology, chose 10 men ages 21 to 43 who stated that they felt unjustly hurt by the abortion decision of their partner. All were single at the beginning of the program, although one married during the program. Eight were employed full-time, and two attended college and worked part-time. Dr. Coyle enrolled the men in a one-to-one educational program that was similar to Dr. Freedman's. Both groups were tested before and after the program. As with the study of incest survivors, the five men who received forgiveness education showed evidence of decreased anger and anxiety as well as increased self-esteem and hope relative to the control group. The men in the control group were then given forgiveness education, and they also were able to forgive and showed evidence of substantial psychological healing.[10]

ARE YOU SEEKING LIBERATION FROM THE EMOTIONAL PRISON?

People who talk with me about forgiveness often say that their resentment was a way of keeping the one who hurt them in a kind of emotional prison. As long as they held onto the anger and bitterness, the other stayed in the jail cell. Over time they began to realize that it was they, themselves, who were imprisoned by the hatred and not the other person. Our hatred affects us emotionally more than it affects the one who hurt us.

Forgiveness is one of the keys to unlocking the door. There is not some automatic "click" that sets you free; the knowledge that you have the option to decide to turn the key can set you free. You must courageously choose to walk out of that cell. Some have lived with the label of "victim" for so long that it's become part of them. They'd rather live in the cell because at least they know what to expect there. Forgiveness beckons you outside and into the future.

Perhaps forgiveness is our best hope for genuine peace between individuals, within families, and among peoples. I agree with the South African religious leader Bishop Desmond Tutu, who faced the most terrible forms of injustice and yet is able to say, "Without forgiveness there is no future."[11]

A POSTSCRIPT ON MARY ANN

I am happy to report that Mary Ann's life is very much on track. As she learned to forgive, she learned to communicate more effectively with Brendan, who began his own journey toward greater maturity. The marriage is intact, and the children are grown, leading responsible lives with spouses and children of their own. In Mary Ann's words,

> The children, now adults, are healthy and mature. They are great kids. I'd like to say perfect kids, but that would be seeing them through the eyes of a mom. They could have borne tremendous scars, but we entered into forgiveness soon enough for all of us to get our lives back. To say that forgiveness is life-giving is absolutely true. Our family is evidence of that.

Certainly she still gets angry. She even has occasions when all the old difficulties come knocking on the door of her mind. She does not let them in for long. She is in control of the anger.

Knowing the power of forgiveness, Mary Ann has been able to informally counsel friends and other family members as they work through times of bitterness and unfairness. Mary Ann is giving forgiveness away, in-between her busy schedule volunteering for civic organizations and giving talks and writing articles on the topic of adolescent health and well-being. She now has the energy, which before was being depleted, to help others.

ENDNOTES

1. The International Forgiveness Institute's web site address is www.ForgivenessInstitute.org.
2. J. S. Wallerstein and S. Blakeslee, *Second Chances: Men, Women, and Children: A Decade After Divorce* (New York: Tichnor & Fields, 1996), 29; J. S. Wallerstein, J. Lewis, and J. Blakeslee, *The Unexpected Legacy of Divorce* (New York: Hyperion, 2000).
3. L. B. Smedes, *Forgive and Forget: Healing the Hurts We Don't Deserve* (San Francisco: Harper & Row, 1984).
4. R. C. A. Hunter, "Forgiveness, Retaliation, and Paranoid Reactions," *Canadian Psychiatric Association Journal* 23 (1978): 169.
5. Ibid.
6. Hunter, "Forgiveness, Retaliation, and Paranoid Reactions."
7. M. E. Kaufman, "The Courage to Forgive," *Israeli Journal of Psychiatry and Related Sciences* 21 (1984), 177–187.
8. R. P. Fitzgibbons, "The Cognitive and Emotional Uses of Forgiveness in the Treatment of Anger," *Psychotherapy* 23 (1986), 629–633; for a review of anger and blood pressure, see S. T. Huang, "Cross-Cultural and Real-Life Validations of the Theory of Forgiveness in Taiwan, the Republic of China" (Madison, University of Wisconsin, 1990).
9. See S. R. Freedman, "Forgiveness as an Educational Goal With Incest Survivors" (Madison, University of Wisconsin 1994); S. R. Freedman and R. D. Enright, "Forgiveness as a Therapeutic Goal With Incest Survivors" (paper presented at the annual convention of the American Psychological Association, New York, 1995); R. D. Enright, S. R. Freedman, and J. Rique, "The Psychology of Interpersonal Forgive-

ness," in *Exploring Forgiveness*, eds. R. Enright and J. North (Madison: University of Wisconsin Press, 1998), 46–62.

10. C. T. Coyle and R. D. Enright, "Forgiveness Intervention With Post-Abortion Men," *Journal of Consulting and Clinical Psychology* 65 (1997), 1042–1046.

11. D. Tutu, "Foreword," in *Exploring Forgiveness*, eds. R. D. Enright and J. North (Madison: University of Wisconsin Press, 1998), xiii.

CHAPTER 2

WHAT FORGIVENESS IS ...
AND WHAT IT IS NOT

Some of you may be impatient. You are suffering and want to deal with your problem immediately, in which case you can turn to Chapter 4, "A Map and Tools for Your Journey," which will guide you through the forgiveness process. On the other hand, you may have questions about forgiveness. You may not be convinced that the forgiveness process is for you. In this case, let me try to answer some of your questions.

Some people are apprehensive about forgiveness because they don't understand what it is. Maybe forgiveness is the Limburger cheese of human affairs; at first it seems offensive, so offensive that we dare not try it. People are afraid that forgiveness means pretending that nothing happened to them. They are afraid that if they forgive they are opening themselves up to being hurt again. They are afraid that forgiving means letting people get away with it. Many people feel that forgiving requires that they forget the offense, which they rightly see as impossible. Many people can't imagine that their feelings toward the offender can ever change.

Although these concerns are understandable, they are not justified because they are a misunderstanding of what forgiveness is. Forgiving begins with acknowledging that we are people who have a right to be treated with respect. Forgiving does not require denying that we have been hurt. On the contrary, to forgive we have to admit that we have been hurt and that we have a right to feel hurt, angry, or resentful. Forgiving does not require denying our feelings. In fact, as we will see, unwillingness to admit that we have been hurt is one of the major impediments to forgiving. We don't have to forget in order to forgive. The forgiveness process will not produce amnesia.

We can't will our feelings to change. Saying "I will not be angry" 100 times may produce exactly the opposite result. But we can take certain actions that will change our patterns of thinking. We might be surprised to discover that our feelings change in response to our actions.

FORGIVENESS DEFINED

Although people considering forgiveness have personal concerns, philosophers and scientists try to examine forgiveness objectively, seeking to explain what it is. Philosophers ask questions such as When we forgive, what exactly are we doing? Are there times when forgiving is the right thing to do? Are there times when forgiving is the wrong thing to do?

During the initial stages of our research, we reviewed ancient and modern writings for a definition of forgiveness. As we scoured the ancient writings, we found stories of blessings of forgiveness or tragedies caused by the refusal to forgive, but few definitions. For example, in the Hebrew Bible, Joseph was left for dead by his jealous brothers, yet he rose to power in Egypt. Having the opportunity to punish those same brothers years later, he instead showed unconditional love, embracing and helping them before they ever repented. Islam's Koran has a somewhat similar story using the same names. In the Christian New Testament, there is the story of the prodigal son, squandering his father's inheritance and then crawling back to the family. To his surprise, his father unconditionally accepts and loves him despite his moral failings. Buddhism has a story of a hermit who is savagely beaten by a jealous king and yet unconditionally accepts the king. I have yet to encounter a story from ancient texts that portrays forgiveness as inappropriate or immoral.

Definitions of forgiveness can be found in modern philosophy. The philosopher Joanna North of Great Britain has written one of the best definitions of forgiveness, and we have chosen to use her ideas as a guide in our work. In my words, her definition of *forgiveness* is

> When unjustly hurt by another, we forgive when we overcome the resentment toward the offender, not by denying our right to the resentment, but instead by trying to offer the wrongdoer compassion, benevolence, and love; as we give these, we as forgivers realize that the offender does not necessarily have a right to such gifts.[1]

Dr. North's definition makes it clear that forgiving begins with pain and that we have a right to our feelings. First, we are acknowledging that the offense was unfair and will always continue to be unfair. Second, we have a moral right to anger; it is fair to cling to our view that people do not have a right to hurt us. We have a right to respect. Third, forgiveness requires giving up something to which we have a right—namely our anger or resentment.

Forgiving is an act of mercy toward an offender, someone who does not necessarily deserve our mercy. It is a gift to our offender for the purpose of changing the relationship between ourselves and those who have hurt us. Even if the offender is a stranger, we change our relationship because we are no longer controlled by angry feelings toward this person. In spite of everything that the offender has done, we are willing to treat him or her as a member of the human community. That person is worthy of the respect due to every being who shares our common humanity.

Forgiveness is a paradox, something that may sound illogical but still works. For example, take the statement "It is more blessed to give than to receive." It sounds silly. After all, *getting* means having more, which should be better. *Giving* means having less, which should be worse. In fact, the person who gives usually comes out of the transaction feeling enriched, while the person who receives feels in some way indebted.

The forgiveness process is full of such paradoxes. For example, it may seem absurd to tell a person "If you want to be free of anger and resentment, give the person who hurt you a gift," but it works.

FORGIVING IS MORE THAN . . .

Accepting What Happened

When the Buddhist ascetic was lying in pain on the ground, did he simply say "Oh well, I am being severely beaten. I guess it's time for me to move on with my life"? The wise man did have a certain transcendent indifference toward his own situation, but also he forthrightly reached out to his torturer, the king. The sage was interested in the king as a person. The same was true for Joseph and his brothers and the father of the prodigal son. There was acceptance, but there was also more. Forgiving goes beyond simply accepting. "Moving on" is not a moral act. One can "move on" with cold indifference.

Ceasing to Be Angry

Ceasing to be angry is a by-product of the forgiveness process. We expect that anger will diminish and resentment will vanish, but cessation of anger is only one part of the process. Focusing exclusively on the cessation of anger as the goal can distort the process. Over time, the forgiver should have a real change of attitude toward the offender.

Suppose a person is hit by a car. The result is brain damage, with no recollection of the injustice and no anger. Has this unfortunate person forgiven the driver? Of course not, because forgiving involves more than accidental anger reduction.

Some people believe that they can simply stop thinking angry thoughts and tell themselves "I will not feel angry." However, there is ample evidence that this technique works only for the mildest of problems.

Being Neutral Toward the Other

Although some believe that freedom from resentment is all there is to forgiveness, I don't agree. I feel that the ultimate goal of the forgiveness process is that the forgiver experience positive feelings and thoughts toward the offender. Of course, I recognize that this may take time. Neutrality may be a step in the process, but it is not the final goal. The Buddhist holy man, who suffered tremendously, was not neutral toward the king. He genuinely wished the king well. Joseph was not neutral toward his brothers; he embraced them with deep love and much emotion. The father of the prodigal son ordered a celebration in honor of the son's return.

Making Oneself Feel Good

There is nothing wrong with feeling good. Forgiving, properly understood and practiced with patience, will increase the forgiver's well-being and emotional health, very dramatically in some cases.

Many people start the forgiveness process because they are tired of feeling bad and want to feel better. Although this is a typical attitude, in most cases this is not the final response. Somewhere along the path, the forgiver decides to give the gift of forgiveness to the offender. At that point, the forgiver moves from a focus on self to a focus on the other, and I have seen over and over that when this happens healing begins.

FORGIVING IS NOT ...

Condoning or Excusing

When we condone, we put up with the abuse by suffering in silence, or we convince ourselves that we deserved the abuse. When we excuse, we are saying that the offense is not worth a quarrel, or we pretend that we weren't injured or that the offender didn't really mean to hurt us. Codependent family members and enablers frequently substitute condoning and excusing for real forgiveness. The wife of the alcoholic says she forgives him for coming home drunk and then lies to his supervisor to cover up his hangover. The battered woman excuses her husband's violence by blaming herself for irritating him. Such actions give forgiveness a bad name, because people come to think that forgiving means allowing yourself to be hit again or to be used or abused again, and this is not true. Forgiving means admitting that what was done was wrong and should not be repeated.

Forgetting

Our brains appear to be designed to remember painful experiences. By remembering the pain and associating it with particular experiences, we hope that we will avoid painful activities in the future. We can forgive, but we should not expect to forget. The forgiveness process will not produce amnesia. Trying to forget is unhealthy. The forgiveness process will, however, change the way you remember the past.

Justifying

Sometimes we realize that we were not wronged, that the person we thought offended us was acting justly. For example, suppose someone stole a car to drive an injured child to the hospital. Upon receiving the car again, the owner recognizes that the "thief" was justified in taking the car. The owner in this case may say "I forgive you," but real forgiveness as I understand it is not necessary.

Calming Down

Some people react to minor offenses with major displays of anger and afterward realize that they had overreacted. Calming down is not the same as forgiving. In some cases, outrage diminishes over time. The incident that seemed so important at the time becomes less important. Although calming down is certainly beneficial, it is not forgiving. Forgiveness does not lessen what happened; it alters how we view the person in spite of what he or she did.

Pseudo-forgiving

Some people find it easy to say the words "I forgive you." They may do so when they mean that no injury was done. In these cases, the Spanish "de nada"—it was nothing—captures the true intention.

Some people use the words "I forgive you" when they have not forgiven at all as a way to control others or to demonstrate their moral superiority. "I forgive you" in these cases means "You are a terrible person who should feel appropriately guilty and don't think I am going to let you forget it for one minute."

The psychiatrist R. C. Hunter regards pseudo-forgiveness as a ploy used by manipulative people to gain control of others. He points out that pseudo-forgivers can be identified by their smug attitude toward the offender, which has nothing in common with real compassion. Dr. Hunter describes a prominent woman who continually and publicly forgave her husband for various offenses, while it was clear to those around her that she was filled with anger and the desire for revenge.

Sometimes people will say "I forgive you" when what they mean is "Don't think you can hurt me." The need to deny that one can be hurt by others is, according to Robert Cunningham, author of *The Will to Forgive,* a symptom of narcissistic tendencies.[2]

A few people use forgiveness as a psychological defense mechanism. These people suffer from emotional difficulties that prevent them from dealing constructively with their own inadequacies. Because they are afraid of being seen as less than perfect, they look for imperfections in others, imagine offenses where there are none, and then insist that they have to forgive. The entire process is designed to keep the attention off their faults. These people will appear to be forgiving, but they will be back next week to forgive someone else.[3]

Forgiveness Is Related to But Different Than Reconciliation

Forgiving is one step in the process toward reconciliation. Reconciliation without forgiveness is often no more than an armed truce in which each side patrols the demilitarized zone looking for incursions by the other and waiting to resume hostilities. Real reconciliation might require forgiveness by both parties, because in many cases there are injuries on both sides. Reconciliation also requires a renewal of trust, and sometimes that is not possible. Reconciliation requires that both parties be ready to resume the relationship, and sometimes only one party is ready to make the effort.

Reconciliation is the act of two people coming together following separation. Forgiving, on the other hand, is the moral action of one individual that starts as a private act, an unseen decision within the human heart. Only as the forgiveness grows does it stream outward toward the offender. One may forgive and not reconcile, but one never truly reconciles without some form of forgiving taking place. If the offender remains unrepentant and unchanged, then reconciliation is impossible. The gift of compassion, benevolence, and love can be offered, and the forgiver can wait in the hope that the other person will change. The gift may be scorned, but the gift retains its inherent value.

ANSWERING SOME QUESTIONS

Let us take a closer look at forgiveness. The deeper your understanding of forgiveness, the more profound your experience of forgiving someone will be. Some of the questions posed below are typical of the ones I get whenever I speak on the topic.

Must I Choose Between Justice and Mercy?

Some people have a problem with forgiveness because they see forgiveness as opposed to justice. We in Western societies have a high regard for the concept of justice. The ancient Greek philosophers, particularly Plato, taught that if a person wanted to live a moral life, he or she had to act justly. The desire for justice is natural. Even small children believe that wrongs should be punished and that good should be rewarded. The legal system enforces justice through laws, courts, penalties, and prisons. In our personal and social lives we are also obliged to treat others with justice, to refrain from causing emotional harm, to respect others' dignity and rights, to keep our word, and to live up to our responsibilities. Thus, a divorced father who fails to pay child support violates the law and is subject to legal penalties. A divorced father who breaks his promise to visit his child fails to live up to his moral responsibility. In both cases, the father has failed to act with justice. The child has a right to be angry.

But justice is not the only option. There are times when mercy is the appropriate response. Offenses can be forgiven, wrongs pardoned, and gifts given to those who don't deserve them. For example, the child who has been deprived of paternal financial and emotional support has a right to justice, but if the father disappears, dies, or refuses to acknowledge the wrong he has done his son, justice is denied. If the child continues to demand justice, he or she will be trapped in anger and bitterness. Even if the father grudgingly pays the financial debt, the child may refuse to forgive the emotional debt and remain trapped in anger. The child has another option: forgive the father. Legal justice may not satisfy the angry heart, but mercy can set a person free even if the offender remains unrepentant.

There is often a tension between justice and mercy, and the decision to forgive does not necessarily resolve this tension. A man who was sexually molested as a child may decide to forgive the man who molested him and still decide to testify against him to protect other children. To say "I have forgiven" and then allow another child to suffer would be to deny the rights of future victims.

On the other hand, the legal system may decide that the circumstances surrounding a crime call for mercy rather than for strict justice. A first-time offender or a young person may be given mercy rather than punishment to the full extent of the law for his or her crime.

Parents often find themselves torn between the demands of justice and mercy. Each offense must be judged, and parents must daily exercise both justice and mercy. For example, if a teenager asks permission to stay out on a school night until 10:00 p.m. and then stays out until 1:00 a.m., a parent may enforce justice by denying the teenager the right to go out at all for a month, but at the same time the parent extends mercy by expressing love toward the child and forgiving the offense. The teenager learns that justice and mercy are compatible. Another parent may choose not to punish the teenager but instead to bring up the disobedience over and over. This teenager receives neither justice nor mercy and will probably fall into sulky resentment and smoldering bitterness, which will lead to additional offenses.

Do Anger and Resentment Differ?

Anger is the primary and in many ways proper response to injury. Anger has a moral quality. For example, in the Old Testament, God is frequently described as angry. In the New Testament, Jesus showed righteous anger on a number of occasions.

Resentment, on the other hand, involves re-feeling the original anger. We remember the injury and re-feel the emotions surrounding the hurt. Anger is like a flame, resentment like a hot coal. Those who build campfires in forests are reminded by Smokey the Bear that before they leave their campsite they should stir the coals even if they appear cold, drown them with water, and then stir them again. Apparently, dead coals can be hot enough to start a fire that will burn down an entire forest. No matter how hot the fire, the coals will eventually become cold, but human memory is capable of keeping an injury alive indefinitely. It is common to find people in nursing homes still seething over offenses that occurred while they were children. It takes direct action to extinguish resentments. The forgiveness process may require us to stir up the coals of resentment, drown them with specific actions, and then stir them again to prove to ourselves that the resentment is no longer a danger to us or to others.

What, Then, Is Involved in Forgiveness Beyond Reducing Resentment?

My study has found that when people successfully complete the forgiveness process, they have reduced or eliminated

- negative feelings toward the offender
- negative thoughts toward the offender
- negative behaviors toward the offender.

Negative feelings can range from continual annoyance and frustration to hatred and rage. Negative thoughts can include ascribing evil motives to the offender or thinking of the offender as a wicked and horrible person or as insensitive and uncaring. Negative behaviors toward the offender can include purposefully avoiding the offender, refusing to talk to him or her, plotting revenge, or bad-mouthing the offender to others.

In addition, those who forgive develop

- positive feelings toward the offender
- positive thoughts toward the offender
- positive behaviors toward the offender.

Positive feelings can range from a very mild sense of liking, respecting, or similar emotion to loving and caring for the person. Positive thoughts can range from just barely wishing the person well to understanding that he or she is a human being who should be respected for that reason alone. Positive behaviors can be something as simple as a smile or as complex as aiding in the offender's character transformation, where this is appropriate.

What Exactly Must I Do If I Decide to Forgive?

If forgiveness involves offering the wrongdoer compassion, benevolence, and love, what is involved? At the appropriate time, the forgiver chooses an appropriate response. You don't have to be afraid that you will have to do something that will put you at risk or invite additional injury.

If you are really angry, have been nursing a resentment for several decades, or have been the victim of a terrible injustice, the very thought of offering your persecutor compassion, benevolence, and love will seem absurd. That is why forgiveness is a process. You can start small—very small. And you don't necessarily have to make personal contact with the person you are forgiving. For example, you might make a deliberate decision to refrain from disparaging remarks about him or her to others. If you are religious, you can offer benevolence by saying a prayer for the offender. If not, you can try to think about him or her in a context broader than the one in which he or she inflicted hurt on you. Isn't the person more than that one act or series of acts against you?

Why Do I Have to Give Compassion, Benevolence, and Love?

Not everyone agrees that forgiveness requires giving the offender an unmerited gift. Howard McGary, a philosopher at Rutgers University,[4] believes that the intention to abandon resentment is all that is required for forgiving. This, according to Dr. McGary, must not be done for selfish reasons, but it can be done for self-pertaining reasons. In other words, although forgiveness must be given unselfishly, the forgiver can recognize that he or she will benefit from forgiving.

Besides helping the self, the forgiver can also foresee benefits flowing to others. For example, suppose a man who is continually angry with his supervisor brings that anger home so that it affects his wife and children. If he forgives his boss, his wife and children will indirectly benefit. It often happens that those who will not forgive for themselves or for the sake of the offender will be motivated to forgive because they see that they hurt others by deciding to hold on to resentment.

Dr. McGary does not believe that compassion, benevolence, and love directed toward an offending person are necessary parts of the forgiveness process. I humbly disagree. If all that is required is the intentional cessation of resentment, then what are we left with when resentment is conquered? Detached indifference? "Writing off" that offender as morally incompetent? Moving from an attitude of resentment to one of casual dismissal of the offender as not worthy of our time? Although these situations might work for some people and might be all that some are initially able to accomplish, I believe, along with Joanna North, Margaret Holmgren, Keith Yandell, and other philosophers, that the forgiveness process can be and should be more. I believe that when resentment leaves, that place should not be left void but instead can be filled with positive feelings. Although this may seem impossible, we have found in our research that in some of the hardest cases people were able to achieve full forgiveness.

A forgiver who offers the limited forgiveness recommended by Dr. McGary may end up replacing resentment with alienation. The forgivers who choose to keep on working at the forgiveness process until they have achieved positive feelings will find that they have in a real way conquered evil with good.

Are People in General Morally Obliged to Forgive?

No. People are morally obliged to be just and to refrain from injuring others. We are not obliged to be merciful. Forgiving is a choice. It is a gift given to someone who doesn't deserve it. Certainly there are religions that say that we are obligated to forgive, but even here the principle of free will reigns. You are free to accept the wisdom or to reject it. The true challenge for the religious person is this: If your faith says that forgiveness is good, what is the underlying moral principle that makes it good? Knowing the answer to that question leads some to switch from a grim obligation to forgive to a joyous privilege to forgive.

Also keep in mind that we have no right to demand that others forgive us simply because we have asked for forgiveness. They are no more morally obligated to forgive than you are.

Is Forgiving Morally Inappropriate If the Offender Does Not Apologize?

Modern philosophers are not in agreement on this question. Joram Haber, for example, claims that we lack self-respect if we forgive unconditionally.[5] Dr. Haber believes that we need to take the time to be resentful and that we take a deeper interest in the offender when we wait for an apology. According to Dr. Haber, by waiting we help the other see the error of his or her ways.

I do not agree. What if the other will not change regardless of your loving overtures? What if he or she remains unrepentant or even flies into a rage when you suggest wrongdoing on his or her part? Does the offender have the right to keep us from forgiving? Do we have to remain angry because the person who hurt us remains unrepentant? This gives too much power to the offender and denies freedom to the victim.

Margaret Holmgren, a philosopher at Iowa State University, believes that the one who forgives shows self-respect because the forgiver refuses to be controlled by the bitterness of that injustice any longer.[6] For Dr. Holmgren, the person forgiving shows respect by being honest with the wrongdoer even if the offender is unrepentant. If the forgiver lets the offender know the extent of the injury, the offender has an opportunity to change. The offender is free to refuse to take advantage of that opportunity, but the person forgiving is free from the burden of anger and resentment. In addition, the forgiver is making it clear that what was done was wrong, should not have been done, and will not be tolerated in the future.

In trying to discourage more injustice, the unconditional forgiver is showing respect for self and for the other, who is seen as someone who could change. Is not every human being, regardless of what he or she did, worthy of respect? When we respect a person's humanity, we are showing respect to ourselves.

Must the Forgiver Trust the Offender?

The simple answer is no. This should put to rest the fear that forgiving opens oneself to being injured again. On the contrary, forgiving is one of the best ways to stop a pattern of repeated injury.

Suppose a woman is married to a compulsive gambler who on many occasions has squandered the family's money. It is appropriate for the wife to say "I forgive you" and "You must get help for your compulsive gambling" and "No more money." Each statement is an act of love. Love wants the best for others, and the best is that they no longer offend. If we are complicit in the offense, as in the case of giving money to a compulsive gambler knowing that he may squander it, then we are not showing love.

Forgiveness is free; trust must be earned. Sometimes trust is never justified. For example, a chronic pedophile should not be trusted with the care of children.

Can One Forgive If the Offender Did Not Intend the Wrong?

Our definition of forgiveness implies that the wrongdoer acted unjustly, but what if he or she had no intention to do so? Although some people believe that forgiveness is appropriate only when the offense is intentional, others believe that it is possible and beneficial to forgive those who have unintentionally wronged us.

People sometimes are seriously injured when no injury was intended. If we begin the forgiveness process by focusing on the question "Have I been injured?" it is not necessary to know for certain that the person who injured us meant to hurt us. The injury may be very real, and we may need to forgive, even if the person who injured us is objectively innocent. For example, Martha was angry at her husband for dying. She knew that he did not intend to get into the car accident that took his life, but she couldn't control her anger. He could have been paying closer attention; he could have slowed down in the rainstorm. Going through the forgiveness process, Martha was able to identify her feelings and visit her husband's grave, expressing forgiveness to him for leaving her alone.

Knowing that the person who injured us did not intend to hurt us can actually complicate the situation. Not only do we feel angry and resentful because we have been hurt, we also feel guilty for being angry and resentful toward an innocent person.

Brad was angry because his parents' time was occupied caring for his seriously ill sister. He was only seven but knew that he was angry when his sister was so sick. He couldn't help feeling that his needs were being neglected. He held onto his feelings of being deprived and to his guilt over his anger. When he married he found himself resenting his wife's care for their children and felt guilty about his feelings. Through the forgiveness process, he was able to forgive his parents and sister, neither of whom intended to hurt him. He was set free from his resentment and guilt.

Forgiving an innocent person is of course different from forgiving a guilty person, because the forgiver must admit his or her guilt, when this is present.

Suppose I Am Wrong, and the Offender Is Innocent?

When people are deeply hurt, they can look for someone to blame. They may connect their pain with the actions of another although pain and the action have no causative relationship. Very often, the anger and resentment in these cases are more powerful and more self-destructive than in cases where the anger is directed at someone who is actually guilty. The irrational nature of the rage may be a defense mechanism against facing one's own responsibility for the situation.

Phoebe harbored deep anger and resentment against her husband's former business partner, blaming him for her daughter's suicide. Phoebe reasoned that the failure of the business had caused stress in the family, which led to her daughter's depression and eventual suicide. In fact, there was substantial evidence that Phoebe's daughter was suffering from adolescent-onset schizophrenia, which was unrelated to the business situation. Phoebe was afraid that she was to blame for her daughter's death and was unable to face that fear, so she displaced her anger onto the business partner who, although guilty of poor judgment, was not to blame for the young woman's death. Phoebe's anger was so all-consuming that it was destroying her health and infecting her remaining children. Trying to reason with her was impossible. The counselor was unable to convince Phoebe of the irrational nature of her anger. Finally, her counselor encouraged her to forgive the business partner, not for causing her child's death, but for causing temporary hardship in the family. Only after she had forgiven was she little by little able to see the situation for what it really was.

Although in most cases objectively viewing the offense and the offender precede forgiveness, in this case objectivity was possible only after the work of forgiveness began. Sometimes people discover as they reach the last phase of the forgiveness process that they were not victims of a terrible injustice, but instead were victims of their own lack of understanding, something they could not see at the beginning.

Are Some People Unforgivable?

Suppose one faces an absolutely unrepentant abuser. This person sees nothing wrong with heaping verbal and physical abuse and, adding insult to injury, tells the victim that the abuse is deserved. Can one offer respect and compassion where it is not wanted? Can one forgive under these circumstances?

Yes. Human history records many examples of horrendous offenses and many examples of heroic forgiveness. Corrie Ten Boom lost her family in the Holocaust and was able to forgive.[7] Her daughter was kidnapped and brutally murdered, yet Marietta Jaeger was able to forgive.[8] Forgiveness is possible even under the most brutal and unfair circumstances.

We should not, however, be critical of those who have not yet begun the process of forgiveness. It would have been unnatural for Corrie or Marietta not to be angry at the murderers of their loved ones. The person who accepts abuse may be accepting the lie that they deserve abuse. No one deserves to be abused, and anger is the proper response to unjust abuse.

No act, no matter how terrible, is unforgivable, but some people choose not to forgive. Respect for the rights of others requires that we respect that choice.

Who Has the Right to Forgive?

Anyone who has been hurt can forgive. But you can forgive a person only for what was done to you. You can't forgive someone on the behalf of someone else. If you owe me $25, I can write off the debt. But I can't tell you that you don't have to pay the IRS the thousands that you may owe them. Marietta could forgive the kidnapper of her daughter for what he had done to her, but she could not tell him that she forgave him on behalf of her daughter. The daughter would have to make that choice herself.

Suppose the Forgiver Is Also Guilty?

Sometimes the forgiveness process is complicated by the fact that both parties have been guilty of serious offenses, which is often the case in family situations. Each offender ruminates over the injuries received. In some cases, the victim commits acts in retaliation that are greater than the original offense. In other cases, the victim wages a campaign of silent sabotage. Very often, forgiving and repentance go hand in hand. Sometimes forgiving precedes repentance because only after the mind is cleared of anger and bitterness can the person objectively evaluate the extent of the injury committed against others. It is common for two people who have been feuding for some time to forgive each other.

Can We Forgive the Dead?

Because people often hold resentments against the dead, forgiving them is not only possible but is appropriate. It should be obvious that the living are being punished by refusing to forgive the dead, but this is not always the case. Many people torture themselves for years because they have yet to release the deceased through forgiving. If one can forgive a spouse who abandoned the family years ago and is living in another state, then why would it be impossible to forgive those who are no longer living?

The forgiveness process, properly understood and used, can free those bound by anger and resentment. It does not require accepting injustice or remaining in an abusive situation. It opens the door to reconciliation, but it does not require trusting someone who has proven untrustworthy. Even if the offender remains unrepentant, you can forgive and restore a sense of peace and well-being to your life. The choice is yours.

ENDNOTES

1. J. North, "Wrongdoing and Forgiveness," *Philosophy* 62 (1987), 499–508; J. North, "The Ideal of Forgiveness," in *Exploring Forgiveness*, eds. R. D. Enright and J. North (Madison, University of Wisconsin Press, 1998), 15–34; related definitions are in R. S. Downie, "Forgiveness," *Philosophical Quarterly* 15 (1965), 128–134; H. J. N. Horsbrugh, "Forgiveness," *Canadian Journal of Philosophy* 4 (1974), 269–282; M. Hughes, "Forgiveness," *Analysis* 35 (1975) 113–117; A. Kolnai, "Forgiveness," *Proceedings of the Aristotelian Society* 74 (1973–1974), 91–106; C. S. Lewis, *The Great Divorce* (New York: Touchstone Books, 1996); and P. Twambley, "Mercy and Forgiveness," *Analysis* 36 (1976), 84–90.
2. B. B. Cunningham, "The Will to Forgive: A Pastoral Theological View of Forgiving," *Journal of Pastoral Care* 39 (1985), 141–149.
3. See ibid.

4. H. McGary, "Forgiveness," *American Journal of Philosophy* 26 (1989), 343–351.
5. J. Haber, *Forgiveness* (Lanham, MD: Rowman & Littlefield, 1991).
6. M. R. Holmgren, "Forgiveness and the Intrinsic Value of Persons," *American Philosophical Quarterly* 30 (1993), 341–352.
7. C. Ten Boom, *The Hiding Place* (Old Tappan, NJ: Revell, 1971).
8. M. Jaeger, "The Power and Reality of Forgiveness," in *Exploring Forgiveness*, eds. R. D. Enright and J. North (Madison: University of Wisconsin Press, 1998), 9–14.

CHAPTER 3

WHY FORGIVE ... AND THE CONSEQUENCES OF NOT FORGIVING

Rather than my answering the question "Why forgive?" I'd like you to write down all of the answers that you can think of. Try to consider your feelings, thoughts, and behaviors and the importance of your relationships. Also, try to focus on the quality of forgiveness itself. What is it about forgiveness that makes it a good thing to do? Take your time, because the question posed is deep and will enhance your understanding about why you might consider forgiving. Continue reading only after you have completed this task.

If you are like most people, your answers fall into eight categories:

1. You forgive to quiet your angry feelings.

2. Forgiveness changes destructive thoughts into quieter, more healthy thoughts.

3. As you forgive, you want to act more civilly toward the one who hurt you.

4. Forgiveness of one person helps you interact better with others. Perhaps your anger with your supervisor has spilled over

to your relationship with your children. Forgiving your boss would be a gift to your children.

5. Forgiveness can improve your relationship with the one who hurt you.

6. Your forgiveness actually can help the one who hurt you to see his or her unfairness and to take steps to stop it. Your forgiving can enhance the character of the one who hurt you.

7. You forgive because God asks you to do so. You forgive as an act of love toward God.

8. Forgiveness, as an act of kindness and love toward the one who hurt you, is a moral good regardless of how the other is responding to you. Loving others, while protecting yourself from harm, is a morally good thing to do.

The first six answers center on the *consequences of forgiving*: The first three answers focus on consequences for *your psychological and physical health*. The next two focus on consequences for *your relationships with others* as you forgive. The sixth answer focuses on the consequences for *the offender's well-being*. The final two answers do not focus on consequences as much as on *the intrinsic quality of forgiveness* as a good thing. Regardless of consequences, some people forgive because they know that it is a morally good thing to do.

Certainly, people forgive for a host of reasons. You may see forgiveness as intrinsically good and also want to rid yourself of the troubling consequences of churning anger. In fact, my own experience with people who forgive is this: At first, people want to harbor anger, thinking that it shows self-respect to remain angry. "He can't do this to me. I won't take it!" Eventually, they come to see that the harbored anger is compromising their personality. They are more surly and hot-tempered than they were before. At that point they want to cast off the anger that is too much to bear. Only later do they come to see the intrinsically good nature of forgiveness.

If you are just beginning to explore the mysteries of forgiveness, then you may be focusing on the various consequences for yourself as a forgiver. You may need some convincing that, in fact, certain kinds of anger are harmful to you. This chapter focuses on the consequences of anger that is held too deeply and too long. Our examination may help you answer the question "Should I forgive?" Please keep in mind, even if you answer yes, that there are other reasons for forgiving that go beyond the consequences for your psychological and physical well-being.

ANGER IN NEED OF CHANGE

When it is as an immediate reaction to injustice, anger is normal and healthy, and no one should feel guilty about experiencing it. Anger is like alcohol: A little bit can be beneficial, but too much of it is a problem, even addictive. Making a decision to embrace forgiveness as a solution to anger doesn't mean that you will never feel angry again, and it certainly does not require the suppression of every angry feeling. Anger has an important place in our repertoire of emotional resources, but not all anger is healthy.

American society is suffering from an epidemic of unhealthy anger. In the late 1990s, as one graphic example, children had shot and killed other children in Pearl, Mississippi; West Paducah, Kentucky; Jonesboro, Arkansas; Fayetteville, Tennessee; Springfield, Oregon; and Littleton, Colorado. Reporters often portrayed the murderers as angry, misunderstood, and bullied by others.[1]

Perhaps more benign but nonetheless troubling, signs of anger gone wild are found in television and radio talk shows where people vent their pent-up anger in public. Programs like the *Jerry Springer Show* encourage parents and children, married couples, friends, and lovers to appear in front of a live audience and express their rage toward one another. Freed from the constraints of civil discourse, the participants not only lash out verbally but often physically. Off-duty police officers are paid to separate the combatants. The audience cheers and claps, egging on the combatants. Although this kind of programming is universally condemned, the ratings remain high, suggesting that many people enjoy vicariously participating in these angry confrontations.

The vast majority of children are not dangerously violent, and most adults do not engage in physical fights with family members either on television or in the privacy of their homes, but destructive anger is all too present in our families, in the workplace, and in our political life.

Anger is an emotion involving feelings and thoughts. Anger affects our bodies. It can sweep over us like a flood. Our hearts beat faster. Adrenaline rushes through our blood stream. We feel strong enough to take on giants. Or anger can be so overwhelming that we feel sick to our stomachs and too weak to move.

My concern here is with unhealthy anger—anger that is disproportionate to the cause, anger that is directed not at the person who has injured us but at innocent bystanders, anger that lingers long after the event, anger that causes self-destructive behavior, anger that destroys families, marriages, and communities.

Most people learn early in life that childish temper tantrums are counterproductive. We discover how to control the outward expressions of the anger. We no longer stand in the middle of the room and scream because we don't get what we want. But being able to control the way we express our anger doesn't mean that we are dealing with anger in a healthy manner. Rather than screaming or lashing out physically at those who have made us angry, some of us learn to lash out verbally, expressing anger through snide comments, cutting humor, or biting criticism. Or we express anger through stony silence, withdrawal, or hostile noncompliance. Although these kinds of anger are more socially acceptable, they are probably even less healthy than a more natural expression of honest anger.

Some anger is mild and transient; like a summer shower, it blows over and is gone. But if you find that your anger hasn't passed away in a reasonable amount of time or if weeks, months, or years after the hurtful event you are still ruminating over the injury, plotting revenge, or feeling the same level of pain, your anger has probably turned into a smoldering resentment. You are a prime candidate for choosing the forgiveness process.

Although a single painful event can lead to intense resentment, most smoldering resentments are caused by a series of small offenses. Even after Mary Ann's husband Brendan had stopped drinking, he still caused resentment. He was incapable of making a request without including a criticism. He would never say "Do you know where my car keys are?" Instead, he said "This house is such a pig sty I can never find anything" or "Why can't you leave my things alone?" And when he found the keys in his back pocket or in the outside of the door where he had left them the night before, he never apologized for the false accusation. This neverending chain of small insults left Mary Ann seething with rage and contemplating divorce, even though Brendan was sober and a good provider and husband.

Other causes of smoldering resentment are unhealed childhood traumas. Children sometimes lack the intellectual and emotional resources to deal with pain. They frequently misinterpret the actions of others. They are capable of substantial anger and often are afraid of their own anger. Children sometimes believe that their angry thoughts are the cause of family disasters. Many people carry unresolved childhood anger into their adult life. A child may have reacted to a traumatic situation by creating a defense, such as displacing anger by yelling at the younger brother. Adult experiences that are similar to the childhood trauma can cause the adult to put up the defense system that helped him or her survive the original trauma. What that person may not see is that the defense system is often self-destructive.

When we think of anger, we may try to classify the kinds of anger by their outward expression: rage, temper tantrums, verbal abuse, physical violence, stony silence. But how we express our anger is not the crucial issue. The forgiveness process is designed to help you deal with anger that has some or all of these characteristics:

- anger that is directed toward a person or other people, not to "fate," circumstances, or inanimate objects
- anger that is caused by a real injustice
- anger that has become a pattern that is not easily broken
- anger that causes you to engage in self-destructive behaviors
- anger that affects your health or well-being.

ANGER AND HEALTH

Several studies have been done about the relationship between anger and health. One problem with these studies is that the researchers do not all define anger in the same way. And too often the research relies on people's self-reports. People fill out questionnaires: How angry were you? How long did you feel angry? However, such questionnaires may not accurately assess the actual levels of anger that a person experiences.

Tina Huang conducted a study in Taiwan,[2] asking 44 adults to recall an incident in their life when they were very angry. They then completed a questionnaire designed to assess the level of anger that they were experiencing. Most people reported low levels of anger. Dr. Huang further asked each person to retell the story of the anger-inducing incident and videotaped their facial expressions as they spoke. A detailed analysis of those expressions revealed that many who had denied anger on the questionnaire were, in fact, very angry. Their faces revealed a pattern of masked anger. It may be that they were hiding their anger from the researchers or that they themselves were unaware of the depth of their own anger.

Researchers using questionnaires may not always be able to distinguish those who are really angry from those who are merely annoyed. Nevertheless, the research on the physical effects of anger has produced significant evidence of the danger of holding onto deep anger.

Blood Pressure

In 1939, Franz Alexander, a medical doctor at the Institute for Psychoanalysis in Chicago, published a paper on the relationship between deep, passive anger—anger turned inward—and high blood pressure.[3] Blood pressure is reported with two numbers: the higher, or systolic, and lower, or diastolic. A diastolic reading over 90 is a sign to health care professionals that there is a problem. Dr. Alexander found that diastolic pressure was higher in those with deep, passive anger.

Later research has supported Dr. Alexander's finding.[4] Robert Harris and his colleagues report that college women with border-line high blood pressure showed higher levels of passive anger than those with normal blood pressure.[5]

Harold Kahn and his research team observed a similar pattern in men in Israel who brooded over unfair treatment at work.[6] We must keep in mind, however, that most who brooded over the unfair working conditions did not develop hypertension. Apparently, some cope with resentment, while others fare less well. Other studies suggest that those who cope well by showing assertion in the face of injustice or who express their anger in a straightforward manner may escape hypertension.[7] A research team headed by H. S. Goldstein and colleagues found that those who expressed anger in stressful family situations had lower diastolic readings than did those who suppressed their anger.[8]

Another study discovered that people who believe that they should express their hostility in an extreme overt manner are more at risk for hypertension than are those who express hostility in a more moderate manner. When presented with a story in which the boss acted unfairly, those who believed that they would confront the unjust supervisor had higher blood pressure than did those who said that they would keep their anger inside.[9] It is possible that the more extreme the anger, not whether it is expressed passively or openly, is the greater risk for damage to health.[10]

Heart Disease

The term "type A personality" was introduced into popular culture by Meyer Friedman and Ray Rosenman in their 1974 book *Type A Behavior and Your Heart*.[11] They found that although coronary heart disease was related to poor eating habits and sedentary lifestyles, stress also plays a large part. Those who are always pressed for time, who are overly aggressive, who are exceptionally ambitious, and who are generally hostile are the most prone to heart disease. Those with intense and abiding anger were most at risk.

According to Redford and Virginia Williams, researchers have abandoned the "type A" explanation and now focus on hostility levels. Hostility, which includes cynical mistrust, intense angry feelings, and a pattern of aggressive behavior, appears to be the real health risk.[12]

A study by R. B. Shekelle and colleagues measured the levels of hostility in 1,877 men working at the Western Electric factory in Chicago in the 1950s. Twenty years later the researchers checked the same men's medical histories to see how many had developed coronary heart disease.[13] As expected, those high in hostility in the 1950s showed significantly more disease in the 1970s. The group with greater initial hostility also were more likely to die than the other group.

Another study looked at hostility, using the same measure as Dr. Shekelle with 225 medical students in the 1950s.[14] Twenty-five years later, the researchers checked to see how many had a history of coronary heart disease or had died from any cause. Those who had higher levels of hostility were significantly more likely to have heart disease and to die earlier. Although these studies report only trends, they do point to the possibility that hostility is related to health problems. More studies need to be done, especially to examine the differences between the men who were hostile and developed health problems and those who were hostile and did not.

In the 1990s researchers began to examine blood flow through the heart, what the medical researchers call the "ejection fraction of the left ventricle." A medical research team placed 18 cardiac patients into mildly stressful situations.[15] These included calculating difficult mental arithmetic problems and recalling an event that was particularly angering. Patients recalling the anger-inducing situation, more so than those in the problem-solving condition, had significantly reduced blood flow through the heart while recalling the angering incident. Although not observed in this study, such restriction can eventually lead to chest pains. The researchers concluded that anger is a stressor that deserves our attention in reducing risk to the heart.[16]

As in the studies on hypertension, we must be careful not to make sweeping statements. Some researchers have found no relation between anger and heart disease.[17] Although these findings may be caused by less-than-perfect measures of anger or hostility, we cannot be sure that faulty measures are the answer. It could be that studies examining hostility years before coronary disease are missing an important factor: Hostile people can learn more serene behaviors years before data are collected on their coronary health. A person who becomes more calm or perhaps more forgiving in the years between testing may have unobserved health benefits.

ANGER AND MORE ANGER

In the 1960s and early 1970s several therapists recommended releasing anger, what they called "catharsis." They observed that suppression of anger or passive hostility caused problems for clients and reasoned that free expression of anger would be more healthy. They encouraged clients to "let off steam," "get it off their chests" and "clear the air."[18] Although the adrenaline output that accompanies the expression of suppressed anger can give a person a temporary rush, if the underlying problems are not addressed, the person is left as angry or even more angry than before. In addition, the person, by venting so intensively and frequently, may have hurt those around him or her. In some cases, people might be trading one dysfunctional method of dealing with anger for another. Some people find that after years of being the victim, they enjoy victimizing others with angry recriminations and blame. Therapists, who believed that venting anger would "clear the air" and allow people to move on in their lives, failed to recognize that some of their clients had learned to use anger as a weapon.

Carol Tavris in her book *Anger: The Misunderstood Emotion* presents a strong case against venting anger as the sole means of emotional healing.[19] She sees venting as potentially dangerous because it gives the angry person an excuse to impose his or her anger on others. Richard Fitzgibbons, who has worked with patients suffering from anger for years, found that excessive expression of anger can lead to even more anger.[20]

The expression of anger is necessary; how we express it and the duration of that expression is the issue. Standing up for one's rights is not only potentially healthy for the individual, but may also create greater fairness in society, as the history of nonviolence against oppression illustrates.[21] Anger helps us assert ourselves in the little, everyday situations in which others take advantage. The philosopher Margaret Holmgren believes that as we are angered at injustice against us, we are showing self-respect in acknowledging that we are worthwhile.[22]

Anger, like other emotions, must be controlled. Suppressing legitimate anger is unhealthy. Continually venting anger is also unhealthy.

ANGER AND FAMILY DYSFUNCTION

Family therapist Virginia Satir has spent years studying family dysfunction[23] and found that anger by one person may lead to illness in another. This happens when one family member engages in a pattern of blaming and fault-finding, which protects the blamer from the criticism of others and leads to emotional and physical problems for those who are the targets.

Social researchers Murray Straus, Richard Gelles, and Suzanne Steinmetz have documented cases in which blaming patterns can lead to even deeper patterns of anger in the home.[24] One person venting anger can make this practice an acceptable norm, leading others to try it. Eventually, family members find that they have permission to express anger toward those in the home but not necessarily to those outside the home. In such cases, expression of intensive anger becomes even more frequent in that home, creating an explosive situation.

Judith Wallerstein, one of the foremost authorities on the effects of divorce, observes that most divorces result from anger and that this anger continues long after the divorce.[25] Children are too often the victims of this anger.[26] Dr. Wallerstein found that the partners would repeat the precise details of the injuries they experienced in exactly the same way they had first told them many years after the divorce. Neither the clarity of the experience nor the pain had lessened in the slightest. The parents often shared their anger with their children, and the children became instruments of revenge against the former spouse. Dr. Wallerstein documented how anger prevents the family members from moving on with their lives.

Some people think that divorce, distance, or death will solve the problem of anger. They assume that if they can just get out of the situation they will feel better. Unfortunately, most take the anger with them and find that years later they are still seething.

ANGER AND COMMUNITY DYSFUNCTION

The beating of the African American Rodney King by four White Los Angeles police officers on the night of March 3, 1991, demonstrates that personal anger can have devastating consequences. Mr. King and a companion had led the officers on an 8-mile high-speed chase. Once apprehended, Mr. King exited the car. Mr. King was asked to lie on the ground. As he refused and rose up from the ground, the officers hit him again and again with their metal batons. The police were angry: perhaps it was work-related stress, perhaps they had family problems, perhaps they had been abused as children, perhaps they had been angry so many times that they now enjoyed the anger-adrenaline rush. Whatever the reason, they turned their anger on Mr. King. What the police did not know was that the entire scene was being videotaped by a bystander.

The video was broadcast on television. The same pictures were played over and over. The community became angry, and when the police were acquitted of wrongdoing, that anger turned into rioting. In the chaos that followed, businesses were looted, buildings were burned, and people were shot.

Anger begets anger. In the former Yugoslavia, Muslims, Orthodox Russian Christians, and Catholics have been fighting one another for centuries. Freed from Communist control, they turned on one another, and we have seen on TV the bodies of slaughtered men, women, and children as they are removed from shallow graves. We have seen the burned villages and bombed cities, and there appears to be no end to the violence in sight. In the Middle East, in Northern Ireland, and in India and Pakistan, innocent people die, and the anger lives on.

Anger over a real injustice can transfer to an entire group and then be transmitted from one generation to another. Revenge too often creates more victims, and the angry victims then demand revenge. One can hope that if people learn how to forgive personal hurts, they will learn to deal with communal anger.

TEMPORARY SOLUTIONS TO TEMPORARY ANGER

Several solutions other than forgiveness have been offered for those who are experiencing dysfunctional anger. Clinicians and researchers recognize the problems caused by intense anger. In searching the published literature on the subject I found seven basic approaches to the problem. It is rare for forgiveness to be mentioned among the solutions.

Catharsis

Those who recommend catharsis encourage their clients to "let it all out" or "get it off your chest." The research on blood pressure and coronary heart disease suggests that catharsis may cause health problems. Several researchers have concluded that this approach may actually intensify temporary anger.[27] Psychologist J. E. Hokanson carefully examined the effects of venting and found some interesting results.[28] Men's blood pressure was lowered somewhat through catharsis, but only if they vented to a peer; venting to an employer, as you might imagine, added to stress. For women, catharsis did not work; cultivating friendlier attitudes proved more effective for them.

One of the few self-help writers still advocating catharsis is John Lee,[29] who distinguishes private and interpersonal catharsis. Because venting directly to another person creates new problems, he recommends "screaming in the car," "beating a drum," and even "breaking glass." Although expressing anger in some form is probably more healthy than totally suppressing it, and expressing it privately better than yelling in public, destruction of property seems to be an extreme approach to the problem.

Relaxation

Several writers recommend learning to relax when faced with extreme anger and stress.[30] Those who promote relaxation as a remedy for anger view anger and relaxation as learned behaviors. They hold that people have learned to be angry when they are hurt and can learn to respond to hurt by relaxing. Specific breathing and muscle relaxation exercises are recommended.[31] According to this theory, because you can't be relaxed and angry at the same time, relaxation should dissipate the angry feelings. Although this technique may work in the short run and be effective for those who are prone to losing their temper for no good reason, relaxation will not solve the underlying problem or heal deep-seated resentments.

Thought Control

Some writers recommend various forms of thought control on the premise that anger is a learned behavior. If our thoughts are the primary cause of our angry emotions, then if we learn to recognize angry thoughts, we can stop angry feelings. A popular technique is to recognize angry thoughts when they first appear and say firmly to one's self "Stop."

This approach may work in the short run, but like relaxation, it does not address or correct the source of the difficulty. If real injustice is the cause of our anger, then that injustice needs to be addressed. Relaxation and thought control can be used as temporary measures or in conjunction with other techniques.[32]

Distraction

When we take our mind off our anger, we can temporarily calm down. In 1918, therapist Frederick Richardson advocated occupying one's mind with other things when temporarily but intensely angry. Reading a good book, writing a neutral letter, and engaging in a hobby are all examples of distraction. Clinical psychologist Robert Kaplan's scientific work supports this view.[33] Redford and Virginia Williams offer helpful hints on how to use distraction to deal with anger but recommend that this approach be used only as a temporary measure.[34] We may, like Scarlett O'Hara in *Gone with the Wind*, decide to think about the problem tomorrow, but eventually we will have to deal with it.

Relaxation, thought control, and distraction are useful when the cause of anger is minor or when someone has to break the anger habit without there being an underlying, unresolved injustice. Once we calm down we often realize that we were overreacting. They can also be helpful when we are so totally traumatized by our injury that we are not able to deal with anything at that moment. Scarlett O'Hara saw her whole world go up in flames and watched men die. She was forced to cope with hunger and fear and didn't have the time or energy to think about what had happened. Scarlett is only a fictional character, but real people eventually have to face their real feelings and deal with their anger. Avoiding pain in order to avoid anger can become a bad habit.

Changing Feelings, Thoughts, and Behavior

A number of writers recommend a broad, systematic approach to chronic anger and also see anger as a learned behavior.[35] Several encourage people who are chronically angry to keep a log of their anger, recording What is the source of my anger? How intense is my anger? How often am I this angry toward this source? How long does the anger last, and how do I express that anger? Keeping the logs helps people realize that their anger has definite patterns; they do not just blow up randomly.

Next comes a process of reframing, or thinking through the exact source of the anger. If an aggressive driver cuts you off in traffic, instead of thinking "That no-good, disgusting person cut me off! I wish I could get back at him," you can reframe the situation, "Perhaps the driver is excessively late for an important meeting. Perhaps he or she is having an exceptionally bad day."

Chronically angry people are then encouraged to find new ways to communicate with others. The point is to channel one's thoughts from aggression to compassion. Chronically angry people can be taught how to deal with annoying situations in a nonthreatening manner. Some people need to learn moral reasoning skills so that they can think through a dilemma and come to a moral solution rather than merely react. Some people need problem-solving skills, and some will benefit from learning how to calm down before they react. Psychologist Suzanne Freedman believes that these approaches are more effective at least in the short run than less comprehensive approaches.[36]

Correcting the Irrational With the Rational

Noted psychologist Albert Ellis advocates a rational–emotive approach to anger reduction.[37] He believes that our resentments are caused by our unreasonable demands that all people must treat us with absolute fairness. Dr. Ellis believes that it is possible to change these unrealistic expectations, so that we no longer expect others to be perfect and realize that what happened to us is not as bad as we thought. We can be annoyed but not deeply resentful.

Dr. Ellis's exclusive focus on perceptions seems to be an effective antidote to anger when there is a mismatch between the actual source of our anger and how we think about that source. When someone fails to make a pre-arranged meeting, our conclusion that he is irresponsible and incompetent may be incorrect and therefore our anger unjustified, but what if our anger is completely justified?

These techniques are based on the assumption that anger is essentially an irrational response, but what if the anger is rational and just? And what if the outbursts of irrational anger are symptoms of a deeper hurt? Sometimes the man who is screaming irrationally at other drivers has been abused as a child or has lost his children in a messy divorce. How can a mother rethink the kidnapping and murder of her child, concluding that her problem is centered primarily in how she is perceiving the atrocity? Is an incest victim going to be helped substantially by learning to deal with annoyances in a nonthreatening manner?

The difference between these techniques and the forgiveness process can be compared with the difference between treating a stress headache and treating a headache caused by a brain tumor. A stress headache may respond to an aspirin, but a brain tumor needs a more aggressive approach. In addition, these anger control techniques may make those who need to forgive feel guilty when they can't learn to control their anger.

Anger is the symptom, but injustice is the cause. The forgiveness process takes care of the symptoms by addressing the cause.

Character Transformation

Redford and Virginia Williams take a unique and interdisciplinary approach to chronic anger.[38] They advocate a multifaceted approach that includes character change. Angry people are encouraged to take a moral approach to problems, to care for others, and to cultivate a more trusting attitude when this is reasonable. They do not advocate blind trust in threatening situations. They encourage reframing annoying situations.[39] They also advocate general altruism, seeing something bigger than themselves in this world, and practicing forgiveness. Altruism might include caring for an animal or becoming involved in community service.

Of course, community volunteer work may not reduce anger expressed toward a particular person for specific injustices, but if our character is transformed, we may alter the way that we handle problems.[40]

ANGER AND FORGIVENESS

Several researchers have studied the effects of forgiveness. Issidoros Sarinopoulos asked about 200 college students and their same-sex parent to fill out forgiveness and anger questionnaires. The more people forgave those who deeply hurt them, the less angry they were.[41] In his doctoral dissertation, Dr. Sarinopoulos further found that the middle-aged parents who did not forgive deep-seated hurts from family members had more physician-diagnosed heart problems than did those who forgave.[42] In fact, the lack of forgiveness was more strongly related to coronary heart disease than was hostility. Tina Huang, in her study of anger and facial expressions, reported that those with the deeper understanding of forgiving were less likely to show masked anger when retelling the story of injustice toward them.[43]

Graduate student Kristy Ashleman, in a study of 30 divorced women, observed that those who forgave the former spouse were more emotionally healthy than those who chose not to forgive. The forgivers had a higher general sense of well-being and lower anxiety and depression.[44] Gayle Reed's research presented similar results. Working with 40 men and women whose former spouse was unfaithful, she discovered that those who were able to forgive and find meaning in their suffering had higher well-being and lower anxiety than those who did not forgive.[45]

Like relaxation training, forgiving others can make us less anxious in the long run.[46] Unlike rational–emotive therapy, forgiveness approaches assume that most people who are fuming over unfairness are perceiving the situation rationally, not irrationally. Forgiveness, properly understood, helps us carefully examine the source and extent of our anger. When someone is exceptionally angry, forgiving can offer an effective antidote.

Most anger reduction techniques that I reviewed, with the exception of the Williams's character-strengthening exercises, focus on anger's *symptoms*, such as countering strong emotions or harmful thoughts. Forgiving requires focusing less on the anger itself and more on the *source* of the anger. When we forgive, we face the fact that another person hurt us.

If you have tried a variety of techniques to help you attain an inner quiet but are still emotionally jumbled and uneasy, perhaps it is time to consider forgiveness. In the chapters that follow I will walk you through the forgiveness process.

ENDNOTES

1. *Time* (May 3, 1999).
2. S. T. Huang, "Cross-cultural and Real-Life Validation of the Theory of Forgiveness in Taiwan, Republic of China" (Madison: University of Wisconsin 1990).
3. F. Alexander, "Emotional Factors in Essential Hypertension: Presentation of a Tentative Hypothesis," *Psychosomatic Medicine* 1 (1939), 173–179.
4. See C. Miller and C. Grimm, "Personality and Emotional Stress Measurement on Hypertensive Patients With Essential and Secondary Hypertension," *International Journal of Nursing Studies* 16 (1979), 85–93; E. L. Diamond, "The Role of Anger and Hostility in Essential Hypertension and Coronary Disease," *Psychology Bulletin* 92 (1982), 410–433.
5. R. E. Harris and colleagues, "Response to Psychologic Stress in Persons Who Are Potentially Hypertensive," *Circulation* 7 (1953), 874–879; see also B. L. Kalis and colleagues, "Personality and Life History Factors in Persons Who Are Potentially Hypertensive," *Journal of Nervous and Mental Disorders* 132 (1961), 457–468.
6. H. A. Kahn and colleagues, "The Incidence of Hypertension and Associated Factors: The Israeli Ischemic Heart Disease Study," *American Heart Journal* 84 (1972), 171–182.
7. See, for example, H. S. Wolff and S. Wolff, "A Study of Experimental Evidence Relating Life Stress to Pathogenesis of Essential Hypertension in Man," in *Hypertension: A Symposium*, ed. E. T. Bell (Minneapolis: University of Minnesota Press, 1951) and H. S. Goldstein and colleagues, "Relationship of Resting Blood Pressure and Heart Rate to Experienced Anger and Expressed Anger," *Psychosomatic Medicine* 50 (1988), 321–329.
8. H. S. Goldstein and colleagues, "Relationship of Resting Blood Pressure."

9. E. Harburg and colleagues, "Resentful and Reflective Coping With Arbitrary Authority and Blood Pressure: Detroit," *Psychosomatic Medicine* 41 (1979), 189–202.

10. Not all studies find a relationship between anger and blood pressure. See for example, M. A. Smith and B. K. Houston, "Hostility, Anger Expression, Cardiovascular Responsibility, and Social Support," *Biological Psychology* 24 (1987), 39–48.

11. M. Friedman and R. H. Rosenman, *Type A Behavior and Your Heart* (New York: Knopf, 1974).

12. R. Williams and V. Williams, *Anger Kills* (New York: Times Books, 1993).

13. R. B. Shekelle and colleagues, "Hostility, Risk of Coronary Disease and Mortality," *Psychosomatic Medicine* 45 (1983), 219–228.

14. J. C. Barefoot and colleagues, "Hostility, CHD Incidence, and Total Mortality: A 25-Year Follow-Up Study of 225 Physicians," *Psychosomatic Medicine* 45 (1983), 59–63.

15. G. Ironson and colleagues, "Effects of Anger on Left Ventricular Ejection Fraction in Coronary Heart Disease," *American Journal of Cardiology* 70 (1992), 281–285.

16. Similar findings are reported by A. Rozanski and colleagues, "Ventricular Responses to Mental Stress Testing in Patients With Coronary Artery Disease: Pathophysiological Implications," *Circulation* 83 (1991), 137–144.

17. See, for example, E. McCranie and colleagues, "Hostility, Coronary Heart Disease (CHD) Incidence and Total Mortality: Lack of Association in a 25-Year Follow-Up Study of 478 Physicians," *Journal of Behavioral Medicine* 9 (1986), 119' and G. R. Leon and colleagues, "Inability to Predict Cardiovascular Disease From Hostility Scores or MMPI Items Related to Type A Behavior," *Journal of Consulting and Clinical Psychology* 56 (1988), 596.

18. See, for example, F. C. Perls, *Gestalt Therapy Verbatim* (Lafayette, CA: Real People Press, 1969); and T. L. Rubin, *The Anger Book* (New York: Collier, 1970).

19. C. Tavris, *Anger: The Misunderstood Emotion, Revised Edition* (New York: Simon & Schuster, 1989).

20. R. P. Fitzgibbons, "The Cognitive and Emotional Uses of Forgiveness in the Treatment of Anger," *Psychotherapy* 23 (1986), 626–633.

21. See M. L. King, Jr., *Strength of Love* (Philadelphia: Fortress Press, 1963).
22. M. R. Holmgren, "Forgiveness and the Intrinsic Value of Persons," *American Philosophical Quarterly* 30 (1993), 341–352.
23. V. Satir, *The New Peoplemaking* (Mountain View, CA: Science and Behavior Books, 1988).
24. M. A. Straus and colleagues, *Behind Closed Doors* (Garden City, NY: Anchor Doubleday, 1980).
25. J. S. Wallerstein, J. Lewis, and S. Blakeslee, *The Unexpected Legacy of Divorce* (New York: Hyperion, 2000); J. S. Wallerstein and S. Blakeslee, *Second Chances: Men, Women, and Children a Decade After Divorce* (New York: Tichnor & Fields, 1996); D. R. Mace makes a similar point, "Marital Intimacy and the Deadly Love–Anger Cycle," *Journal of Marriage and Family Counseling* 2 (1976), 131–137.
26. G. E. Gardner, "Aggression and Violence: The Enemies of Precision Learning in Children," *American Journal of Psychiatry* 128 (1971), 77–82.
27. See R. DeCharms and E. J. Wilkins, "Some Effects of Verbal Expression of Hostility," *Journal of Abnormal and Social Psychology* 66 (1964), 462–470; and R. M. Kaplan, "The Cathartic Value of Self Expression: Testing Catharsis, Dissonance, and Interference Explanations," *Journal of Social Psychology* 97 (1975), 195–208.
28. J. E. Hokanson, "Psychophysiological Evaluation of the Catharsis Hypothesis," in *The Dynamics of Aggression*, eds. E. I. Megaree and J. E. Hokanson (New York: Harper & Row, 1970).
29. J. Lee, *Facing the Fire: Experiencing and Expressing Anger Appropriately* (New York: Bantam Books, 1993).
30. See Lee, *Facing the Fire;* M. McKay and colleagues, *When Anger Hurts* (Oakland, CA: New Harbinger, 1989); and R. Potter-Efron, *Angry All the Time: An Emergency Guide to Anger Control* (Oakland, CA: Harbinger, 1994).
31. Please see M. McKay and colleagues, *When Anger Hurts,* for examples.
32. R. Williams and V. Williams, *Anger Kills.*
33. R. M. Kaplan, "The Cathartic Value of Self Expression."
34. R. Williams and V. Williams, *Anger Kills.*
35. Examples include R. Novaco, *Anger Control* (Lexington, MA: Lexington Books, 1975) and B. Glick and A. P. Goldstein, "Aggression

Replacement Training," *Journal of Consulting and Development* 65 (1987), 356–362.

36. S. R. Freedman, "Anger and the Value of Catharsis: A Developmental Analysis of Differences in Expression, Intensity, Causes, and Duration" (Madison: University of Wisconsin, 1991); S. R. Freedman and R. D. Enright, "Forgiveness as an Intervention Goal With Incest Survivors," *Journal of Consulting Psychology* 64 (1996), 983–992.

37. A. Ellis, *Anger: How to Live With and Without It* (New York: Citadel Press, 1977); A. Ellis and W. Dryden, *The Practice of Rational–Emotive Therapy* (New York: Springer-Verlag, 1987).

38. R. Williams and V. Williams, *Anger Kills.*

39. R. Novaco, *Anger Control.*

40. See also E. Larsen, *From Anger to Forgiveness* (New York: Touchstone Books, 1992).

41. I. Sarinopoulos, "Forgiveness in Adolescence and Middle Adulthood: Comparing the Enright Forgiveness Inventory With the Wade Forgiveness Scale" (Madison: University of Wisconsin, 1996).

42. I. Sarinopoulos, "Forgiveness and Physical Health, (Madison: University of Wisconsin, 1998).

43. S. T. Huang, "Cross-cultural and Real-Life Validation."

44. K. A. Ashleman, "Forgiveness as a Resiliency Factor in Divorced or Permanently Separated Families" (Madison: University of Wisconsin, 1996).

45. G. Reed, "Forgiveness as a Function of Moral Agency in the Context of Infidelity and Divorce" (Madison: University of Wisconsin, 1998).

46. Scientific evidence can be found in Al-Mabuk and colleagues, "Forgiveness Education With Parentally Love-Deprived College Students," *Journal of Moral Education* 1 (1995), 173–179; C. T. Coyle and R. D. Enright, "Forgiveness Intervention With Post-Abortion Men," *Journal of Consulting and Clinical Psychology* 65 (1997), 1042–1406; S. R. Freedman and R. D. Enright, "Forgiveness as a Therapeutic Goal" (paper presented at the meeting of the American Psychological Association, New York, August, 1995); and J. H. Hebl and R. D. Enright, "Forgiveness as a Psychotherapeutic Goal With Elderly Females," *Psychotherapy* 30 (1993), 658–667.

Part II

THE PROCESS OF FORGIVENESS

CHAPTER 4

A MAP AND TOOLS FOR
YOUR JOURNEY

Anger need not leave us helpless. Just as an antibiotic can be an effective antidote to infectious disease, forgiveness can be an antidote to dysfunctional anger and debilitating resentments. The research we have done at the University of Wisconsin–Madison demonstrates that people can forgive, and when they do, many find relief from the effects of harbored anger.

For many years we have been running a seminar on forgiveness for faculty, students, and people in the community. The seminar has been dedicated to looking into all aspects of forgiveness. Over the years we have received input from numerous sources. We have searched for stories and case studies of forgiveness in classic and contemporary, religious and secular literature. We have tried to clarify what is involved when one person forgives another.

As our work progressed, we began to develop a model for forgiveness that is divided into phases. Within the four phases we have, at the moment, identified 20 guideposts in the process. I say "at the moment" because when we tested our original model on real people with real anger we found that we had to change some of the guideposts, so perhaps in the future we will make other changes. Our model is not something carved in stone—it is not the Ten Commandments or even the Twelve Steps—rather it is the product of our observation of what works.

We see forgiveness as a process to be used when dealing with particular kinds of anger and resentment. We chose the word *phase* for the major divisions of the process because we felt that it expressed the gradual nature of the change experienced by those who use the forgiveness process. The word suggests a gradual change, for example, the moon is described by scientists as going through phases, each night slightly changing. So we see people as gradually changing. Also, the forgiveness process is rarely a one-time event. Often, no sooner is forgiveness completed with one offender than you may see other areas where forgiveness is needed. And because injuries and injustice can happen at any time, you will probably need to use forgiveness in the future.

We used the term *guidepost* rather than *step* to describe the parts of the phases because we did not want to cause confusion for those who are already using a step program and because these guideposts are not steps that one must take in an inflexible order. Those familiar with 12-step programs know that taking the steps in sequence is important and that all steps are essential for full recovery. Within the four phases, the guideposts do not always have to be addressed in order, and for some people some of the guideposts will not apply to their situation. The first eight guideposts are rather like a checklist. Those forgiving need to ask themselves "Is this a problem for me? Have I been doing this?"

Our group and some researchers learning from our group scientifically tested the four phases of forgiveness with elderly women hurt by injustice,[1] teenagers deprived of love from at least one parent,[2] incest survivors,[3] men hurt by the abortion decision of their partner,[4] and fifth graders experiencing difficulties with inner-city poverty.[5] Many of those participating in the studies learned to forgive and experienced powerful emotional healing when they used the process. In fact, the results exceeded our expectations.

THE MAP

As I present the model of forgiving, readers should keep in mind some important points. We do not all forgive in the same way. Some people may need to examine carefully each guidepost of the model, while others skip guideposts without hampering their forgiveness effort. We all heal from injustice at different rates. Some may forgive deep injustice in a few weeks, others may take a year or more. The deeper the hurt, the more time may be required. Certain guideposts will be more relevant to your circumstances. Those guideposts that appear to be especially important to you should be traversed with the greatest of care and preparation.

Some of the guideposts will be more difficult than others. This is typical, and so you need not become discouraged when you find it slow going at times. Do think carefully about each guidepost. Sometimes people are in denial and will insist that they don't need to look at a particular area when, in fact, that is exactly where they need to look.

The forgiveness process is not rigidly fixed. Having addressed a particular guidepost at one phase in the process, you may be surprised to discover that later you have to go back and revisit it, this time with a transformed attitude. Deep anger and resentment are rarely caused by a single occurrence. The deepest hurts often involve destructive relationships that lead to other destructive relationships, and the layers of hurt have to be peeled away one at a time. Because each person's experience is uniquely individual, each person's forgiveness process will also be uniquely individual.

Very often a person will forgive at one level and then months or even years later get angry all over again. Often the surface anger was hiding deeper hurts, and these could be addressed only when the person was strong enough to confront the real source of the problem. So, it is important not to be discouraged if anger comes back; it just means that there is probably something or someone else you need to forgive.

Forgiveness is a skill. The more you forgive, the easier it gets. Practice really does make perfect. Of course, forgiveness is more than a skill—it is an attitude of goodwill and a moral virtue that develops. It even becomes part of your identity, part of who you are, as you begin to incorporate it into your life. Forgiveness has a way of transforming your character and relationships as you understand and practice it.

Forgiveness as Hard, Sometimes Painful, Work

Forgiving is not a quick fix. It is hard, sometimes painful, work. Serious emotional wounds require serious medicine. If you are reading this book because you need to heal, then you should monitor the level of pain you are feeling. Just because you can skim this book at a single sitting doesn't mean that you can complete the forgiveness process in an afternoon. The book is like a road map that you review before you make a cross-country journey so that you know where you are going. Once you get on the road, you need to read the map at each junction to check your direction.

Your Motivation to Forgive

Throughout this book, I emphasize that forgiveness is something we give to those who have hurt us. It is, however, important to remember that people don't start the forgiveness process wanting to give those who hurt them a gift. Some people want revenge. Some want the offender to beg for forgiveness or suffer some terrible humiliation. Others simply want to wipe out of memory the painful event and the person who caused it. If a person were already filled with generous sentiments toward his or her tormentor, then he or she would not need the forgiveness process. What then is the motivation for beginning the process?

You want your own pain to stop. You want to be able to heal and move on.

When professor Suzanne Freedman and I began to test the forgiveness process on incest survivors, every one told us they would never forgive the perpetrator. They also told us that they believed our research was doomed to failure. They thought that these honest admissions would make them ineligible for participation. They were all sure that we would not want them in our study. They were surprised when we assured them that they were actually the kind of people we were looking for.

With the incest survivors, as with the other groups, we found that although the original motivation was self-preservation, the forgiveness process helped the survivors eventually move beyond themselves to give those who had injured them the unmerited gift of forgiveness. This is a paradox of forgiving:

As we reach out to the one who hurt us, we are the ones who heal.

So don't be ashamed or deterred if your initial motivation is self-preservation. This is a perfectly normal response to deep injury. It is not a contradiction with the definition of forgiving. It is simply a developmental step along the way.

If at this point you are asking yourself "Why should I begin the forgiveness process?" it's OK if you choose one of the following motivations:

- I am tired of feeling this pain and want it to stop.
- I don't want to go on letting this person hurt me.
- If I forgive, I will feel better.
- If I forgive, maybe I will become physically or psychologically healthier.
- I don't want to give this person the satisfaction of hurting me.

Your Worldview and Forgiveness

When forgiving, people invariably try to fit forgiveness into their worldview. Everyone has a worldview, in that we all have ideas about justice, mercy, love, God, eternity, and morality. A worldview answers the "big" questions of life, such as How did humanity come to be? In other words, Who or what was around to make us? What are people like at the core of their being? Are people basically good, basically bad, or perhaps neutral as society makes us good or bad? How do you change, becoming more good? Where do you ultimately go when you die?

As you develop your answers to these questions and form a worldview, you may notice that you use certain methods to support your ideas. Some people rely on faith, a belief in what they cannot see. Others rely more on reason, what makes sense to them as they think through the questions logically. Still others rely mostly on experience, focusing on what works as they fail and succeed and learn the hard lessons of life. Still others try to rely mostly on facts and science as their guide. You may use all of these ways of knowing to different degrees but may rely mostly on one or two of them.

Our worldview has been formed in part by our families, the culture we were brought up in, the religion to which we belong, and the philosophical ideas to which we have been exposed. Some people have consistent worldviews; they have chosen a particular religion or philosophy and make decisions based on their beliefs. On the other hand, some people have worldviews that lack consistency. For example, they may insist that they are believers in a religion that recommends and fosters forgiveness yet believe equally strongly that forgiveness is a sign of weakness.

We specifically sought out people with very different religious and philosophical worldviews so that we could design a forgiveness process that could be used by as many people as possible. Our goal was to develop a process that was usable by theists and non-theists. Although we believe that the process is useful for everyone, there are some people whose worldview rejects forgiveness. Those whose worldviews are filled with cynicism and skepticism may find that forgiveness is incompatible with their view. After all, if the one who hurt you cannot or will not change, why reach out to the person at all? If forgiveness is for wimps, why bother? Although one cannot generalize about every person who subscribes to a worldview that promotes anger, skepticism, and revenge, it is possible that some people are attracted to these ideologies because they were injured and don't want to forgive.

Although it is not necessary for you to have a consistent worldview before you begin the forgiveness process, it can help. The well-known psychologist Erik Erikson believed that a consistent worldview is essential if a person is going to accomplish anything of value.[6] If you don't have a consistent worldview when you begin the forgiveness process, you may find that your view will become more coherent as you move through the process.

Phases of Forgiveness

The Guideposts for Forgiving gives an overview of the four phases of forgiveness. Let's look briefly at each.

GUIDEPOSTS FOR FORGIVING

PHASE I—UNCOVERING YOUR ANGER

- How have you avoided dealing with anger?
- Have you faced your anger?
- Are you afraid to expose your shame or guilt?
- Has your anger affected your health?
- Have you been obsessed about the injury or the offender?
- Do you compare your situation with that of the offender?
- Has the injury caused a permanent change in your life?
- Has the injury changed your worldview?

PHASE 2—DECIDING TO FORGIVE

- Decide that what you have been doing hasn't worked.
- Be willing to begin the forgiveness process.
- Decide to forgive.

PHASE 3—WORKING ON FORGIVENESS

- Work toward understanding.
- Work toward compassion.
- Accept the pain.
- Give the offender a gift.

PHASE 4—DISCOVERY AND RELEASE FROM EMOTIONAL PRISON

- Discover the meaning of suffering.
- Discover your need for forgiveness.
- Discover that you are not alone.
- Discover the purpose of your life.
- Discover the freedom of forgiveness.

PHASE 1—UNCOVERING YOUR ANGER. To forgive, you must be willing to examine how much anger you have as a result of someone else's unfairness toward you.

Realizing that you are angry can be very painful, but forgiveness is not about pretending that nothing happened or hiding from the pain. You have suffered and need to be honest with yourself about that suffering.

PHASE 2—DECIDING TO FORGIVE. Forgiveness requires a decision and a commitment. Because this decision is such an important part of the process, we have broken it down into three parts:

1. turning your back on the past,
2. looking toward the future, and
3. choosing the path of forgiveness.

PHASE 3—WORKING ON FORGIVENESS. Simply making a decision to forgive isn't enough. People need to take concrete actions to make their forgiveness real. This phase culminates with the giving of a moral gift to the one who hurt you, which we will see in chapter 9.

PHASE 4—DISCOVERY AND RELEASE FROM EMOTIONAL PRISON. Unforgiveness, bitterness, resentment, and anger are like the four walls of a prison cell. Forgiveness is the key that opens the door and lets you out of that cell. What will you find when you get outside? Frankly, I can't predict what will happen in each individual case. I do know that the vast majority of people who forgive with whom I speak are much happier outside of their prison than they were inside. In fact, I can't think of one person who, having gone through the forgiveness process, wants to go back into the prison of resentment. But being on the outside often involves adjustments and a new way of thinking and living. You may find that forgiving helps you mature. You may gain new insights into the meaning of suffering. You may find that you are able to become the person you have always wanted to be.

For some people, the change is so gradual and natural that they may not notice how profoundly they have been changed. Therefore, I feel that it is important for people to reflect on how forgiveness has changed them. In this book, you will be meeting people who have reflected on the change from anger, fear, and hatred to compassion, benevolence, and love. When you get to Chapter 10, notice the positive changes that these people experienced.

Choose a Companion for Your Journey in Forgiveness

Do you have someone to support you during the forgiveness process? Forgiving someone is interpersonal as we reach out to the one who hurt us. You need to have someone you can talk with about each aspect of the forgiveness process. This person should not be the one you are forgiving.

Please don't do this alone. Anger and resentment can trap us in a cycle of negative thinking, self-justification, shame, and guilt. Another person, one who is sensitive and who has experienced forgiveness, can help sort things out. Without that other voice, we can just go round and round, telling ourselves the same lies over and over again, because we don't know they are lies. For example, we might condone a verbally abusive person, thinking that he or she is not so harsh. Or, we may exaggerate a parents behavior, thinking that he or she is evil, when, in fact, that parent was only applying fair discipline. A supportive person may help you discern an offender's right and wrong actions more accurately.

Consider the very complicated life of Camille, 62 and widowed. Her life was ruled by her anger toward her stepmother, who had controlled the family with an iron hand. When Camille's mother died she was sent to live with her kind put poor paternal grandparents. When Camille's father remarried, Camille was devastated at being taken away from the only home she had ever known. No one acknowledged her feelings of loss. Her stepmother was outwardly very generous, but the gifts were poisoned with the demand that Camille be grateful for being saved from her lower class grandparents by being allowed to live in the supposedly vastly superior surroundings of her stepmother's home. Camille was not allowed to speak of her dead mother. When her dead mother's family came to visit, Camille's stepmother did not allow them to tell Camille who they were. When Camille's father divorced her stepmother, the stepmother adopted Camille. When the stepmother remarried, Camille was told to accept the stepmother's husband as her father, and when Camille had children, her stepmother insisted that the children not be told that he was not their real grandfather. When their real grandfather came for a rare visit, the children were not told who he was. What was amazing about this situation was that although Camille recognized that she was angry at her stepmother, she was so under the control of her stepmother that she believed she was wrong for feeling angry and that her stepmother's demands were entirely justified. She kept her intense anger from others, and even from herself, for decades.

It was years later, after Camille told the story to a friend, who expressed outrage, shock, and horror at the injustice of the situation, that Camille was able to realize the full extent of the injustice she had suffered. She was able, with the friend's help, to get beyond her guilt for not feeling grateful, to understand the toll that this situation took on her family, and to begin the forgiveness process.

THE TOOLS: KEEPING A JOURNAL

I'd like you to consider keeping a journal of your progress as you work through the material at the end of this chapter and in Chapters 5 through 10. A journal is a telling of your story—who you are, who the people are that accompany you, the contexts in which the story unfolded, complications and conflicts, and the resolutions. A journal is a record of your experiences each day in your story. As Anne Hazard Aldrich, who has written a helpful book, *Notes from Myself,* on the art of journal-keeping, puts it, "A journal lets us THINK IN WRITING and thus lets us see the full dimensions of our lives."[7]

For those of you who may be hesitant about journal writing, let me offer a few words of encouragement. Keeping a journal allows you to look into your past, examine your present, and plan for the future. It is not stuffy, analytical writing, but can blend quiet reflection with more free-form impressions and a "pouring out" of emotions, confusions, and frustrations. It is sometimes hard to see our areas of growth unless we have markers in time, which you will have as you enter the date each day. The dated entries will help you gauge the progress that you, indeed, are making. In addition, journals can be a source of both healing and fun.

> In a journal one can purge all the emotions that were bottled up during the day. Once you start, you will be amazed at just how much has been contained in the dialogue of your days. It is revelatory, therapeutic, and a great deal of fun to let loose in words, and your journal is the best, and sometimes the only, place to do it.[8]

Journals have been written for centuries. There are spiritual journals, such as Augustine's *Confessions;* journals for emotional healing, such as Kathleen Adams's workbook *The Way of the Journal;* those focused on travel, such as Alexis de Toqueville's impressions of his visit to a new country in *Democracy in America;* and those recording personal experiences during a deciding moment in history, such as *Mary Chesnut's Civil War.*

Mrs. Chesnut, married to a prominent brigadier general during the fall of the South, reflected on the battles, the smoke, and the ruins as counterpoint to an antebellum gentility that she knew and lost. Her journal entries of anxiety and frustration are in stark contrast to her family portrait that shows a poised, elegant Southern belle with a velvet burgundy dress trimmed in lace and a string of pearls placed just so around her neck for the artist's brush to capture. Mayhem hid behind this loveliness and order, when the 42-year-old plantation owner wrote at a particularly historic moment, dated April 22, 1865:

> Colonel Chad Jones came with a dispatch, a sealed secret dispatch. It was for General Chesnut. I opened it.
> Lincoln–old Abe Lincoln–killed–murdered–Seward wounded! Why? By Whom? It is simply maddening, all this.
> I sent off messenger after messenger for General Chesnut. I have not the faintest idea where he is, but I know this foul murder will bring down worse miseries on us.
> Mary Darby says: "But they murdered him themselves. No Confederates in Washington."
> "But if they see fit to accuse us of instigating it?"
> "Who murdered him?"
> "Who knows!"
> "See if they don't take vengeance on us, now that we are ruined and cannot repel them any longer."[9]

Her day was filled with tension, discussion, giving orders. She was able to sort out some of the implications of this bad news for her very way of life in her writing.

If you decide to pursue the journal writing, please consider 10 principles below that may be helpful.[10]

- *Principle 1.* Select a journal appropriate to your tastes and lifestyle. Will you select a blank-paged book? If so, try to get one that lays flat on the table as you write. Will you be making your entries on your computer? If so, will you be putting the ideas right onto the hard drive or using a disk? The disk is easier to keep private, but over time any disk can deteriorate. Certain software programs can check the health of your disk.

- *Principle 2.* Prepare before writing. I will give you a series of questions following certain material. Please take the time to review the chapter and think about the question before responding.

- *Principle 3.* Set aside a time for writing. Some like to write upon rising in the morning when all is quiet and the mind is fresh. Others prefer late evening. Whatever time fits your schedule, it may be best to do the writing at about the same time each day to get into a routine.

- *Principle 4.* Find an appropriate place to write. Where is there a sense of quiet and peace to which you can adjourn?

- *Principle 5.* Try to record the gist of your concerns, not every detail. Writing in a journal should not be a contest to see how many specifics you can record in one sitting. Recall Mary Chesnut's entry the day she received the news of President Lincoln's assassination. She did not record every thought or feeling, dialogue, possible consequence. Her ideas were punctuated with the essential dialogue and the basic consequences that might follow. She was probably exhausted at day's end anyway, too tired for detailed entries.

- *Principle 6.* Pace yourself. Do not feel that you must fill a certain amount of space each day. Let the words come as naturally as possible. When you have had enough or are tiring, set the journal aside. You can always continue at the same spot tomorrow.

- *Principle 7.* Give yourself permission to write. As Ms. Aldrich suggests, "Writing is clarifying; it is not an impenetrable mystery to be avoided."[11]

- *Principle 8.* Consider the issue of privacy. A journal kept on a computer disk is easier to store away from other people than is a book. For the more traditional book, place the words "Confidential" or "Private—Please do not open" on the cover. However, privacy does not mean that you isolate yourself in the writing. Feel free to discuss aspects of your entries with others as you deem appropriate.

- *Principle 9.* Consider the care of the journal, now and in the future. How will you store it now so that it does not get ruined in any way? How do you wish others to deal with the journal when you are gone? You might consider putting instructions about the dispersal or disposal of the journal in your will, for example.[12]

- *Principle 10.* Be sure to assess your emotional well-being. Journal writing can be emotionally painful when working on issues of forgiveness. Please be sure to assess how anxious, depressed, or angry you are with the one who offended you. If your negative emotions are getting the better of you, please do not handle them alone. Seeking professional help is always a good idea when you are feeling overwhelmed.

Where to Start

It is best to start with one person and one injury or pattern of injury. Usually, the person who is considering forgiveness knows exactly whom they need to forgive and for what.

There is, however, one thing you should consider before you decide whom it is you have to forgive and for what. Is this the first time that this injury has happened to you? When we have been seriously hurt as children, we often find that we are drawn into similar situations. For example, if our father failed us, we may seek out father figures with the same faults, trying to get what we missed and getting hurt again and again. In these cases, although we may be feeling extremely angry at the most recent in this string of faulty father figures, the root of our anger is our father, and he is the one we need to concentrate on.

Susan, 45 and a mother of five, had been humiliated by her fourth-grade teacher, and every time she had to confront a matronly woman in authority, she would feel again that humiliation and react to that woman in a way that would produce a counter-reaction and an additional humiliation. She was continually at war with her children's teachers. Enraged over the latest confrontation, she tried to apply the forgiveness process and realized that her anger was disproportionate to the offense. When she thought about it, she remembered how she had been humiliated as a child, how she had wanted revenge against her teacher, and how she was afraid that her children would be hurt as she had been. By forgiving her teacher first, she was able to forgive other teachers and to deal with current problems rationally.

PREPARATION

To prepare for the forgiveness process, ask yourself the questions below. I recommend that you read through the rest of the chapter first and then consider going back to each question in your journal. It may take a few days to work through this material in written form because you are just getting started and because these original musings may lead you into considerable reflection.

Who Hurt You?

Sometimes we are angry with a group of people, but in most cases serious resentment focuses on an individual. If you have any doubt, just imagine the person who offended you sitting in a chair next to you. How do you feel?

Cecil, 59 and a banker in a rural area, was so angry at his son, who worked at the only gas station in town, that he refused to fill up his car's gas tank there. Instead, he made trips to the next town, 10 miles away, whenever the gas gauge was half-full. Such self-defeating behavior is a clear symptom of the need to forgive (or at least to get a more fuel-efficient car!).

Although there is no one right place to begin the forgiveness process, in general most people begin with the person with whom they are the most angry. Another strategy is to start with childhood injuries and work toward the present, because patterns of anger and resentment often begin in childhood and affect adult relationships.

How Deeply Are You Hurt?

In one of our studies, we asked college students and middle-age adults to describe their feelings after the most recent incident of injustice.[13] For the older adults, the deepest hurts occurred within the family. They were more likely to report being injured by their spouse, children, parents, and close relatives. For the college students, the most frequently reported hurts were from boyfriends or girlfriends. Those who were deeply hurt by loved ones were more likely to experience heightened anxiety and psychological difficulties than those hurt by acquaintances or strangers.

Which Situation Will Be Your Focus?

Once you have chosen the person you need to forgive, it is helpful to focus on a single offense. Often the first deep wound in the relationship is the best place to start. It is natural to be thinking about what happened yesterday or last week, but if a particular relationship has been troubling for a long time, it is more profitable to go back to the roots of that trouble. This failure to go back to the roots is one reason people say "Well, I tried to forgive and can't." Resentment is a weed in our emotional life that has to be pulled out down to the roots. Cut off the visible leaves, and it will only come back stronger in 20 different places.

Mary Ann, whom you met in the first chapter, likened her forgiveness process to the work she had to do on a rock garden. Poison ivy had gotten into the garden. No matter how many times she tried to cut it down, it just came back. Finally, she took the entire garden apart, removed all the plants and set them aside, dismantled the rocks and pulled out every bit of the root. The poison ivy was finally defeated.

What Are the Specifics of the Incident?

Forgiving someone for a specific injury may be best accomplished if you first remember the event in detail. What time of day was it? Were you outside or inside? Was it a hot sunny day, a cold rainy night? What was the other person wearing? How did he or she speak with you? Was he or she harsh, or dismissing, or even indifferent? If the event was a life-changing trauma, the remembrance will not, in most cases, be too difficult. Some women remember the color of the flowers in the wallpaper of the room where they were sexually molested 50 years after the occurrence.

Who Was at Fault?

Is it possible that you may have contributed to the situation? Discuss this with your companion on the forgiveness journey. Your anger and pain may have clouded your judgment about your own guilt. A good rule to follow is that if you feel terribly guilty, you probably were at fault, and if you feel completely innocent and absolutely justified in your anger, there is a good possibility that you may not be.

At some point in the forgiveness process, you may want to seek forgiveness for the wrongs you have done, even if your wrongs are 1% of the problem and the other person's wrongs are 99% of the problem. But you don't have to do that now, because if you try to apologize to someone you are still angry with, you may start another argument and then have another thing to apologize for.

Did you do anything to spark a confrontation? Were you both guilty of insensitivity? Were you both having a bad day and, perhaps, was the person not altogether unfair? In other words, if you are to forgive, you must determine whether your resentment is justified.

Even if you were having a bad day, even if you did make someone angry, please keep in mind that you are not responsible for the way that he or she expressed that anger. You are not re-sponsible for another's deep lack of respect or aggressiveness or violence. If he or she was unfair, despite your own reactions, then you may consider forgiving. Of course, under certain circumstances both of you may need to forgive each other.

Was the Person Truly Unfair?

The fact that you felt hurt doesn't mean that you have been the victim of injustice. For example, tensions were running high at the insurance office lately. Bill told Mike that he was acting selfishly, ignoring all but himself. As a result, the work that needed to be done was slowed. Mike, upon hearing all of this, felt betrayed, resentful, and embarrassed. He had been doing his fair share, he thought. As time passed, he reflected carefully on the apparently harsh criticism, concluding that Bill did him a favor because, in fact, he had been in his own world as of late. The feedback Mike received could have been delivered a bit more gently, but he needed to hear it. Bill, in the final analysis, was not acting unfairly; Mike, in his own view, had nothing to forgive. He, instead, rolled up his sleeves and worked harder.

Are you misunderstanding something in the relationship? Are you jumping too quickly to the conclusion that the person was unfair? Are your expectations too high, and if you lowered those expectations would you conclude that no forgiveness is necessary? Is there a good reason why the person acted as he or she did? Is pardoning, condoning, or excusing a more appropriate response to this situation, or do you need to forgive?

Once you decide that forgiveness is in order, then you can begin the process.

ENDNOTES

1. J. H. Hebl and R. D. Enright, "Forgiveness as a Psychotherapeutic Goal With Elderly Females," *Psychotherapy* 30 (1993), 658–667.
2. R. Al-Mabuk and colleagues, "Forgiveness Education With Parentally Love-Deprived College Students," *Journal of Moral Education* 24 (1995), 427–444.
3. S. R. Freedman and R. D. Enright, "Forgiveness as a Therapeutic Goal" (paper presented at the annual meeting of the American Psychological Association, New York, August 1995).
4. C. T. Coyle and R. D. Enright, "Forgiveness Intervention With Post-Abortion Men," *Journal of Consulting and Clinical Psychology* 65 (1997), 1042–1046.
5. S. Hepp-Dax, "Forgiveness Education With Inner-City Fifth-Grade Children" (New York: Fordham University, 1995).
6. E. Erikson, *Identity, Youth and Crisis* (New York: Norton, 1968).
7. A. H. Aldrich, *Notes From Myself: A Guide to Creative Journal Writing* (New York: Carroll & Graf, 1998), p. 6.

8. Ibid, p. 17.
9. C. V. Woodward, ed., *Mary Chesnut's Civil War* (New Haven, CT: Yale University Press, 1981), p. 791.
10. These ideas come not only from me, but also some come from A. H. Aldrich, *Notes From Myself,* and C. Baldwin, *One to One: Self-understanding Through Journal Writing* (New York: Evans, 1991).
11. A. H. Aldrich, *Notes From Myself,* p. 15.
12. The idea of future care of the journal is from C. Baldwin, *One to One.*
13. See M. J. Subkoiak and colleagues, "Measuring Interpersonal Forgiveness" (paper presented at the annual meeting of the American Educational Research Association, San Francisco, April 1992) and "Measuring Interpersonal Forgiveness in Late Adolescence and Middle Adulthood," *Journal of Adolescence* 18 (1995), 641–655.

CHAPTER 5

ACKNOWLEDGING YOUR ANGER

PHASE I: UNCOVERING YOUR ANGER

How have you avoided dealing with your anger?

Have you faced your anger?

The first phase in the forgiveness process involves uncovering anger. You can't begin to forgive until you have discovered the nature and depth of your anger. Anger can compromise your life. In this phase you need to examine, as honestly as possible, the amount of hurt you harbor as a result of the injustice.

Phase 1 of the forgiveness process presents you with a series of questions about anger and other emotions. For some of you, these may seem silly, because anger is all you are able to feel at the moment. But even if this is the case, you may be aware of only a part of your feelings. Your anger may be blocking out other feelings such as shame and guilt. On the other hand, you may be so afraid of your anger that you have not allowed yourself to feel at all. The guideposts are designed to help you begin dealing with the anger.

There is no one correct way to respond to these questions. One way to approach the process might be to read through the entire chapter first without making journal entries to get a feel for the kind of questions I am posing. Then go back to each section and answer the questions in your journal. Also, if after you have given serious consideration to a particular section its questions are not relevant to your situation, feel free to skip it and proceed to another section.

Take your time. You might want to focus on just one section a day. Although there is nothing wrong with making journal entries for two or more sections in a day, please pace yourself. Some people have a tendency to drive at the journal writing for the first day or two. After all, you've finally decided to face your emotional pain head on. Yet, approaching the writing is somewhat like starting a new physical exercise routine. Early enthusiasm can lead to stiff and sore muscles, diminishing the joy of the task. Try to ease into the writing as you would a new exercise regimen.

As you read, you will encounter different people in this and later chapters who tell their own stories about unfair treatment and their own recovery from it. The vast majority of these brave souls wrote down their stories for me as part of our research at the university. I include their stories, with their permission, so you can see the kinds of entries they made. You may gain some helpful insights for yourself from how others have encountered forgiveness.

Now, let us consider the first question.

HOW HAVE YOU AVOIDED DEALING WITH YOUR ANGER?

Common Defense Mechanisms

Defense mechanisms are shields that the mind constructs to protect itself against feelings such as fear or anxiety. Pain hurts. Because most people don't enjoy feeling pain, they try to avoid it. Psychologists have discovered that people use denial, suppression, regression, displacement, and identification with the aggressor to deal with feelings they are afraid to face.

DENIAL. Denial involves convincing yourself that nothing bad actually happened. Denial can temporarily protect you from shock or even despair. It allows you to rally your psychological resources before confronting the trouble. Temporary denial can be healthy, but pretending that nothing happened when something has or that you haven't been hurt when you have is unhealthy.

Trudy, 35 and the mother of three young children, adored her father when she was a child. He constantly praised her achievements and sacrificed to see to it that she had fashionable clothes and the best educational opportunities. But Trudy's father also engaged in inappropriate behavior toward her. When she was 8, he refused to put a lock on the bathroom door and frequently came into the bathroom when she was bathing. He touched her inappropriately on a number of occasions. Trudy tried to avoid giving her father these opportunities, but at the same time she convinced herself that she was just imagining that her father was showing an unacceptable sexual interest in her. She denied that his behavior was wrong.

As she grew up, she refused to acknowledge the pain that his behavior caused her. She frequently found herself crying hysterically for no reason. Trudy was 30 before she was able to admit what her father had done, because she loved him and did not want to lose the support she received from him. It wasn't until she faced how much this behavior hurt her that she was able to forgive him. After she forgave him, she stopped crying "for no reason."

Sometimes we deny because we do not wish to confront the person who has hurt us. Maria, 22 and a waitress, was in a relationship with a cocaine addict who was stealing money from her to support his habit.[1] Maria was afraid of facing her anger and the injustice because acknowledging both would require action that Maria was unwilling to take:

> I experienced denial of how much it hurt me. I explained it away by saying it was because of a drug addiction. I thought that if I admitted how much it hurt me, I would have to let him go because I would lose respect for him.

David, middle-aged, slightly balding, and a bit overweight, leans over his graphic design work. He is in a wheelchair as he relates his story for a monthly magazine. Working out of his home 10 years ago, he encountered a crazed customer who insisted that David had somehow "ripped him off." The customer stormed off, and David thought that the threatening showdown was over. Alone in his living room, he looked up from his work, and there was the disgruntled customer, now a gun-wielding madman, who confronted, shot, and paralyzed the helpless freelancer.

In his attempt to recover from the paralysis, David ignored his wrath toward the gunman. He was not the kind of person who was revengeful or even deeply angry, he told himself. As he tried to live a denying life from his wheelchair, failing to see the warning signals of his own despair, David eventually became depressed, alienating his own family. His wife left him. In anger and alone, he sometimes swirled his wheelchair around the darkened living room, perhaps hoping to hit those who were burning in his imagination and memory. Bitterness became his companion, until a friend boldly pointed out that he was wallowing in self-pity. The confrontation served, in part, to break the denial.[2] "I needed to get outside of myself," he realized. Over time, he recalls, "I began investing time and love in other people's lives."[3]

SUPPRESSION. Denial entails convincing yourself that nothing happened; suppression involves pushing thoughts about the event from consciousness. Those who use suppression to deal with injustice and pain try to distract themselves. Suppression prevents healing.

Mary Ann suppressed her anger toward her husband Brendan. During the day, she would escape into the fantasy world of soap operas, but at night she worried as the hours rolled by and he still wasn't home. Her anger grew until she was on the verge of hysteria. When Brendan walked through the door drunk, she said nothing. On weekends she pushed the bad thoughts out of her head and acted as though everything were perfect. It was not until she faced his unfairness and her own emotional pain that Mary Ann was able to overcome her anger and forgive.

REPRESSION. Sometimes an event is so traumatic that the injured person will thoroughly repress all memory of it. This kind of selective amnesia is more likely to occur if the victim is a child. Some women who were sexually abused as children repress all memories of it for years or even decades.[4]

There has been substantial debate over the question of repressed memory. It may be that certain therapists who were themselves sexually abused as children have assumed that women showing certain symptoms of dysfunction are doing so because they have repressed the memory of childhood sexual abuse. These therapists appear to have encouraged—some would say "pressured" —their clients to "remember" incidents that may or may not have taken place.[5] A few notorious cases of false accusation have created confusion over whether people can actually forget traumatic incidents or whether, years later, they simply make up what never happened. Evidence shows that such repression does exist, but each case needs to be looked at carefully.

How do you know if you are repressing the memory of a

terrible trauma? If you are irrationally and absolutely terrified of some location or activity, or if you hate someone for no apparent cause, you may want to consider the possibility that you have repressed a traumatic memory and discuss the matter with a qualified therapist. Although you can't forgive what you don't remember, if you do remember something, you can forgive. It is possible that the forgiveness process will help you separate the false memories from the real ones.

DISPLACEMENT. Displacement occurs when people transfer angry feelings from the person who has hurt them to someone else. For example, a man holds onto anger against his mother because, when he was a child, she was unreasonably controlling. He now is temperamental toward his wife. Every time she makes the smallest suggestion, he accuses her of trying to control him. The wife is angry at her husband but afraid that he will leave her if she shows anger, so she tries to control her son. When he follows his father's example and rebels against her control, she displaces the anger she feels toward her husband onto her son. The son, in turn, displaces his anger against his mother onto his younger brother. Displacement allows anger to be transferred from one generation to the next.

Chad, 26 and a graphic designer for a small company and an art education major at the university, relates a classic case of displacement toward his father Stanley. Three years ago, his mother Harriet died of cancer. Two years ago his father, with whom Chad still lived, revealed the secrets that Harriet had been married previously and that she had numerous affairs while married to him. Throughout their marriage, Stanley and Harriet had six children in between the breakups and threats by Harriet that she would abandon the family. At the time he heard these revelations, Chad was recovering from a nasty flu, which only intensified his displacement. He recalls

From that day on, I hated my mom. I began calling my mom names such as "pig" and such. My Dad didn't like it much, but I kept saying all these things about my mom. I liked it that he was getting angry. I kept doing it. I wanted him to be mad. I began telling him how foolish he was for thinking he needed her. I never felt guilty for anything I said that day.

In later chapters we follow Chad's progression toward forgiveness.

Kristy Ashleman, a university graduate student, assessed the relationship between levels of forgiveness and family functioning. She studied 30 divorced or permanently separated women and 30 of their children ages 10 to 13, one from the family of each woman. She found that

- The more that the mother forgave her former spouse, the less she used harsh or negative behaviors toward the children when disciplining them.
- The mothers who forgave the least seemed to displace their anger onto the children through harsh parenting.[6]

REGRESSION. Regression involves engaging in behavior that is considered understandable in a child but is inappropriate for an adult. Children can also regress to earlier stages of development as a way of dealing with anger. The adult who seeks to be continually nurtured but who refuses to nurture others may be showing regression. Adult temper tantrums are another form of regression. If one acts like a child, then one may end up solving the problem as a child would. A person who uses regression to deal with pain does not deny the hurtful reality but avoids making mature decisions about how to deal with that pain.

Lawrence, 32 and an executive, was known for his hard work and mature attitude at the office, but behind closed doors at home, he flew into a rage whenever his wife Martha or their two children did not behave in ways he wanted. Once, when Martha confronted him that he was not doing enough around the house to help her or the children, he ripped the toaster out of the wall socket, flung it to the floor, breaking it, and then stormed out of the room. His temper tantrum mirrored the ones he had as a child, when we was coddled and spoiled by his parents. Lawrence eventually had to acknowledge his narcissistic tendencies, which helped ease the regressive behavior that was tearing his family apart.

IDENTIFICATION WITH THE AGGRESSOR. A victim identifies with the aggressor by imitating the behavior of the abuser. This destructive form of handling anger is sometimes observed in men who have been abused as boys. The boy who is beaten becomes a bully in school or abuses his girlfriend or wife. Men who sexually molest children were themselves often repeatedly sexually molested as children. Abusers frequently pick out children to abuse who are the same age as they were when they were first abused.

✎ **Journal Entry**

- Have you been using a defense mechanism to deal with the hurtful event? In your journal, discuss how you tried to distance yourself from the anger, hurt, and anxiety. We tend to fall back on the defenses we've used previously. So, if you can identify your primary defense, you may be able to gauge when you are starting to use it.
- Are you currently using a defense mechanism to prevent yourself from confronting injustice? Why do you think so?
- Does your use of a defense mechanism actually hurt you? Make a list of the possible ways in which the defense has gotten in the way of your emotional healing.
- Are others adversely affected by what you do? Again, try to

make a list of the people who have been hurt and specifically how they are hurt by your pattern of anger or defense.

HAVE YOU FACED YOUR ANGER?

In this phase you only have to identify the ways in which you are using defense mechanisms to avoid facing injustice and your anger. You don't have to change these behaviors. These behaviors are habits that you have learned and practiced. These are the walls you have spent years building. Because you built them to protect yourself from anger and injustice, you can't dismantle them until you have dealt with the anger and injustice.

What you need to do at this point is look over the walls and face your anger and the injustice. Look at the ways anger has harmed you. Look at all you have deprived yourself of to hold onto your anger.

Anger can vary in intensity and duration. When it is deep and long lasting, anger can make us miserable. How deep is your anger? How long have you been living with it?

Carol, 32 and a homemaker who had a wide circle of friends through her neighborhood and civic involvement, had just given birth to a third son. To her friends, she had the ideal marriage to Elliot, a handsome, responsible husband who was an excellent provider. He willingly supported all of her helpful activities within the community. Yet, as the months progressed, he became increasingly resentful of her fatigue and time spent with the baby. Her husband grew increasingly unsupportive of her, eventually abandoning the family and engaging in an extramarital affair. As if that weren't terrible enough, his sexual adventure led to a tryst at a nearby lake, where he accidentally drowned. Carol was caught in an emotional firestorm. At first she had to struggle just to be aware of her anger. Only later could she confront that anger so that it slowly left her.

I was immediately thrown into a state of shock, denial, anger, and beyond all, shame. I had to take sleeping pills just to make it through the night that first couple of weeks because of the tremendous gut-wrenching, sick, heavy feeling in the pit of my stomach. I couldn't eat or sleep.

Carol was traumatized by a tragedy. Other people suffer from a pattern of anger that can be traced back to childhood experiences. Jerrod, 35 and a lawyer with a friendly but somewhat sad countenance, found that he was harboring resentment toward his mother because she deprived him of love and affection. He also resented his brother, who received what Jerrod considered to be unmerited maternal love and affection:

Although I cannot say I hated my mother, I think I very clearly resented her. This, combined with other things that occurred in my childhood, made me believe that I could never please my mother, that she took no real pride in me or my accomplishments. I felt many times that I had done things that . . . deserved special recognition, but my mother just ignored, disregarded, or minimized. Although I would not classify myself as a difficult adolescent, my mother and I argued more and more, and I always felt that she tried to force me into a mold, always asking why I wasn't like my older brother. The resentment extended to my older brother, who I began to feel took advantage of his position in the family and my mother's affection and ignored me unless it was to his advantage.

✎ Journal Entry

Once you acknowledge your anger, you need to evaluate it rationally. As you write, please consider talking over your insights with your forgiveness companion. Remember, becoming aware of your anger is difficult work. Share your burden with your confidant.

- Is your anger focused on a single recent event, a pattern of events, or a childhood trauma? In your journal, address the variety of people and circumstances that anger you. Try to aim for the gist of your anger here, not minute details, because this could become a laborious task.

- Even if you listed many people and multiple causes of anger, these can form the basis for more forgiveness once you've worked through forgiving the one particular person. Now focus on the one person whom you began to describe in Chapter 4. Please read what you said about the one who will be the focus here. Is there anything you'd like to add in the journal about this person at this time?

- Would you describe your anger toward this person and the one hurtful event on which you are focusing as mild annoyance, implacable hatred, or somewhere in between? Please rate your anger on a 1 to 10 scale, with 1 being "not angry at all" to 10 being "as angry as I can possibly be." When you are ready, please enter this number in your journal. You may wish to highlight this rating by circling it, for example, so that it is easier to find in the future. As you progress through the forgiveness process, I will occasionally ask you to again rate your anger on the same scale and compare the latest entry with this first one.

- How long have you been angry or resentful over this particular matter? This is part of your story, the context in which you were hurt. Has the anger deepened or eased across time?

- Write down the words that come to mind as you reflect on the person and the day in which the unfairness occurred. Try to examine patterns of thought as expressed in the writing. What words seem to emerge frequently?

- Are you angry at someone who reminds you of someone who hurt you a long time ago? Who is this other person or these other people? Have they hurt you, or are you displacing your anger? Sometimes it is helpful to carry on a written dialogue with yourself when you are unsure of the answer. One side is your rational self; the other is your angry, displacing self. Try this exercise in your journal to see if displacement emerges as you write the dialogue.

- Is your anger childish, or are your reactions immature? Why do you say this? What is your evidence for this?
- Does your anger make you feel anxious or afraid? Spend some time recording your feelings that emerge from the anger. What are these feelings like? When do you tend to feel this way?

Remember that anger can be healthy. Anger can motivate us to take action, to right wrongs, to stand up and face problems, to fight for our self-esteem. When you are wronged or see some injustice, you have a right to be angry. Anger becomes a problem when, instead of taking action, you let your anger settle into an ongoing resentment. It is problematic when you seek revenge rather than justice. It also is problematic when you are too afraid to act and fall into denial, suppression, or repression.

- As one step in confronting your anger, please take the time to review what you've written in your journal from the entries in Chapters 4 and 5. Write a one- to two-page letter to the person, *one that you do not send.* Try to express succinctly to the person the learning that you have gained so far. Let the person know why you are angry, how angry you are, and the struggles you've endured because of the unfairness.

If you feel that anger is controlling you, if resentment borne out of another's unfairness is causing self-destructive behavior, then you need to use the forgiveness process. If you feel out-of-control because of the anger, it is important to talk with your companion on this journey. Try to set aside time each week to meet and discuss your progress toward emotional healing. Let him or her help you assess the depth of your emotional pain. Consider seeking professional help if your emotions are deep and long lasting and you believe that such help is warranted.

Regardless of how you are reacting, I'd like you to put the book down now for a while. Take a rest from the work. You can continue once you feel refreshed, perhaps tomorrow or even the day after that. Be sure to acknowledge your achievement that you have begun to take action.

ENDNOTES

1. This is the first verbatim entry from our research at the university. All names have been changed to protect the person's identity.
2. D. V. Kiel, "I'm Learning How to Forgive," *Decisions* (February, 1986), 12–13.
3. Ibid, p. 13.
4. D. L. Eastin, "The Treatment of Female Incest Survivors by Psychological Forgiveness Processes" (Madison: University of Wisconsin, 1989) p. 233.
5. For a discussion of these controversial cases, see L. V. Cheney, *Telling the Truth* (New York: Touchstone Books, 1995), especially pp. 163–174.
6. K. A. Ashleman, "Forgiveness as a Resiliency Factor in Divorced or Permanently Separated Families" (Madison: University of Wisconsin, 1997).

CHAPTER 6

CONFRONTING THE DEPTH OF YOUR ANGER

PHASE I—UNCOVERING YOUR ANGER

Are you afraid to expose your shame or guilt?
Has your anger affected your health?
Have you been obsessed about the injury or the offender?
Do you compare your situation with that of the offender?
Has the injury caused a permanent change in your life?
Has the injury changed your worldview?

Having begun the journey of forgiveness, you may feel that you've done enough work to last a lifetime. This is a normal reaction, because forgiveness is difficult, tender territory. It is important to discern ways in which anger has complicated your life. Such insight may help motivate you to forgive, and forgiveness may be a key to your well-being.

ARE YOU AFRAID TO EXPOSE YOUR SHAME AND GUILT?

Victims can feel ashamed and guilty because they have been victimized. They are afraid that people will blame them. They may believe that they are, in part, responsible for their own victimization.

Shame

People who divorce may feel that old "friends" are now whispering about them, wondering "What did he or she do to cause the divorce? Isn't it a shame?" Victims of sexual abuse sometimes believe that people see them as "damaged goods." People who have been fired feel that co-workers are blaming them for incompetence. John Patton, a pastoral counselor, believes that this kind of shame is a common complication to the forgiveness journey.[1]

When the Chicago newspapers reported her husband Elliot's death and the circumstances surrounding it, Carol was overwhelmed with feelings of shame. She felt like taking the children and running away.

At age 43, Michael, a construction worker in a large city, seems older than his years because of the burdens of anger he has carried for so long. He can still recall vividly the day 26 years ago when his father falsely accused him of using drugs. When Michael insisted on his innocence, his father turned Michael toward the sun so that his vision was obscured, then bashed him across the head. As he lay defenseless on the ground, Michael was filled with shame. He felt that if he had been a man, he would have stood up against his father's violence. Although this was not the only time Michael had suffered at his father's hands, this incident encapsulated a history of abuse. For almost 30 years Michael allowed his life to be controlled by feelings of anger and shame.

Rose, a 19-year-old college student whose parents immigrated from Mexico, was traumatized when her alcoholic father threw a knife at her, hitting her in the chest. Because the knife hit handle first, she was not seriously physically injured, yet the incident left her emotionally scarred. Like many abused children, Rose blamed herself for the abuse:

This experience shattered my self-confidence. . . . I felt that my father was saying I was bad and unworthy. . . . I distanced myself from my friends and was embarrassed about my situation. I had a sense of shame which I showed by walking with my head down. Later in life I denied that it bothered me, but now I can see that it affected me greatly.

Cindy, a 25-year-old who works with handicapped children, was deeply shamed by her live-in partner Adam. After a serious argument with him, Cindy left for the afternoon and sought refuge at a friend's house. Adam, however, stormed into the house and demanded to speak with her. "This is not a good time to talk," she insisted. He then threw a glass against a wall. As she recalls,

> He then started pushing me around the room, and I fell over a chair. He forced me to stay on the ground while he squeezed my forearms and told me we were going to talk. I managed to get him off to one side and said, "Let's go outside." When we got to the door, I told him to go on out because I had to grab something. Then I locked the door.

She and her friend called the police, who came immediately. Cindy had to endure the shame of such a fight in front of her best friend and then reporting it to the police, with neighbors watching and wondering.

In his studies of shame, psychologist Gershen Kaufman identifies three common reactions people experience when shamed.[2]

1. *Feeling rage and contempt for the one who shamed them.* The anger associated with shame is added to the anger one feels over the original offense. Carol had been angry at her husband, and now she was also angry at the newspaper reporters for publicly revealing her shame.

2. *Striving for power.* The shamed person tries to dominate others to protect himself or herself from further shame. The boy

who is continually shamed by his father might become a bully at school.

3. *Disproportionately blaming the offender.* The offender is seen as the cause of all the troubles the person faces. The injured party may think "If only this hadn't happened, I'd be happier, more successful, more fulfilled in life."

✎ Journal Entry

Do you have shame? Write a few paragraphs or perhaps a page in your journal in which you tell your story of shame. As you did with anger, after you have written your entry and read it, please rate on a scale of 1 to 10 the amount of shame you believe you have. Let 1 stand for "no shame at all" and 10 stand for "an extreme amount of shame."

What, exactly, is the cause of the shame? In your opinion, are people truly judging you badly, or are you speculating about this? Write a paragraph describing what you think others are saying or thinking about you.

Is your pride getting in the way of accurate perceptions, or are you accurately perceiving others' views of you? Consider Dr. Kaufman's three common reactions to shame. Do any of them describe your current reactions? How are you responding to yourself and others, given the amount of shame you have?

Because shame can be a barrier to facing anger and forgiving, if you have much shame (say, an 8, 9, or 10 on the scale), you need to expose your shame to the light of day by telling one person the whole story. You need to hear yourself telling all the details and discover that no matter how embarrassing the situation, you are still lovable. If the story is really terrible, you may want to choose a professional, whether a therapist or a member of the clergy, with whom you can reveal your shame, because they are specially trained to deal with big secrets. Catholic priests, for example, must be willing to die rather than reveal a secret that they have heard in the confessional.

Perhaps you can start sharing details of your experience with your forgiveness companion. If your degree of emotional pain is so intense that you think professional help is necessary, then together discuss the appropriate person. Review your story before you see another person so that you have the necessary detail to aid his or her guidance.

Guilt

Shame is the fear of what others will think when they find out what has happened to us. Guilt is how we feel about ourselves when we realize that we have violated our own standards of right and wrong. When we forgive, sometimes we have acted as an offender as we lash out at the other person. Sometimes we act so insensitively toward the other that we are left with feelings of guilt because we behaved wrongly.

We must be careful to distinguish between real guilt and false guilt. One way to distinguish between them is how they make us feel. Real guilt often makes us feel angry. The pain and humiliation of realizing that we have really hurt another person is often so overwhelming that we try to throw off the pain by blaming someone else. Most people can endure only a few seconds of real guilt.

False guilt is often a reaction to anger toward someone we need or love. We are hurt and angry when a person we love hurts us, but we are also afraid that our anger will provoke additional injury. We are afraid of our anger, so we turn our anger on ourselves and feel guilty. This false guilt may seem easier to deal with at the time than real anger.

Suzanne Freedman, a professor at the University of Northern

Iowa, points out that survivors of abuse and violence frequently experience feelings of guilt.[3] Incest survivors, for example, may convince themselves that the experience was their fault because they didn't resist or tell. They may even come to believe that they were willing participants. A survivor may have wanted her father's attention. Her father may have told her that it was her fault. In her mind she may have known that something was wrong but was unable to protect herself. According to Dr. Freedman, survivors need to realize that an offender's betraying act was his or hers alone.

Julie felt guilty over being sexually abused by her brother. She had known what they were doing was wrong, but in their dysfunctional family, any affection, no matter how inappropriate, was better than nothing. After Julie forgave her brother, she was able to look at the situation as an adult. Her counselor asked her to look at her own 8-year-old daughter: "Do you think that this child should be expected to resist her older and stronger brother?" Julie had to admit that she would never consider a child morally responsible for being the victim of abuse.

✎ Journal Entry

In your journal, write down the question "Am I guilty of some wrongdoing toward the person who hurt me?" On the left side of the page, please write down instances in which you may have acted unfairly. Opposite each entry on the right side, please answer the assertion that you were unfair. Try to show how you, in fact, were acting reasonably under the circumstances. In those situations in which you have no defense for your behavior, acknowledge that in writing. Once finished, examine those instances in which you had no defense. These may be your areas of guilt.

Then rate on a scale of 1 to 10 how offensive your behavior

was in each instance you were unfair, with 1 being "very mildly offensive" and 10 being "extremely offensive." The number of times you were unfair is an indication of the quantity of inappropriate behaviors in which you engaged. The ratings will give you an indication of the quality of your unfairness, which may be even more of an indicator of guilt than quantity. For example, one incident of unfairness that rates a 10 may be more guilt-inducing than five very mild offenses toward the other person. Take some time to sort out your pattern of wrongdoing, if any, and the amount and intensity of the patterns.

If you believe that you are genuinely guilty, then you might consider confessing the nature of your wrong behavior to the offended person. If he or she is unavailable, talking to a support person may prove helpful. Making amends, where this is possible, should also be considered. However, even if you acted wrongly toward the person, this does not exonerate him or her from the wrongdoing toward you. In other words, you do not cancel your act of forgiving just because you, too, were unfair.

HAS ANGER AFFECTED YOUR HEALTH?

Many people find that angry feelings compromise their health. Anger requires energy, and if all of your energy is going to thinking about the offense and the offender, there may be none left over for just living. Anger affects the levels of adrenaline in your body, and this in turn affects every organ. Anger can make you ill. It can make you sick to your stomach, give you a headache, or make you tense.

Patti, 28 and a freelance writer, was struggling to keep her marriage together and her children healthy. It was not easy. Her husband seemed increasingly indifferent and the children's interactions with one another were becoming more and more strident as tensions in the home swelled. Her anger and resentment drained her energy to the point that she was unable to work for more than 30 minutes without feeling exhausted. She dragged herself out of bed in the morning, took naps during the day, and then couldn't sleep at night. She sought medical help for chronic fatigue, but the tests revealed nothing. Blood tests don't discover resentment. She changed her diet, took up drinking coffee, then gave up coffee, but nothing worked. Her anger simmered while her health faltered.

Anthony, 35 and a public school teacher, was denied a promotion he thought that he deserved:

> What was unusual, now that I think back, is that I tried to simply let out my anger. Especially upon going to bed for the night, I would think about the principal and what happened. I'd get angry, thinking this was a good thing to do. You know, get it off my chest. Instead of my anger lessening, my bedtime ritual became just that—a ritual in which this principal would habitually be in my thoughts at bedtime. Anger at this time of day became regular, and the anger built up over time rather than lessened. It got to the point that I would fantasize about punching him out. It felt good for awhile, but I didn't realize that this increased my anger all the more.

✎ Journal Entry

Reflect in your journal on these questions:

- How much of your energy is devoted to defense mechanisms or negative thinking? How much is left for living?
- Suppose that you have 10 units of energy each day to help you do all that you must. How many of those units of energy are used in "stewing" about the person you are considering forgiving?
- Are you tired of being tired?

HAVE YOU BEEN OBSESSED WITH THE INJURY OR THE OFFENDER?

Some people can't seem to get the injury or the offender out of their minds. They find that they dream about or think about the person without even meaning to do so.

Carol's husband would not have died if he had not been involved in an adulterous affair. The injustice was compounded by the fact that he left her alone with a newborn and two older children. Even though some friends encouraged Carol to consider herself lucky to be rid of an unfaithful husband, Carol was not rid of Elliot. The memory of the offense was her constant companion. During the day and at night she suffered from a recurring nightmare:

> I think everyone who goes through a trauma replays the event just to make sense of it. Whenever I heard sirens, it would set off the memory of that day. I also had a recurring dream for about three years after Elliot's death. I had left home in Illinois with the kids, because nobody had ever found Elliot dead or alive. In the dream, I moved to a cabin in Northern Wisconsin amidst forests and rolling hills. He shows up one day, driving toward the house on the dusty drive, in an old Ford pick-up. He stops and demands to see the kids and takes them all with him. I end up with no one. I've lost all that ever mattered to me. I'd always wake up crying but then relieved that the kids were still with me and asleep in the house.

Michael, who had been falsely accused of using drugs and beaten by his father, also experienced frightening nightmares:

> I did have extremely violent nightmares in which I shot people, beat them. . . . Very often a storm of bullets would be fired at me, people would attack, but never was I hurt. These dream sequences lasted for about 22 years.

Decades of this kind of pain is tragic, but it is not rare. When therapist Judith Wallerstein began her study of families going through divorce, she wanted to find out how long it took for them to heal. At the end of five years, she found that most hadn't healed, so she extended the study to 10 years and then to 15. By then the children were grown and starting life on their own, and yet for many the pain and anger were still very real and debilitating.

Have you been thinking over and over about the event? Do you replay the event when you wake up in the morning, while in the car, while at work, while you are trying to go to sleep, in your dreams? Do you bring the subject up in conversation? Have you gone a whole day without thinking about it once? If not, you may be obsessing over the injury.

✎ Journal Entry

To see the pattern of your thoughts, keep the journal readily available for one day this week. Try to be aware that day of each time the person or the event settles into your mind. Make a note of this in the journal. Write down the time of day the thought occurred, what you were doing, and the nature of the thought. End the entries the next morning, just in case you had a dream that should be entered. Then examine the patterns in three ways:

- Were you engaged in particular activities when you thought about the person and the event? If so, are they the kinds of activities you might have shared with the person? In other words, sometimes places and activities are associated with particular people. Is this true in your case? If you find that you begin thinking about the person in certain situations, you might want to practice forgiveness in these very same situations once we introduce the forgiveness exercises in the coming chapters.

- What is the nature of the thoughts? Are they aggressive thoughts in which you condemn the person? Are they simply thoughts of you being together? Try to get a sense of the quality of the thoughts and images. The more aggressive the thought, the more forgiveness may be needed.

- How many times did you enter something in the journal that day? This will give you some indication of the frequency of thinking about the person compared with how often you think of other things. Thinking a lot may be related to any depleted energy you may be experiencing. Forgiving the person may quiet the thoughts and restore energy.

DO YOU COMPARE YOUR SITUATION WITH THAT OF THE OFFENDER?

If the offender has prospered while you have suffered, this disparity in circumstance may become another cause of anger. This is common when the pain continues for a long time. David sat paralyzed in his wheelchair, day after day, comparing his state to that of the gunman, who was walking. David became psychologically depressed as he thought how he was sentenced to life imprisonment in his chair while the gunman was free. Such comparisons create new reasons to be angry.

Although comparison can be depressing, it can also be a positive step. David Eastin and Suzanne Freedman, both of whom did their doctoral research at the University of Wisconsin–Madison, point out that comparing yourself with the one who hurt you is a positive step, because the forgiveness process requires focusing on the offender.[4] You may discover that the offender is not as well off as you may imagine. He or she may be afraid of being found out or of losing his or her self-respect. The offender may be suffering, even if it is not apparent.

At the same time, you may wish to examine your own thoughts about yourself. Sometimes we view the injury accurately but exaggerate or distort the consequences. Bitterness can affect our thinking. Are any of your thoughts about your situation exaggerated? Are you saying "Because this happened, I will never be happy again"? Are you feeling that you are worthless because of what happened? Even if we have been injured, we are free to make choices. If we have allowed the injury or anger at the offender to control our lives, we—and not the offender—are responsible for that choice. If we are responsible, we can change.

✎ Journal Entry

In your journal, please reflect on the comparisons you may be making between you and the one you wish to forgive. State one of his or her advantages and one of your disadvantages. Then, challenge the perception to see if it is true. Keep up this pattern until you have examined most or all of the ways in which you feel that the other is now better off than you.

Next, take some time to see those areas in which he or she is worse off than you because of what he or she did. I will not ask you at this point to do anything special with this knowledge. Just knowing about it is sufficient for now.

HAS THE INJURY CAUSED A PERMANENT CHANGE IN YOUR LIFE?

David was permanently disabled by his injury. Carol could not bring her husband back or wipe out what he had done. Michael couldn't get his childhood back. The greater the loss, the more difficult forgiving may be. On the other hand, sometimes the pain is so terrible that the person is driven to find release and may be willing to consider anything that promises to help—even for-giveness.

Sometimes the fact that the injury is going to have permanent consequences is not initially apparent. Doctors may hold out hope for recovery when the injury is physical. When the injured party realizes that the injury is permanent (such as death or some phys-ical loss), the injured party may become angry all over again. In such cases, the injured party, who may have initially forgiven, may have to repeat the forgiveness process.

Therapist Henry Close described a client who was sexually assaulted and refused to forgive because she had a strong need to see herself as a virgin. As long as she refused to face what hap-pened, she was unable to forgive and therefore was caught up in self-destructive anger. Only when she faced the fact that she was no longer technically a virgin and integrated this into her view of herself was she able to forgive and be free.[5]

Sometimes people have to go through a grieving process to deal with a permanent loss. Those who try to forgive before they have accepted and grieved permanent losses may find that they have to forgive again.

✎ Journal Entry

In your journal, please reflect on the issues here. If there are any permanent losses for you, please list one and describe how it has affected you. You may need to just let out the feeling, knowing that you are moving toward the constructive activity of forgiving. Then, list another loss and follow a similar writing pattern. As you write, you may not feel at all like forgiving under these circum-stances, but keep in mind that such a reaction is normal. Grieving over loss is necessary if you eventually are to forgive and experi-ence emotional release.

HAS THE INJURY CHANGED YOUR WORLDVIEW?

When we are deeply injured, our view of the world can sometimes change. Injustice can cause people who were optimistic and trusting to become cynical and embittered.

Michael reacted to his father's violence by becoming distrustful of others. He rejected religion and other institutions as a way of repudiating his father, who was a police officer with religious beliefs:

> I was aware at this time of trusting no one. I was wary, defensive, and self-protective. I also tried to eliminate any aspect of dependency on other people. I had no interest in religion or any group, as none had offered any protection from my father's abuse. I also got rid of God in my worldview, except as a crutch used by others.

Cindy, who was treated unfairly by her partner at her best friend's home, generalized her anger to all men:

> After the relationship ended, I was very angry and resentful. These feelings were extended to other men for about a year. This made me think that maybe I would never be able to trust or accept a man into my life again. This realization was very upsetting. Prior to the hurt, I had a worldview that life was good, and I was doing well in my life. Following the hurt, my view changed drastically at first. The first year I was down on the whole world. No one was as good as they seemed. The world was not great. But later I came to realize that my world just got messed up for awhile, but it really was pretty great, and I was able to get my original perspective back.

Felicia was continually belittled by her mother. She reacted by adopting her mother's rigid, critical worldview. At age 53, she generally disliked and mistrusted people:

I was intolerant of weaknesses in myself and others. Now, as I finish working through my emotional recovery, I feel more confident and am making friends. When things "go wrong" it is no longer a major crisis. I'm learning to say, "Oh well, things happen. Tomorrow will be better." I used to say, "I can't do anything right; I'm hopeless!" I used to fall apart and take it personally if my car had a flat tire!

Felicia's initial worldview, following the constant criticism from her mother, was to imitate her mother's intolerance. As she forgave, she softened and came to see that people make mistakes. She realized that she doesn't have to control other people's behavior and tries to be tolerant when others do not conform to her expectations.

After giving birth to her third child and after losing her husband, Carol began to search for a new worldview. Eventually her search led her to a Christian church, where she felt her questions were answered and her suffering understood and accepted. The love she found there helped her overcome her feelings of shame.

Those who have been injured have to deal with the existence of evil in the world, not as a philosophical problem but as a lived reality. Social work professor Beverly Flanigan has observed how those experiencing injustice tend to alter their "just-world" view to accommodate instances of unfairness into their philosophy.[6] Some people react to injustice by trying to find a spiritual answer, others reject the spiritual. Some people get angry with God. Some are terrified when they realize that there are things they can't control. In some cases, the new worldview is more realistic, but in other cases, the person embraces a generalized bitterness toward many or even most people. Forgiveness can be instrumental in reversing a worldview that embraces bitterness and pushes goodness aside.

✎ Journal Entry

Before entering into the work of actually forgiving, write an essay describing your worldview before the hurtful event and how it has changed following the event. Compare and contrast where you've been and where you are now on such questions as

- What are people in general like?
- Who am I?
- How do I change for the good?
- Why am I here? What is the purpose of life?
- Why is there suffering in the world? How is suffering eased?
- What do I believe about how the world operates and my place in it?
- Where do I go when I die?

Once completed, try to discern the changes from your past to your present. Has your worldview changed? Is it a more pessimistic or optimistic philosophy of life now? If more optimistic, has the experience of the hurt strengthened you? If more pessimistic, which I find is typical immediately following deep hurt, then you are experiencing yet another layer of pain from the injury. On the positive side, a pessimistic worldview is not a permanent change. As you forgive, you may find that your worldview once again changes, this time for the good.

Are you prepared now to consider forgiving the one who hurt you? Emotional pain is a great motivator for seeking solutions to problems. Consider answering the following questions in your journal.

- Is anger present when you think about the incident?
- Is your anger still intense months or years after the offense?

- Is anger making you sick and tired?
- Do you continually think about the offense and the offender?
- Do you believe the offense has changed your life for the worse?

Let us go further in the forgiveness process.

ENDNOTES

1. J. Patton, *Is Human Forgiveness Possible?* (Nashville, TN: Abingdon, 1985), pp. 39–64.
2. G. Kaufman, *Shame: The Power of Caring* (Cambridge, MA: Shenkman , 1980).
3. S. R. Freedman, "Forgiveness as an Educational Choice With Incest Survivors" (Madison: University of Wisconsin, 1994), pp. 217–219.
4. D. L. Eastin. "The Treatment of Female Incest Survivors by Psychological Forgiveness Processes" (Madison: University of Wisconsin, 1989); S. R. Freedman, "Forgiveness as an Educational Choice."
5. H. T. Close, "Forgiveness and Responsibility: A Case Study," *Pastoral Psychology* 21 (1970), 19–25.
6. B. Flanigan, *Forgiving the Unforgivable* (New York: Macmillan, 1992), p. 128.

CHAPTER 7

COMMITTING TO FORGIVE

PHASE 2—DECIDING TO FORGIVE

Decide that what you have been doing hasn't worked.
Be willing to begin the forgiveness process.
Decide to forgive.

In this chapter you will consider whether or not to forgive the person who hurt you. You will be asked for a *commitment* to forgive the person. As with any commitment, this one will challenge you to see the forgiveness process through to the end, including the hard work entailed in forgiving someone. Remember, however, that the work will ultimately free you.

DECIDE THAT WHAT YOU HAVE BEEN DOING HASN'T WORKED

Recall Michael's story, in which his father falsely accused him of drug use and then hit him. Michael's unpleasant dreams convinced him that how he was dealing with his anger wasn't working:

I repressed my feeling of betrayal toward my father for many years, but I remained plagued by difficult dreams. I believe I simply matured through these feelings in a rather slow fashion, though I had grown quite tired of having them for several years. I have always been a mostly cheerful, good-natured person who likes jokes, so the dreams seemed very out of place in my life. It didn't take a Freud to figure out where they came from.

Michael realized that in his dreams he was becoming like his father, a prospect that frightened him. Michael wanted to be the cheerful happy person that he had been as a child.

Deciding that you must change course involves a change of heart. Gloria, in her mid-30s and struggling to keep her relationship with her husband alive, explained to a counselor how she believed that the persistent sadness she was experiencing was related to sexual abuse by her father when she was a child. She ended her comments with the statement "I can never forgive him."

The counselor replied, "Yes, you can. Forgiveness involves a decision. You are free to make that decision and begin the process of forgiving him."

Gloria was stunned. It simply hadn't occurred to her that forgiveness was possible. The counselor pointed out that Gloria's current situation needed a solution. There was every reason to believe that forgiveness would change things for the better. The idea that she could forgive and that forgiveness would change things resonated with Gloria.

Carol, whose husband publicly cheated on her, experienced a change of heart when she joined an active Christian church. She was encouraged to be open about her suffering:

> With my commitment to this program and my growing love for Jesus, it became clear to me that I had to become honest with myself and my second husband. With the disclosure of the truth, doors opened for me. I could feel the burden fall. It wasn't so bad letting

others know of my secret, and I began to realize that Elliot's sin was no reflection upon me—he chose his behavior.

Hiding the pain and shame hadn't worked, but being open and sharing with others represented a change of heart. Even though Carol had not yet forgiven Elliot, her new worldview, coupled with a newly found honesty, began to show positive results.

Ask yourself honestly, Is what you have been doing working? Are you happy? Are you at peace? Are you optimistic? If not, isn't it time to try a different course? If revenge, anger, and bitterness are not making you happy, isn't it time to turn this whole thing around?

✎ Journal Entry

In your journal, describe your current emotional state regarding the person who hurt you. Let yourself know, as honestly as possible, your true feelings. List the solutions you have attempted in the past and an assessment of how effective those proposed solutions have been. Rate each solution that you previously had attempted on a scale of 1 to 10, with 1 being "a very ineffective solution for you" and 10 being "a great solution for you." Once finished, please look at the number of solutions you've tried and how effective they have been for you. Is it time for a change?

You can make a decision to move in a different direction. To do this you may also need to change your worldview. Does your worldview allow you to deal with injustice in a constructive, healthy way? Does your worldview make room for a compassionate approach to others? If you believe that people cannot or should not forgive, you may need to rethink that assumption.

We tend to develop our worldview from our past and current experiences. Sometimes there are inconsistencies between what we *have* believed and what we *want* to believe. Consider the case of Jorge, a middle-age executive who grew up in a family that religiously attended worship services but who considered revenge to be a virtue. His father had lived by one unchanging maxim, "Never forgive," and had taught his children that they had an obligation to hold a grudge. Jorge obediently attended religious services with his family, he prayed daily, but he never internalized his religion's teaching on the importance of forgiveness. He frequently expressed his absolute determination never to forgive his son-in-law for the failure of his daughter Alicia's marriage, although the couple themselves had made peace with one another and realized that they were both at fault.

Jorge was emotionally locked into anger. He ignored its effect on himself and others. Whenever the grandchildren came for a visit, he blanched whenever they mentioned their father. In all likelihood, the grandchildren were picking up the subtle message that the mention of their father's name led to anger and tension in their grandfather's house. This certainly is not the kind of message that Alicia wished to convey to her children.

Jorge was shocked when Alicia pointed out to him that the prayer he said every day included a requirement that he forgive those who had injured him. He responded angrily, "Who do you think you are, telling me I have to forgive!" To forgive, he would have had to be willing to reject his father's worldview, and he was not willing to do that. Alicia was not willing to spread hatred to her children. She, therefore, had the hard decision to make: Do I continue bringing the children to visit their grandfather, or do I preserve my former husband's and the children's father's good name? For now, she chose the latter and ended visits to the grandfather's house.

The theology professor Lewis Smedes writes, "Surrendering the right to revenge can be equated to surrendering the right to carry the weight of the world on your back." According to Dr.

Smedes, "Forgiveness offers the best hope of creating a new fairness out of past unfairness."[1] It is sad that some people refuse to let go of anger even though anger brings them only unhappiness and grief.

✎ Journal Entry

Consider writing another essay, this time for someone who is unfamiliar with your particular worldview. Explain to him or her what your philosophy or set of beliefs stands for. Try to let this uninformed listener truly understand your position. Tell the person why you hold to this view, why it is important to you, why it makes sense to you. As you do so, consider those particular points in your worldview that are getting in the way of your forgiving. Also remember those points that are of help to you in forgiving.

The purpose of this exercise is to have you understand your worldview so clearly that you can see the strengths and weaknesses of your belief system, discerning those beliefs you may need to change from those you need to keep. Reviewing the material on worldviews from Chapters 4 and 6 may be helpful to you here.

Remember that your worldview is what you really believe, which may not always be congruent with the teachings of the religion you espouse, with what society tells you is important, or with what close friends recommend. Try to explain to the person how compassion, patience, and understanding toward others play a part in your view.

BE WILLING TO BEGIN THE FORGIVENESS PROCESS

Once you are able to recognize the faulty beliefs and failed strategies you used in the past, you can look to the future and consider the possibility of a different course. If you choose forgiving as the way to solve your current problem, you will go down one path and reject other approaches. Those who have chosen this path have found freedom and peace. Although there are no guarantees, there is genuine hope that forgiveness will make a change in your life. Are you ready to take that chance?

Change can be scary. That is why at this point you are encouraged to consider a willingness to forgive before you make the decision to forgive. Those who have found freedom from compulsive and self-destructive behaviors through participation in 12-step programs will notice a similarity between this point and step 8: "Made a list of all persons we had harmed, and became willing to make amends to them all." This connection to the 12-step programs is accidental. We weren't thinking about the 12 steps when we came to see the importance of a point involving willingness to forgive. However, the fact that the highly successful 12-step program also calls for a moment when those following the steps ask themselves "Am I willing?" suggests that people have a need to pause before they take a serious step. Exploring your willingness can take a brief or a prolonged time.

Helen, 35 and a file clerk, did not earn enough money to make ends meet on her own salary. She continued to fume at her ex-husband for suddenly leaving her. Five years after he left, by her own admission, Helen was bitter and tired. When her friend Rebecca suggested forgiveness, she was overwhelmed with the difficulty of it all. As Helen saw it, she would have to abandon resentment (and bitterness), work on seeing her husband in a new light, feel something positive for him, and cease condemnation. It seemed too much. Then Rebecca asked, "Would you be willing to simply wait for awhile and think about forgiveness as a possibility somewhere down the road?" This, she thought, she could handle.

In the coming weeks, Helen spent time thinking about what forgiveness is and the costs to her of forgiving and not forgiving.

She examined for herself the differences among forgiving, condoning, excusing, and forgetting. She asked herself, "Am I willing to continue thinking about this?" She asked out loud to Rebecca, "Is forgiveness an option for me?" Rebecca waited patiently, knowing that the choice to accept or reject forgiveness was Helen's. In the end, Helen decided to try forgiveness.

Chad, whom you met earlier, was not willing to consider forgiveness as an option toward either his mother, who had many affairs while he was growing up, or his father, who told him of his mother's exploits when he was in his early 20s. Yet, when his brothers and sisters finally approached him, entering into deep discussions about forgiveness, he was willing to consider forgiving his father:

> Talking to my brothers and sisters definitely helped shape my choice for forgiveness. They were all for forgiveness. They even tried to get me to forgive my mom. I was so mad at them for making such a suggestion! There was no way I would ever forgive my mom. I did consider forgiving my dad, however, for dumping this news on us. I realized that he was trying to do what was best.

✎ Journal Entry

Are you willing to consider forgiveness? If so, it is time to review what, exactly, it is that you are considering. In your journal write a paragraph or two detailing what forgiveness is, what it is not, and what it is more than. Here give details. Please write your own definition of forgiveness without looking back at the information in Chapter 2. Try to capture the essence of the definition as well as some important points about what forgiveness is not and what it is more than.

Once you've completed this exercise, please read again the material in Chapter 2. As you read, jot down points in which you and I disagree. There are two forms of disagreement. In one, you may not have included something I did include only because you forgot to write it down. Or, you included something that I may simply have missed. In other words, from what you can tell, we are not disagreeing on a basic meaning of the word *forgiveness*. Let's call this type of disagreement *benign omission* to signify that we are not disagreeing on some ideological, philosophical, or theological level. A second area of disagreement is that I may have put something down and you deliberately avoided it because you consider the idea wrong. Let us call this kind of disagreement an *important difference*.

Let's start with your and my definitions. Where do we differ? Do we differ, as far as you can tell, because of some benign omission by one of us? If, for example, I said that forgiveness includes empathy and compassion toward the offending person and you left it out, do you wish now to include it in your definition? If so, please add it. This would be one example of a benign omission that is easily altered.

Now examine our definitions for important differences. Are there any? What is the nature of the difference? A typical important difference is in the challenge that you offer compassion, benevolence, and love toward the one who hurt you. You may reason that you do not feel like offering these, that you never will feel like offering these, and so they are not part of what forgiveness is. Please consider this challenge, if in fact we are disagreeing on this point: How you feel now may not be how you feel later. Also, your feelings need not be the driving force behind the definition. The meaning of forgiveness may exist independently of how you are feeling about forgiveness at any given time.

My point is this: If you disagree with me about any aspect of the definition of forgiveness, what is the primary source of our disagreement? I think that the primary source should be that you have an excellent argument about why I am incorrect in my definition. The primary source should not be that you simply don't prefer to think about forgiveness in the way it is presented. If you are frustrated about any disagreement over our definitions, please express that in the journal and try to discern the nature of the disagreement: a benign omission or an important difference.

When you are ready, please go over the material you've written about what forgiveness is not and what it is more than. Do we disagree anywhere? Are the differences the result of benign omission or an important difference? Are you willing to include those areas of benign omission, thus adding to your paragraphs about the meaning of forgiveness? If I have benign omissions, I hope that you will take the time to write me so that I might deepen my understanding of forgiveness.

If we have important differences, it is time to ask why again. Please work with the disagreements until you are satisfied that your definition is as accurate and complete as possible. I ask this because the exercises to follow in this and later chapters are directly based on the definition that I laid out in Chapter 2.

Once the definition is clear for you, I urge you to take the time to write it again in the journal. Now, read that definition with our current question in mind: Are you willing to consider forgiveness as an option? You now should have a clear idea about what it is that you are considering. The definition of forgiveness is your guide. It is a definition to which you may refer a number of times in the future.

DECIDE TO FORGIVE

Forgiving is a choice, one you are free to make or to reject. Even if you begin, you can stop the process if forgiveness seems irrelevant or too painful for you. You can take it up again when you are ready.

The philosopher William Neblett considers one's commitment to forgive to be the heart of the process.[2] Committing to forgiving does not mean that you have completed the undertaking but instead that you have made a good beginning.

Gail, a 32-year-old homemaker and mother of three, was burdened with chronic anxiety. Upon waking, she would feel a tension in the back of her neck. Upon rising, she would feel unsafe, wanting to run away. Her behavior and occasional mood swings were difficult for her family. She became afraid that her husband might leave her and take the children. She sought counseling from a score of therapists, but none of them were able to help. Finally, she approached a counselor who explained as part of their initial session that he used forgiveness as part of the emotional healing process.

Gail was confused. What does forgiveness have to do with neck tension, with feeling unsafe? The therapist explained that such tension can be the result of deeply seated, subconscious anger toward a family member now or in the past. As the sessions progressed, Gail discovered that she had burning anger toward both parents, who were short tempered, verbally insensitive, and were not loving toward her as she grew up. She reacted to the idea of forgiveness with disdain, adamantly insisting that there was no way she would ever forgive her parents. The counselor did not push the issue. Gail left the session determined to hold onto her anger.

She decided instead to work off her anger at the counselor by taking a long jog through the woods near her home. After an hour, she stopped and in the quiet beauty of the forest thought to herself, "Why not try forgiveness, everything else has failed." Gail was prone to impulsive gestures, and so she blurted out in the still of the forest, "I forgive you, Mom and Dad, for all you did to me when I was a child." Almost immediately, she felt a sense of freedom.

But the work of forgiveness had only begun. For the next three years Gail and her counselor rode a roller-coaster of emotional ups and downs as Gail revealed a history of abuse from her parents. Later the counselor admitted that if he had known the full extent of the abuse Gail had endured, he might never have mentioned forgiveness. But Gail had tasted freedom and was determined to be completely free. She refused to stop the process until she had forgiven each and every incident of abuse. Ten years later Gail occasionally feels anxious, but her marriage is strong and she has, with serenity, faced a number of family crises that might have tested even the strongest woman. For her, there is no going back to anger and bitterness.

The pastoral psychotherapist Robert Cunningham, in his reflections on forgiveness, points out that we need to approach the work of forgiveness with an attitude of willingness rather than a willfulness.[3] *Willingness* is a receptivity to taking the time to let the forgiveness process work itself out and not try to control or force the process. Those who approach the forgiveness process with a God-centered worldview will expect to wait for God. Others may understand that any natural healing process takes time. Sometimes the process takes time because we start the process thinking that we have a particular problem with a particular person and then discover layers of resentment that must be peeled away one by one.

When we show *willfulness* toward forgiving, we are saying that we will be the sole determiner of how and when the process is complete. Such reasoning is bound to fail, because healing takes time. You wouldn't expect a broken leg to heal instantaneously. The healing of emotional injuries also takes time.

The commitment to forgive includes a willingness to put aside any claim to revenge, even in its most subtle forms, against the one who hurt you. This includes the revenge of condemning the offender to people who do not need to know about the offenses. Some people want to rush out and confront the offender with forgiveness, but they are more interested in forcing the offender to listen to a catalogue of complaints, charges, and crimes than in offering real forgiveness. Some people say they are forgiving but are actually using the words as a means of revenge, of showing their moral superiority because, after all, they can "forgive."

In your case, are you willing to make the commitment to forgive the one who hurt you? The decision requires patience and perseverance on your part. Are you ready to do the work that forgiveness requires?

Please keep in mind that I am asking you here to take only this step: Try to refrain from subtle revenge toward the person by not condemning him or her to others, by not snubbing him or her, or by not leveling any other insult. You can even take this step with a deceased person as you refrain from dragging his or her name through the mud when in conversation with others. I am not suggesting that you stop talking about him or her entirely. After all, you may need to discuss the person with a confidant or a counselor, but the point here is to work on getting rid of subtle forms of revenge.

Please notice that this guidepost does not require you to add anything positive, such as compassion, benevolence, or love, toward him or her right now. Even though I see these positives as part of forgiveness, I do not see them as part of the decision to forgive.

✎ Journal Entry

Take some time to reflect on refraining from subtle revenge in your journal. What do you think of this idea? Are you willing to change in this way? You might want to structure this written exercise as a kind of debate. State a good reason for going ahead with forgiveness, and then answer it with any doubt or concern you may have. Continue the writing until you have exhausted the back-and-forth discussion. What do you conclude at the present time? If you are ambivalent about forgiveness, I would suggest that you lay aside the journal and this book and take a break from the idea of forgiving. You can come back later, even another day, and continue with the pro-and-con writing until you choose to take the step toward forgiving.

Once you are willing in a general way to refrain from subtle forms of revenge, I'd like you to reflect in your journal on the specific ways in the past that you, in fact, have been unkind to the person. Are you willing to put these behaviors aside? If so, you have progressed far. You are on the way to forgiveness.

ENDNOTES

1. L. B. Smedes, *Forgive and Forget* (2nd edition) (San Francisco, CA: Harper, 1996), p. 55.
2. W. R. Neblett, "Forgiveness and Ideals," *Mind 83* (1974), 269–275.
3. B. B. Cunningham, "The Will to Forgive: A Pastoral Theological View of Forgiving," *Journal of Pastoral Care 39* (1985), 141–149.

CHAPTER 8

GAINING PERSPECTIVES

PHASE 3—WORKING ON FORGIVENESS

Work toward understanding.

✎ Journal Entry

Up to this point, the focus has been on you and your anger. Now we turn around the perspective, focusing on the one who hurt you. To begin, write as true a story as possible in your journal describing the person who hurt you. There are no guidelines for this—simply describe what the person is like.

EMBELLISHING THE STORY

This chapter is about your perception of the other's life story. As we begin to understand the other through his or her story, our perceptions can be narrow. We focus only on a few aspects of the offender's personality or we dwell on what he or she did to us without seeing that there is a richer story for us to understand.

If you have decided to forgive, then trying to embellish your story of the person, by viewing him or her through a wider perspective, can help turn your intention into reality. Sometimes the decision to forgive is enough. Suddenly, perhaps miraculously, the heart changes, insight comes into the situation, and the offended person feels free from the resentment and bitterness. However, in most cases, change takes work and time. Adding to your story about the other becomes part of the work of forgiveness.

I will be asking you for details about the person that include

- what life was like for him or her when growing up
- what life was like for him or her at the time of the offense
- what your relationship with him or her has been like in a broad sense
- what he or she is like when you see his or her true humanity using a *global* perspective
- what he or she is like when you take what the philosopher Keith Yandell calls a *cosmic* perspective, seeing him or her in a spiritual, religious sense.[1]

The decision to forgive is a wonderful way to open up the heart and the mind. Those who focused on their anger before making a decision to forgive often find that, after making the decision, they are able to view the offender in a new light. Lewis Smedes describes this process as "seeing with new eyes."[2]

Although sometimes it may seem that offenders are irrational and their actions are senseless, in most cases, offenders act as they do for reasons. These may not be justifiable, but they may be understandable. Understanding the forces that drive offenders is an important aspect of the forgiveness process. However, understanding why someone has injured another person does not mean that we condone or excuse the offense.

Let's take some time to see the expanded perspectives that

others have achieved as they struggle to forgive. Then we can focus on your situation.

TAKING THE PERSONAL PERSPECTIVE

After making the decision to forgive her mother, Mary Ann focused on her mother's past, what it was like for her while growing up. She was able to see that her mother Marion was a victim of her grandmother Margaret. She was able to see how her grandmother was, in turn, a victim of her great-grandfather and in-laws.

Grandmother Margaret's mother had died when she was 14. Her 20-year-old cousin came to help out with Margaret and the other children. Before the year was out, the cousin was pregnant by Margaret's father. They married quickly, but there was gossip. Margaret reacted to the situation by denying that anything untoward had happened between her father and cousin. Until the day she died, she refused to admit what her father had done.

Margaret rushed into marriage at 18. Her in-laws constantly criticized her. During the Great Depression, Margaret's husband lost his job and was unable to find another. He sat around the house thinking up get-rich schemes that never panned out, and Margaret was forced to support the family while at the same time keeping up the facade that they were a successful middle-class family. She succeeded by lying and demanding that her children lie.

Marion was a top high school student, anticipating college, when the economic depression ruined her plans. She was angry and had chronic low self-esteem. She tried desperately to please her mother, but no matter what she did, it was never enough. Margaret constantly criticized Marion's children, and Marion reacted by lashing out at Mary Ann and her sisters. The more Mary Ann thought about her mother's childhood, the more she understood what her mother had suffered. These insights made Mary Ann more determined to deal with her anger before she passed it on to her children.

Gertrude, age 44 and a receptionist at the local used car dealership, was singled out by her family for abuse and mistreatment. After years of harboring a self-destructive anger toward her mother, Gertrude was able to understand how her mother had suffered at the hands of her own mother, an angry and unhappy person, how her grandmother had experienced humiliation as a servant, how her great-grandmother had endured poverty and oppression, and so on back through history. This helped her eventually feel compassion for her mother which, in turn, diminished her anger and enabled her to forgive.

Chad, whose father only recently confessed Chad's mother's series of affairs, reacted with a closed-minded coldness at first toward his father, who kept the secret hidden for years. Forgiveness was out of the question for a father who was so weak. Yet, over time, Chad had this to say:

> In my eyes, my dad became the strongest man I've ever known. He's been through so much in his life, and he never falls down. It takes someone very strong to experience the pain he's felt in his marriage and continue to raise six unaffected, responsible children. He suddenly became the most amazing person to me. When I put myself in his shoes, it becomes easier for me to understand where he was coming from [in not telling us sooner]. He didn't want us growing up hating our mom. It's hard to imagine what it must have been like to live with these secrets. He's always been a loving father, and it must have been extremely difficult to play this charade. I think sympathizing with my father's point of view aided in the forgiveness process. Instead of being selfish and mad that he lied to us, I started understanding his pain and sense of no other options.

When Carol began the work phase of forgiveness, she was able to see her husband Elliot with "new eyes":

He once told me that he was never touched as a child, and he would make sure that his kids were hugged all the time. I now realize that he never dealt with his childhood, and all the resentment, anger, and frustration had come out with his intensified addictions. I felt a new sense of what he longed for as a little boy.

A new perspective aided Carol in revising her negative feelings, thoughts, and behaviors into more positive ones. However, she did not excuse or condone Elliot's hurtful actions as she expanded her perspectives of him.

For Rose, whose alcoholic father wreaked havoc in their home, healing began as she reflected on his childhood:

I definitely saw my father differently. Instead of a mean guy, I began to see him as someone who went through a terrible childhood. For example, my grandfather made my father feel unworthy by calling him names. My father, as a result, couldn't deal with the world and turned to alcohol. My thoughts of sympathy replaced resentment and anger. This view allowed me to forgive more easily than I would have.

Jerrod's reflection about his love-depriving mother shows a similar pattern:

It became clear to me, growing up in the Depression and being part of a large family and stepfamily, that my mother had to suffer a number of hardships early in her life, as well as being required to assume substantial responsibility for her younger siblings before she may have been prepared intellectually to do so. My mother has said things about her family that indicated that there was little affection shown in her family from parents to child. My mother always remained loyal to her mother, but she seemed to be a loner in many ways, finding it necessary to mask her feelings in public to protect herself.

We can also ask what life was like for the offender at the

time of the offense. For example, Felicia resented her mother for being "totally emotionally absent" during Felicia's childhood. When she thought about how, during those crucial years, her father suffered from tuberculosis and her mother from depression and an obsessive–compulsive disorder, her attitude toward her mother changed:

> Without the changed view, there could have been no forgiveness. When I saw my mother as she really was, I felt very sorry for her —she must have been so sad, lonely, and trapped by her illness and by our family's lack of financial resources and by my father's illness. Not to mention the physical burden of taking care of two little girls in a rural home with no phone or running water and electricity which was not dependable. She never got help and suffered for years, and talked honestly to no one.

Jerrod also resented his mother's lack of attention and was able to forgive when he began to understand the difficulties that she faced:

> The pressures of working at a job she really did not enjoy and a strong sense of duty drove her. I think it was hard for her to show affection. Also, her first son was relatively easy to handle and was a popular child. Having unexpected twins, and especially a second son who was so much different than her first son, I think, was hard on her. Being, in some ways, a difficult child, while also evidently the brightest child, I think caused her no small degree of aggravation. . . . She tried the best she could and loved me in her own way.

Notice that Jerrod not only expanded his story by focusing on his mother's pressures at the time, but also by seeing his relationship with his mother in broader terms. He saw that she loved him as best she could, despite her occasional failings.

Anthony, the teacher who was denied a promotion, also

found it easier to forgive his principal by reflecting on the pressure that the administrator was under at the time:

> I started to see the principal as scared. He said "no" to my promotion at a time of deep budget cutbacks. There was even a piece in the newspaper at the time saying he was not a strong leader. I began to see that he was afraid for his own job. Maybe his get-tough letter to me was a way to show himself that he was a strong leader. He did this in the wrong way, but I saw a different person —someone who was unsure and made a very bad administrative decision because of it. After all, he is a person, one who is fallible, prone to mistakes, but a person nonetheless.

Anthony doesn't condone the principal's actions. He still believes what was done was wrong, but he can see the principal as a vulnerable person whose fear led to the apparently unjustified decision not to promote him. Not only did Anthony expand his story about the principal by putting the offensive incident into perspective, but also he took what I call the *global* perspective. He saw the principal as a person, as a member of the human community, who erred but who still had a humanity worth respecting.

Sometimes people understand themselves better as they try to understand the hurtful situation. This was the case with Cindy, as she struggled to make sense of her partner Adam's temperamental display at her friend's house:

> As I tried to understand Adam, I saw myself in a new light. My life was no longer attached to his, so why should I carry around this hate and anger? I saw him as the man who was not always in control and that meant he was not to be a part of my life. This aided my forgiveness, because it paved the way for me to see my own life clearly.

Another way to work toward understanding is to ask yourself if it is possible to separate the offense from the offender. Sometimes we may suffer a terrible wrong from a person who in many other ways has been good to us. Can we balance the wrong done against the good? This doesn't excuse the wrong, but it can help us understand that the offender doesn't hate us.

Jerrod, who still believes that his mother's child-rearing behavior was wrong, now can say "she has done her best to try to raise me, and she does love me."

Maria, whose husband was arrested for cocaine possession, had to separate the person and the act in two ways. First, she was able to forgive, despite knowing that what he did was wrong, and second, she forgave while being quite hesitant to enter into the relationship again until he showed definite signs of changing his ways.

> I watched him struggle once he was released from prison. He was trying to make things right in his life. I could see this. I also saw how much he was hurt by the fact that he had done this to me. At the same time, I tried to understand the circumstances under which he grew up—adopted and [of mixed race]—being taunted by people who were prejudiced. This had to hurt him deeply. What made it very hard is that everyone around me kept saying that I shouldn't forgive him. No one was supportive. They were very judgmental, but at the same time, I could see him struggle very hard to forgive himself.

Sometimes understanding leads to a different conclusion. Not every offender is a victim. Kendra was sexually abused and physically threatened by her uncle, who was a petty criminal. Also, Kendra was devastated when, years later, her aunt admitted that she had known what her husband was doing but did nothing about it because she didn't want to lose her economic security. Neither relative showed the slightest remorse. For Kendra, understanding involved recognizing that some people choose evil for so long that evil becomes a part of who they are. The physician M. Scott Peck wrote about this phenomenon in his book *People of the Lie*. Those who confront offenders who appear to be without a normal sense of guilt may find insight in Dr. Peck's book.[3]

Michael, whose father physically abused him, found that understanding did not change his perception of his father as a violent man:

> I'm disappointed that my dad has never apologized for his behavior. I've tried very much to understand why my dad was so violent, and I know he was the victim of violence. I cannot, in all honesty, say that my view of my father has changed significantly over the years except that he is no longer a physical threat to me. I don't think my perceptions of him aided in my forgiving. I forgave him to help myself primarily, but I'm sure he is glad to know that I hold no grudge.

Psychiatrist R. C. Hunter observed that sometimes it may be obvious that the forgiveness process may not be complete.[4] This may be the case with Michael. He may have forgiven his father as far as he is able at this time, but perhaps after a number of years pass he may be able to understand his father in a way that he cannot now. Sometimes people like Michael's father break down on their deathbed and ask for forgiveness or give some sign of repentance. Even if repentance never comes, Michael still may be able to deepen his forgiveness.

TAKING THE GLOBAL AND COSMIC PERSPECTIVES

In some cases the actions are so evil and the offender so unrepentant that there is no way to understand them based on an examination of the person's past or even the pressures of the present. The offenders in such cases refuse to respect the rights and inherent value of other human beings. Their actions are offenses against humanity and must be repudiated and condemned. In these cases the *global* and *cosmic* perspectives may be helpful.

Bernice, 23 and a volunteer for a nonprofit peace organization, had worked tirelessly in a Southeast Asian country repairing the homes of people who were poor. She was working out of a sense of charity and good will, not for money. After many, many hours of back-breaking construction work, a band of rebels from a nearby community pillaged and burned the homes that Bernice had so painstakingly tried to restore. She was devastated. She never before or after encountered the faceless marauders who burned the homes and then escaped into the night. What were the childhood situations like for the rebels? What current political troubles might have precipitated this response from them? Bernice wasn't sure.

She had a very difficult time forgiving those who destroyed the homes. Whenever she saw her impoverished friends' faces, she got angry. After much internal struggle, Bernice began to see the invaders as human, not as enemies to be written off. Certainly she continued to view their actions as wrong, but she did not see them as villains who should be destroyed. She came to understand that their lives were even more impoverished—not in a monetary sense —than were her friends. She never respected what the rebels did, but she slowly began to recognize and respect their humanity. They, too, need homes to live in. They have aspirations, needs, and desires. They are fully human.

Bernice's understanding, with the aid of the global perspective, has brought her a long way toward forgiving. But what of those people who cannot see the other's humanity? If we are so offended by the evil done that we see these offenders as less than human, then we can fall into the same evil. By granting to the offenders the status of a human being, we repudiate the idea that human beings can be treated as less than human. This perspective of seeing people as less than human can be destructive, as Martin

Luther King, Jr., understood. At the time when his own house was being firebombed and his children were being threatened, he wrote

> The chain reaction of evil—hate begetting hate, wars producing more wars—must be broken, or we shall be plunged into the dark abyss of annihilation. . . . love is the only force capable of transforming an enemy into a friend. . . . By its very nature, hate destroys and tears down; by its very nature, love creates and builds up.[5]

This does not, of course, mean that we look the other way when evil comes or that we legally pardon offenses because we must love our enemies. Punishment in its proper context is appropriate and just and may lead to a change of heart in even the most offensive offenders.

The *cosmic* perspective is fascinating to observe in those who forgive. In my experience, the vast majority of people who work through forgiveness take this kind of perspective. My experience is consistent with a Gallup Poll taken in 1991 in which 83% of more than 900 respondents claimed that they needed God's help to forgive.[6] What the cosmic perspective looks like, of course, depends on the spiritual or religious beliefs of the person who is doing the work. We have maintained a neutrality in our programs on issues of spirituality and religion so that each person can choose his or her own path. Consider Marietta Jaeger's poignant ideas toward an inmate who was accused of murdering her daughter Susie:

> I readily admit that I wanted to kill this man with my bare hands. . . . By this time, however, I had finally come to believe that real justice is not punishment but restoration, not necessarily to how things used to be, but to how they really should be. In both the Hebrew and Christian Scriptures whence my beliefs and values come, the God who rises up from them is a God of mercy and compassion, a God who seeks not to punish, destroy, or put us to death, but a God who works unceasingly to help and heal us, re-

habilitate and reconcile us, restore us to the richness and fullness of life for which we have been created. This, now, was the justice I wanted for this man who had taken my little girl.

Though he was liable for the death penalty, I felt it would violate and profane the goodness, sweetness, and beauty of Susie's life by killing the kidnapper in her name. . . . I was convinced that my best and healthiest option was to forgive.[7]

Dr. King, again when his family was being threatened, took not only a global but also a cosmic perspective when he wrote

We love men not because we like them, nor because their ways appeal to us, nor even because they possess some type of divine spark; we love every man because God loves him. At this level we love the person who does an evil deed, although we hate the deed that he does.[8]

✎ Journal Entry

Are you prepared to write the story of the person who hurt you, focusing on whom he or she was, is, and may become? When I use the word *story*, I do not mean that you should make up a fairy tale about how wonderful the person is. In this sense a story is an attempt to be as accurate as possible about the person and his or her conflicts and complications in life.

I once heard someone describe forgiveness as "only substituting good thoughts about the person for the bad." To me, this is creating a fairy tale, as if we can't stand to live with ideas that the person is imperfect, mistaken, or even cruel and indifferent. Let's try to take up the challenge of seeing the person in more detail, in a broader context, to expand what we know about or at least how we think about him or her. Consider five questions.

- *Question 1—What was life like for him or her when growing up?* In starting your narrative in the past, try to sketch the child and the adolescent before you sketch the adult. Most people know well the one who hurt them because most of the betrayals and hurts come from those close to us. Do you recall, from the person or from others, what struggles were endured as a child? Try to describe some of the incidents that you know in such a way that you enter into the child's world. Was the person frightened or confused? Was he or she deeply hurt from others' actions? Did he or she cry? Try to write about three or four events in the person's past. Then describe his or her vulnerability that seemed to flow from these difficulties.

At this point be sure not to confuse forgiveness with condoning or excusing. The person's hardships should not become your hardships.

Some of you will not be able to answer this or questions 2 and 3 because you do not know personally the offender. You may wish to go directly to questions 4 and 5, which focus on the global and cosmic perspectives.

- *Question 2—At the time of the offense, what was life like for the person?* Was he or she under considerable pressure? If so, from what? What were the circumstances of his or her story when the hurtful event took place? Try to imagine what he or she was thinking. This sometimes can be discerned by what was said or by actions. Try to understand how he or she was feeling.

Can you see any vulnerability here, as you did when focusing on the child? In your opinion, might the person's reactions at the time of the event be a spillover from childhood patterns? A child who witnesses temper tantrums by a parent, for example, can become temperamental as an adult.

Take time to muse on some of these questions, realizing that forgiving is not the same as condoning.

- *Question 3—Are you able to tell the story of your relation-ship with this person in a broader sense than the offense itself?* How long have you known the person? What has he or she been like during the good times? Was it all bad, or are there some good images that come to mind? Try to describe at least three incidents in which the person showed good judgment or strong character. These are not substitutes for what happened to you. After all, forgiveness takes place in the courageous context of your acknowledging the other's unfairness. Even so, I'd like you to see the person's good qualities.

  In Chapter 6 I asked you to jot down your impressions of the ways in which the offender is worse off now than you as a result of the hurtful event. Please review your writing there. What is life like for him or her because of what happened? Again, my point is to help you see a person who genuinely is a *person*.

- *Question 4—What is the person like in the global perspec-tive?* Recall that a global perspective zooms the lens out much further than within your household, workplace, or other set-ting. The global perspective challenges you to see the person as a member of the human community, which sometimes can be difficult, especially if you've "written off" him or her.

  When I talk to people about those they are trying to forgive, I see that the would-be forgiver is sometimes hesitant to ac-knowledge the other as a genuine human being. The potential forgiver at times seems to espouse a modern-day version of the "flat earth" theory. In other words, the one who is con-sidering forgiveness would like to take the offender by the nape of the neck, march him or her to the farthest reaches of the realm, drop the person off the face of the earth, and listen until he or she lands in another principality far from earth. If I am describing you, take heart; you are not alone. What we need to do now is change this attitude.

I am not asking you, in taking a global perspective, to welcome the person back as a spouse or employer or anyone else who is close to you. Certainly, as you forgive you may reconcile, but that is not our present focus. I am asking you if you can see the offender as a member of the human race, one who belongs on this earth, just as you do, one who deserves a place to live and air to breathe.

Try to work with this global perspective until you see the offender as fully human and deserving of respect because he or she is human. This is not easy. It may be helpful at this point to review your responses to the first three questions and then write about what makes the person human and what your response should be in light of this knowledge.

- *Question 5—What is the person like as you take a cosmic perspective?* Recall that the cosmic perspective focuses on spiritual or religious outlooks. If you do not have a spiritual or a religious perspective, you may decide not to answer this question. Most people, however, do incorporate this view into their philosophy of life.

 I deliberately use language that is not specific to any one religion, so my images may be a bit vague. Try to place my questions within your existing worldview so that you are as concrete and specific as possible in your answers.

 What is your concept of the divine? Many see the divine, the higher power, God, as love. How does God see the person on whom you are focusing?

 What does your worldview have to say about redemption, or how a person is transformed toward the good in this life or enters into an afterlife? Is the person who hurt you redeemable? I am not asking for your opinion or judgment on this issue. Instead, what does your worldview have to say on the matter? All monotheistic traditions, for example, have means through which even the worst people can be redeemed. This image of good and evil along with transformation is a powerful one and has pervaded literature, theater, and cinema. Take some time to see whether the person is redeemable relative to your belief system.

Can you see the person as a member of your spiritual or religious tradition? I am not asking whether you think that he or she will ever go to church or enter the synagogue. Instead, I am asking if you can see him or her as a part of the divine plan, as belonging to a wider group than your family, workplace, or even the global community of those living on earth right now. Muse about this possibility.

Is it possible that you may see him or her in an afterlife? Some of you are thinking that heaven won't be much fun if this turns out to be true, but please bear with me. If you believe in an afterlife and if the other person might, just might, be there, then you may have some work to do in forgiving and reconciling. What would you say to the person? What might you say to the person now so that the tensions are all wrapped up before the meeting in the hereafter? This person may be important to the one you call God. If this is true, how does this alter your perception of the person?

Finally, many spiritual or religious people do not see themselves as self-sufficient but instead as needing help from the divine. Is this true in your case? If so, what help do you need and how are you going to get it so that you can forgive?

PUTTING THE PIECES TOGETHER

It is time to integrate the varied perspectives you now have of the person who hurt you. Please read again your answers to the five questions, then consider this: How has your view of the person changed as a result of answering the questions? What work still must be done to deepen and broaden your story of the person?

ENDNOTES

1. K. Yandell, "The Metaphysics and Morality of Forgiveness," in *Exploring Forgiveness,* eds. R. D. Enright and J. North (Madison: University of Wisconsin Press, 1998), pp. 35–45.
2. L. B. Smedes, *Forgive and Forget: Healing the Hurts We Don't Deserve* (San Francisco, CA: Harper, 1984).
3. M. S. Peck, *People of the Lie* (New York: Simon & Schuster, 1997). C. S. Lewis's *The Great Divorce* (New York: Touchstone Books, 1996) offers a similar insight.
4. R. C. A. Hunter, "Forgiveness, Retaliation, and Paranoid Reactions," *Canadian Psychiatric Association Journal* 23 (1978), 167–173.
5. M. L. King, Jr., *The Strength to Love* (Philadelphia: Fortress Press, 1963), pp. 51–52.
6. M. M. Poloma and G. H. Gallup, Jr., *Varieties of Prayer: A Survey Report* (Philadelphia: Trinity Press, 1991).
7. M. Jaeger, "The Power and Reality of Forgiveness," in *Exploring Forgiveness,* eds. R. D. Enright and J. North (Madison: University of Wisconsin Press, 1998), pp. 13–14.
8. M. L. King, Jr., *The Strength to Love,* p. 50.

CHAPTER 9

BUILDING POSITIVE FEELINGS, THOUGHTS, AND BEHAVIORS

PHASE 3—WORKING ON FORGIVENESS

Work toward compassion.
Accept the pain.
Give the offender a gift.

Your next step is to examine the feelings that may be emerging as you see differently the one who hurt you. The new, more positive feelings will take some time to develop. Do not try to rush or force them. Allow the process of forgiving to unfold, but at the same time stay open to the positive developments that may be budding.

WORK TOWARD COMPASSION

At the beginning of the forgiveness process, the idea of feeling compassion, empathy, or love toward the offender may have been unthinkable, but after a person has decided to forgive and has worked on understanding, a change in feelings is possible.

I believe that working toward empathy and compassion is

important because the alternative is "nonfeeling" toward the offender. Nonfeeling is not a healing emotion.

You may decide that a variety of emotions are appropriate for your situation. *Empathy* happens when we feel the same feelings as another person. We are angry with them, sad with them, happy with them. Martin Hoffman, a psychologist at the University of Michigan, claims that empathy develops when people come to understand others. Once forgivers see the offender as a person who has suffered, they are able to imagine what the offender went through and how the offender felt.[1] In contrast, *sympathy*, not empathy, occurs when we feel for the other. We see their anger and feel sorry for them.

Empathy, in turn, may generate a sense of compassion toward the other. *Compassion* means suffering with the other person. Compassion is a tender-hearted response to empathizing with another person. Some people may feel that sympathy in the form of pity for the offender is the most that they can muster. Compassion takes time to develop.

Perhaps it is easier to experience empathy or sympathy with someone whom we have loved or do love, but we can feel compassion toward acquaintances, as Anthony did when he forgave the principal who did not give him a promotion:

> I was aware of some changed feelings toward the principal. As I saw him struggling in his job, I actually began to feel sorry for him. Liking him surprised me because prior to this, I had written him off.

Anthony was surprised that he was able to move from bitterness to caring.

Maria was able to feel empathy and compassion toward the partner who stole from her:

> Yes, I tried to put myself in his shoes all the time. I tried to under-

stand how he was also hurt by the fact that he hurt someone that he loved. I tried to understand the circumstances under which he grew up—adopted and [of mixed race]. He experienced a lot of prejudices from people growing up. He was abused by his biological mother. I always tried to cut him slack and have compassion for him based on his life experiences. This did help me to forgive him.

As you work on understanding, positive feelings toward the offender may emerge, but sometimes they don't emerge, and sometimes it takes time for feelings to change.

✎ Journal Entry

Write down the feelings that you are experiencing toward the person at the moment. Feelings can be fleeting, so your writing may reflect varied and changing emotions.

Examine what you wrote. Do you see any sign of positive emotions? Are the emotions as negative as when you began reading this book? Have you moved from deeply angry to more neutral emotions?

If you have come this far in the process and you still feel as angry as you did at the beginning, you may not be forgiving the right person. Sometimes we are exceedingly angry at a person who has recently hurt us because this present hurt is in some way similar to a hurt we experienced as children. In these cases, we need to start over again, this time forgiving the injuries we sustained as children.

Do this free-form writing for a few minutes each day over the next week. Try to see changes in patterns of feelings as you write, whether the negative emotions expressed are lessening in amount and intensity and whether the positive ones are increasing in amount and intensity. Please keep in mind that you cannot will the negative emotions away so easily and usher in the positive ones whenever you wish.

Also, consider trying an exercise in guided imagery developed by psychologist Craig Humphrey.[2] He has found a way to make compassion exercises concrete by focusing on the heart.

In a quiet place where you will not be disturbed, sit in a comfortable chair. Close your eyes and take a few deep breaths. While relaxed, concentrate on your heart, its warmth, its sense of well-being. When you are ready, think of a person with whom you have an excellent relationship, one that is free of deep conflict. Slowly bring him or her into your heart. You might want to think of an affirmative thought such as "I hope that [name him or her] has happiness and peace." What do you feel?

Repeat the exercise thinking of the one who has hurt you. When relaxed, focus on your heart and slowly bring the person into your heart with a positive affirmation. Do not feel discouraged if the first few times you feel annoyance and not peace. This approach takes time to learn. You do not switch from feelings of anger to ones of kindness and peace just because you've tried the exercise a few times. Record your reaction to this experience in your journal.

The approach is akin to classical conditions. Ivan Pavlov, a preeminent Russian physiologist who turned to psychology early in the 20th century, found that his laboratory dogs would begin to salivate whenever Dr. Pavlov brought food to them. He eventually sounded a bell before bringing in the food. As the dogs learned to associate the sound of the bell with the food, they began to salivate at the sound of the bell. Even when no food was forthcoming, the canines drooled as the bell sounded.

You are no dog, and your situation is not about bells and biscuits, but the principles of learning are similar. You may have begun to associate feelings of anger, annoyance, or even hatred at the image of the one who has hurt you. As you imagine him or her in your mind, you don't salivate as Pavlov's dogs did, but you may have come to associate the image with your anger. Taking the image of the person into your heart may lead to a new association, one of relaxation and warm well-being, when thinking of him or her.

Of course, you must still distinguish feelings of well-being and actually being well when interacting with the person. Offenders who refuse to change destructive ways cannot be trusted. You will have to distinguish feelings of well-being associated with the person that are part of the forgiveness process and appropriate behaviors when in interaction with the person that are part of reconciliation.

Learning takes time and effort. If this imaging exercise is disturbing to you, then shut off the image. You may not be ready for this exercise. What is nice about Dr. Humphrey's approach is that it can be practiced by anyone regardless of religious and spiritual beliefs. The image of the heart as a center for love and kindness is, shall we say, at the heart of many religious and humanistic traditions.

On a scale of 1 to 10, please rate your degree of compassion for the person who hurt you, with 1 meaning "absolutely no compassion," and 10 meaning "tremendous compassion." Record this rating in your journal.

ACCEPT THE PAIN

What do we do with the pain we experience? We have seen that we can't deny it and expect it to go away. We have also seen that pain has a terrible way of growing and multiplying—being communicated down the generations from mother to daughter and father to son—and how years after the offense the pain can be just as sharp and just as debilitating. We have seen how pain can lead to self-destructive behavior. Maria's partner tried to cover his pain with cocaine. Carol's husband masked his need for love and affirmation in the compulsive search for sexual pleasure. Felicia's and Jerrod's mothers withdrew from their children; Michael's and Rose's fathers attacked. All had been hurt and had transferred their pain to others.

If we forgive, we have to deal constructively with our pain. We certainly don't want to pass that pain onto others. One major motivation for forgiving is the fear that children will inherit their parents' anger and that cycle of pain, anger, and offense will go on and on.

So, what can we do with the pain? We can accept it.[3]

In Phase 1 we uncovered the ways that we try to deny or avoid anger and pain. Now we are ready to face the offense with all its pain and grief. When someone dies, we grieve because we are losing the future. We will have to live through all the tomorrows without the one we love. When we forgive, we may need to grieve for all the days we lost because of the offense.

We may never have really cried for ourselves. For example, children who are sexually abused rarely cry or show any emotion. They keep it all inside, denying their feelings and the horror of what is happening to them. During the forgiveness process, many victims of child abuse cry for the first time. Mary Ann found herself crying for herself and for her mother and for all the possibilities that were forever lost. She wept for several days, but when the grieving was over, she felt free for the first time of the pain that she had hidden deep in her heart.

An incest survivor told me that as she "absorbed the pain," her identity changed from victim to survivor. People who are hurt are like sponges. The sponge soaks up water; you "soak up" the pain. Over time, the water evaporates out of the sponge until it is dry once more; the pain you absorb slowly dissipates until you are free from it.

When you absorb the pain, you do not seek pain, but you do accept it as it comes. As you stop hiding from the pain, you discover that you can handle the pain, and then it lessens. You become stronger and don't have to transfer the pain to someone else. In accepting the pain, you give a gift to those around you, who may have been uninvolved in the incident of hurt. Carol was well aware that Elliot's pain had been transferred to her and that if she did not accept that pain, she might transfer it to her fatherless sons:

> Along with the realization of Elliot's pain over his childhood came my commitment as a parent to love my little boys in any way I could and to show them how valuable they were to me.

Carol's point about the intergenerational transfer of pain is acknowledged by psychotherapist Allen Bergin:

> Is it important, then, for somebody, sometime in the history of a pathological family, to stop the process of transmitting pain from generation to generation? Instead of seeking retribution, one learns to absorb the pain, to be forgiving, to try to reconcile with forebears, and then become a generator of positive change in the next generation. The therapeutically changed individual thereby becomes intergenerationally transitional by resisting the disordered patterns of the past, exercising an interpersonally healing impact, and then transmitting to the younger generation a healthier mode of functioning.[4]

Maria recognized that accepting the pain was an emotional and not a rational process:

> I accepted the pain by allowing myself to feel the feelings that I felt and not analyze why I felt the way I did. Then I kept telling myself that it happened, I feel pain, and to simply allow myself to go through all of the emotions and not to control them.

Michael was able to accept the pain caused by his father's brutality:

> My forgiveness has involved some absorption of pain. My experience has forever altered how I see the world, how I view trust, and how defensive I am in the face of a threat. But I would characterize most of my forgiveness as more cathartic than absorptive. It was more a release of direct accountability and blame.

Anthony also was able to accept his own pain:

> I guess you could say that I accepted the pain. I decided not to let that incident get in the way of my own humanity. I was not going to let that incident turn me into a cynic, hurting my family or my relations with fellow teachers. I was not even going to let the incident stand in the way of my caring about the principal as a professional or as a person. I decided to stop all the anger, which I now saw as unnecessary garbage in my life.

Jerrod, reflecting on the process of forgiving his mother, learned to accept the pain:

> I think I have accepted the pain as part of a process involving other painful experiences that led me to forgive my mother. In the past two years I have been laid off as a result of a corporate restructuring, lost my wife to a sudden illness, and changed my life direction. The support of my mother and father and the remembrance of my wife and what she would have wanted me to do as a result of her death have caused me to resolve that I had to move on and not become mired in depression or excessive self-reflection. I had to get on with my life and not hold grudges against those who might have caused me pain.

Rose found that absorbing the pain helped her to forgive the partner after he stole from her:

By "absorbing" the pain I was able to move on with my life. I went to AA meetings for families of alcoholics, and I began to see that these programs helped out a great deal. They helped not only me and my family, but also the program helped my father.

Carol found that admitting the pain and sharing it with others helped her to heal:

The memories and the sadness over the whole event are still there, but my life is no longer centralized around any of the past feelings of the shame, anger, etc. I'm actually proud of myself that I chose to listen to the opportunities God placed before me (He was extremely active during my grief, with the direction He was giving me). I met the challenge, and I feel very much loved and valued for what I had learned through this experience.

Felicia grieved for herself and for her mother, but being able to grieve led to freedom:

I felt pain, both for myself and for my mother, as I confronted our pain. Does this make sense? Rather than feeling that I absorbed the pain, I felt relieved and freed.

For everyone in this book, accepting the pain was a pivotal step in forgiving. It gave some the strength to move on despite the pain. For others, it was central in positively changing a worldview toward greater caring for others. When we deny the pain or pass the pain onto others, we block our own healing and are afraid of the pain. We build up defenses to protect ourselves, but these defenses prevent the healing process. When we finally allow ourselves to hurt, to grieve, and to mourn, we are free and can begin to heal.

✎ Journal Entry

Have you gotten to the point where you have accepted the pain so that you do not pass it along to future generations? In your journal write about what it means, in your case, to accept the pain that the offender imposed on you. How difficult is it for you to accept that pain? Rate the level of difficulty or ease on a scale from 1 to 10, with 1 being "very difficult to accept the pain" and 10 being "extremely easy to accept the pain." We will refer to this rating later in the book.

Does your worldview have any helpful images about accepting or absorbing pain? Ancient religious traditions have many stories of bearing the pain on others' behalf. Can you think of role models from your belief system that may help you bear the pain that you did not deserve?

Consider discussing your insights with your forgiveness companion. Accepting the pain of what happened can, by itself, be a painful experience. Together you might want to explore what it means to bear pain and how you are going about it. Ask your companion for feedback on your progress.

GIVE THE OFFENDER A GIFT

This point in the forgiveness process may surprise some. Why should we give the offender a gift? We are, after all, the injured party. The offender owes us, we don't owe anything. But by giving a gift to the one who has hurt us, we break the power that person has over us. Taking the concrete step of giving a gift to the offender finalizes this phase of the process. Technically, giving a gift is not of emotion only, as implied by the chapter's title. I include it in this chapter, however, because the giving of or at least the desire to give a gift often flows from transformed feelings.

At this point in the process you need to consider what kind

of gift would be appropriate in your situation. One incest survivor who I know decided to show generosity and love to her father by sending him a birthday card. This was a big step, because they had not communicated in any way for years.

The gift given need not be a physical object; in most cases, it will be a gift of moral love. The gift can take many forms, depending on the circumstance. Another incest survivor visited her ailing father in the hospital. She gave the gift of time, sitting for long hours by his bed. She eventually began to help with his care, feeding him during meals. Soon after she forgave and reconciled, he died. She recalls what a gift the forgiving was to them both; forgiving after he was gone would have been more difficult. For both of these women, the forgiveness journey, culminating in the gift-giving, took about one year.[5]

Anthony chose to reach out to his principal with an expression of thanks for the good things the man had done:

> When I was able to forgive, I found myself reaching out in a genuine way to my principal. He just recently retired from his job. I was able to ... thank him for his support on other projects I was involved with. I could thank him with a genuine spirit of enthusiasm. He has decided to remain in this community, and I've spoken with him. He is genuinely interested in my teaching, and I am sincerely interested in his transition in life.

For Michael, the gift was allowing his father to visit with his family:

> He visited me and my wife and son for a week this year, and for the first time in our relationship he listened to things I had to say with respect. We talked about many things from family and sports to politics and philosophy. There were no obvious outpourings of affection or deep conversations about the past. Being together was the gift.

Jerrod also has given the gift of time, coupled with comfort for his mother:

> My mother has said that I am much more patient with her and that we get along much better and can communicate much better. I do not feel the anxiety in dealing with my mother that I used to have. I used to avoid her because we would always end up fighting. I have at times found myself comforting or providing support for her, something I could not have done earlier.

In some cases, the person who has hurt you is dead. You could take flowers to his or her grave. You might say something good about the person to others. Some newspapers publish remembrances of the dead, and you might place a small ad in memory of the person who injured you. You shouldn't be insincere and say things about the deceased that aren't so. You might instead choose to do something for the offender's children or make a donation to a charitable organization in the name of the deceased.

Your own situation is unique, and so your gift will be unique. There is no need to feel rushed in giving it. Sometimes the opportunity will appear spontaneously. In other cases, you may plan your gift. You may say to yourself, "I am not ready today, but three months from now I will send this person a greeting card."

It is important to remember that although giving the gift is good for you, the gift should also be good for the offender. You shouldn't use the gift as a means of revenge. For example, publishing a memorial ad in the newspaper that announces your forgiveness of the person for all the terrible things that he or she did to you would not be an appropriate moral gift.

It also is possible that the other person will reject your gift. If he or she is unaware of how much you were hurt or is still boiling angry at you, then the person may not be receptive to what you have to offer. No matter—you can give a gift of loving kindness without letting him or her know that you have forgiven.

The giving of the gift should be separate from the work of reconciliation. The gift should not come with a card that says "I forgive you for all the terrible things you did to me," unless the person has specifically asked for forgiveness, and you had previously refused to forgive or ignored the request. Even then, your forgiveness should be as generous as possible.

After Mary Ann forgave her mother, they were reconciled. Mary Ann's mother was still prone to irrational outbursts, but Mary Ann refused to allow these episodes to destroy their relationship or injure her mother's relationship with the grandchildren. A few years later, Mary Ann's mother, realizing that she was losing her short-term memory and terrified of being kept alive on machines, asked Mary Ann to consider the possibility of never putting her into a nursing home. Mary Ann was able to give her mother the gift of that request. Five years later, Mary Ann's mother had lost almost all of her short-term memory. She stopped eating and was hospitalized with severe dehydration. The doctor explained that the family had no choice but to put her in a nursing home. Mary Ann told him that she had made a solemn promise that her mother would not be put into a home, and she intended to keep it.

She called hospice services and made arrangements to care for her mother at home. However, when she returned to the hospital to pick up her mother, the doctor said that inexplicably her mother's condition had deteriorated significantly and she would live no more than 48 hours. Mary Ann felt extremely grateful that she was able to be at her mother's bedside during the last few hours and to uphold her request.

✎ Journal Entry

Make plans for the gift-giving in your journal. Make a list of the kinds of gifts that may be good for the person. Be specific. For example, if you say, "I will try to show love to the person," what does that mean in your case? Will you smile at him or her? Give a hug? Prepare a nice dinner? Send a note? Help with a chore? Speak kindly about the person to others? Then evaluate each idea in light of how you feel about such a gift. This back-and-forth process should continue until you believe that you've found the right gift for the person and one that you feel comfortable giving. You may need to do this exercise again when you feel more creative and good ideas quickly come to mind.

ENDNOTES

1. M. L. Hoffman, "Empathy, Social Cognition, and Moral Action," in *Handbook of Moral Behavior and Development* (Vol. 1: Theory) (Hillsdale, NJ: Erlbaum, 1991), pp. 275–301; "The Contribution of Empathy to Justice and Moral Judgment," in *Readings in Philosophy and Cognitive Science* (Cambridge, MA: MIT Press, 1993), pp. 647–680.
2. C. W. Humphrey, "A Stress Management Intervention With Forgiveness as the Goal" (Cincinnati, OH: Union Institute, 1999).
3. The idea of accepting, or bearing, or "absorbing" the pain, as one forgives, was first introduced by M. E. Kaufman, "The Courage to Forgive," *Israeli Journal of Psychiatry and Related Sciences* 21 (1984), 177–187, and by A. E. Bergin, "Three Contributions of a Spiritual Perspective to Counseling, Psychotherapy, and Behavioral Change," *Counseling and Values* 33 (1988), 21–31.
4. A. E. Bergin, "Three Contributions of a Spiritual Perspective," p. 29.
5. S. R. Freedman and R. D. Enright, "Forgiveness as an Intervention Goal With Incest Survivors," *Journal of Consulting and Clinical Psychology* 64 (1996), 983–992.

CHAPTER 10

EXPERIENCING DISCOVERY AND RELEASE FROM EMOTIONAL PRISON

PHASE 4—DISCOVERY AND RELEASE FROM EMOTIONAL PRISON

Discover the meaning of suffering.
Discover your need for forgiveness.
Discover that you are not alone.
Discover the purpose of your life.
Discover the freedom of forgiveness.

Working toward forgiving is not the whole story. As you complete your work, you will begin to discover the ways in which the forgiveness process changes you. The changes take place because of what you have done. This phase is designed to focus your attention on how forgiving is changing you now and how it will change you in the future as you make new discoveries about yourself and forgiveness.

DISCOVER THE MEANING OF SUFFERING

Psychotherapist Victor Frankl was a victim of the Nazis. He experienced the horrors of the Holocaust firsthand. Afterward, he developed a worldview and an approach to psychotherapy that squarely confronts the problem of suffering. He believes that people can find meaning in the most terrible suffering. Dr. Frankl does not believe that people should accept injustice. He totally supports action to reduce or eliminate evil, but he recognizes that no one can change the past. Although efforts to prevent an evil like Nazism from ever again threatening the innocent are important, such efforts cannot eradicate the evil that has already occurred.[1]

For Dr. Frankl, people can't change the past, but they can change their attitudes toward the injustice and suffering by finding meaning in what happened.

Did you learn anything from your unjust experience? Did it make you a stronger person, a more morally sensitive person, a person who is more mature or more courageous or more peaceful? Did others somehow gain because of what you endured and how you matured? Dr. Frankl summarizes the search for meaning this way:

> The noblest appreciation of meaning is reserved for those who, by the very attitude which they choose to this predicament, rise above it and grow beyond themselves. What matters is the stand they take —a stand which allows for transmuting their predicament into achievement, triumph, and heroism.[2]

Dr. Frankl believes that suffering can be integrated into the larger context of one's life. Bearing pain leads to an acceptance, and the suffering becomes less painful.

Russian novelist Alexander Solzhenitsyn discovered that in the bleak horror of a Siberian labor camp, a prisoner could find meaning, even if was only in performing well a seemingly trivial task. In his book *The First Circle,* Mr. Solzhenitsyn describes a busy room in which four prisoners were getting ready to celebrate a holiday in the midst of boredom and anxiety about being shipped to a hard-labor camp. They resist the officers, even the imprisonment itself, by maintaining their dignity. As one prisoner, "the designer," was readying his socks for sewing, another prisoner, Adamson, gave explicit instruction about the proper manner for mending as a way to combat the boredom and as a way to teach a lesson—resist totalitarianism, without fear, by being neat and focused on your daily routine. Adamson says to the designer,

> Darning is effective only when done conscientiously. God save us from a formalistic approach. Don't hurry. Put stitch after stitch and cross-stitch everything twice. One of the most common mistakes is to use rotten loops at the edge of a torn hole. Don't economize, don't save bad parts. Cut around the hole. Have you ever heard the name Berkalov?[3]

Mr. Adamson then went on to teach a lesson about a calm, defiant, old artillery engineer, Berkalov, who, upon the day of his arrest, continued to darn his socks as the police sought and arrested him. The moral meaning: Find courage and dignity by continuing to persevere in the little things of life when chaos and immorality are chasing you.

Each person finds meaning in a different way and in a different place, but no matter how terrible the suffering, there is always some meaning to be found.

Jerrod, in reflecting on the meaning of his suffering, saw the experience as something that strengthened his values:

> Looking back and regretting what I have done, without learning from it and moving on with my life, will only result in more problems. I have decided to live my life according to my values and that bad things can happen to anyone, regardless of how "good" or "bad" they are. The important thing is to go on with your life and help other people . . . even if they sometimes fail to appreciate it or treat you badly.

Jerrod is now less concerned with others' negative judgments and more confident of his own values.

Maria, after working through her partner's theft to support his cocaine habit, reflected,

> it proved to me that I am capable of forgiving someone that does me wrong. I am capable of letting go of hurt and seeing past it. That says a lot about me.

Maria's suffering gave her the opportunity to see herself as a forgiving person. She fits Dr. Frankl's description of people taking a bold stand, "transmuting their predicament into achievement, triumph, and heroism."

As people struggle toward meaning, their quest sometimes culminates in a grander, more overarching philosophy of life that Dr. Frankl calls "supra-meaning," which is similar to a worldview. Carol's search for meaning is one example of the development of a supra-meaning. Carol found an entirely new way of looking at the world as she refined her view of injustice and anger:

> With forgiving the hurts in my life came the realization that a lot of people are walking around without even knowing how to be successful at resolving their pain. I've seen how easily people hurt each other daily, in "put downs," "slams," or "better than you" attitudes. I understand how dysfunctional behavior causes pain to those you love and how unresolved grief can turn to bitterness. When I see an angry person, I am no longer intimidated, but sad because of how they are limiting themselves. When people are angry, bitter, and self-absorbed, they cannot be creative and open to new experiences. They are bound by their limited paradigms. They cannot grow to know life to its fullest.

Forgiving led Carol to many new insights. For her, forgiving is a key to healing. She seems almost sad that others do not yet see this way. She can stand against others' anger now, whereas before she was intimidated. Forgiving has opened doors of creativity and growth for her, and she is convinced that it can do the same for others.

✎ Journal Entry

In your journal, please reflect on these questions:

- How does your own worldview explain suffering?
- Can you see your suffering in the larger context of your life? If so, explain how your suffering has made you a better or a more mature person.
- What, specifically, have you learned and gained from your experience and from the forgiveness process?

Even if you see the suffering as providing no useful end for now, please keep in mind that forgiveness is a journey. Any conclusions of suffering's uselessness may not be the final word. If, on the other hand, you see meaning, this may begin the process of actual healing. Finding meaning in your suffering can lighten the burden of absorbed pain and enhance the clarity of positive changes in your life's journey.

DISCOVER YOUR NEED FOR FORGIVENESS

It is not uncommon for someone who begins forgiving to realize that he or she has been in the undesirable position of offender in the past. How did you feel when you realized that you had done wrong? How important was it for you to be forgiven? Did you want to be written off by the one you offended? What was it like when you received forgiveness?

Such questions often prompt sympathy for the one who hurt you, as Bobby Cunningham, a psychotherapist who specializes in pastoral care, noted.[4] The willingness to further explore forgiving as an option may arise, and empathy and compassion may deepen.

It would be false in many cases to conclude that your imperfections are the cause of the other's insensitivity. We must avoid this kind of reversal while, at the same time, realizing that we are imperfect and in occasional need of forgiving from others. If a false sense of guilt begins to arise, you should revisit the discussion of guilt in the uncovering phase of forgiving in Chapter 6. A legitimate journey of forgiveness involves seeing with greater clarity, not more clouded distortions.

✎ Journal Entry

Can you recall an incident (not necessarily involving the one who hurt you) in which you hoped to be forgiven? What was it like being on the receiving end of the gift? How might these insights aid your forgiving? Tell this story in your journal.

Turn to Chapter 14 for more on asking for and receiving forgiveness.

DISCOVER THAT YOUR ARE NOT ALONE

Forgiving need not take place in isolation. The pain you feel may seem cloistered deep within you so that it seems inaccessible to others. When you accept the pain, it can seem as though you shoulder the pain by yourself. Yet, it can be borne with others.

Rose sought help in forgiving her father through Alanon family group meetings designed to help those with an alcoholic family member. As she recalls

By going to meetings, I realized I wasn't alone in any part of my "journey." This helped me greatly, as I had more confidence in that I was doing the right thing.

Felicia, who struggled to forgive her "emotionally absent" mother, has profound gratitude for the therapists who listened to her and accepted her. It was caring counselors who stood with her. Because she had sensitive counseling, she was able to move along the path to acceptance, forgiveness, and emotional health.

For Maria, help came in the form of support networks, where she could talk over her problem with others who had similar experiences. The growth of the self-help movement and the extension of the 12-step approach into many areas of suffering means that many people adjusting to various problems can find help.

Those who seek such support should approach group participation carefully, because occasionally a group can veer away from its founding principles. Tricia, 27 and a graduate student, had been an active member of an Alanon group in one state. In the group she had been encouraged to forgive her alcoholic mother and alcoholic husband and found tremendous healing. However, when she moved to another state and sought out another Alanon group, she found that this group was dominated by several women who discouraged forgiveness. They spent a great deal of time at each meeting airing resentments against their former spouses. After a few meetings, she realized that these women resented her suggestions to members that they could forgive. Tricia left the group and found support elsewhere.

✎ Journal Entry

In your own case, do you have or seek support in forgiving? What is the nature of the support? Do those who support you have a good grasp of what forgiveness is? How do you know this? Has your companion aided your forgiveness? In what ways?

DISCOVER THE PURPOSE OF YOUR LIFE

I was a bit surprised when many of the incest survivors in our program expressed an interest in becoming helpers to other survivors.[5] Before the program, many were understandably preoccupied with their own pain. After considerable healing was realized, they wanted to give back to others. I understood then that people begin to see new directions in their lives following deep hurt and recovery.

Finding *purpose* differs from finding *meaning*. When people find meaning in suffering, they come to a new understanding about what happened in the past. They put the suffering in perspective, knowing that they've learned something valuable from the experience. Finding purpose not only changes your attitude toward the future, but also provides direction.

Carol was determined to love her children and to not transfer her pain and anger to them. She also found a new desire to speak to teenagers about sexual abstinence and marital commitment so that others would not have to go through the same experiences as she did.

Anthony found a new approach in family and work:

> I'll tell you this. A new purpose now is to never let anger control me ever again. I thought I was somehow empowered by my anger . . . I now realize it was tearing me apart. A new purpose? Yes, to be more forgiving across the board.

Rose, the college student hurt by her alcoholic father, also is determined to avoid resentment and anger:

I think now I care more about talking through problems, and I avoid fights as I think nothing is worth (real) fighting or at least drawn out fighting.

Mary Ann found that through conversation she could help others to forgive. Her own experience gave her insight. She would notice anger and unforgiveness in others and reach out, sharing her own story, encouraging friends, acquaintances, and sometimes even strangers to forgive.

✎ Journal Entry

Take some time to contemplate your purpose in life. What new purpose may be developing that involves how you interact with others? This may be part of your unfolding story.

DISCOVER THE FREEDOM OF FORGIVENESS

Freedom comes with a price. That price includes courageously confronting our anger, being able to label someone's behavior as wrong, humbly accepting that someone hurt us deeply, and working on changing our thoughts, feelings, and behaviors toward the person who does not necessarily deserve all of this. With time, our work and the support of others can begin to bear fruit. We can feel freer and even more mature. Let's look again at the writings of many of those who we've followed throughout this book.

Consider Rose's reflection at the end of her forgiveness journey:

> When I realized that I had forgiven my father, I did feel released. I was able to let go of the hate, and that made me a happier person, as I could think about other things—not dwell on the past. My

father lives in his own little world, so he wasn't affected by this; however, my friends and family noticed the change. Because I was happier in general I was able to put more into my positive relationships. Being a happier person is the major benefit I received from forgiving.

Michael describes his sense of well-being in terms of his dreams. Following his father's physical abuse, he had been tormented with two decades of nightmares in which he hurt others:

I began very quickly to lose episodic nightmares and began to dream more happily in color. If my father was affected by my forgiving him, I think it was in knowing that I don't hold any grudges, what's past is over.

Felicia describes her change after she forgave her mother:

Yes! Release and liberation, emotional and physical. An internal peace, relaxation, openness, acceptance of myself and others. A new sense of purpose and exploration. No more excessive alcohol use. Better eating and exercise patterns—lost about 20 pounds. I'm enjoying life and its challenges more. Also, seeing the beauty around me instead of "burying" myself with my eyes closed! Since both of my parents are deceased, they were not affected.

Cindy, whose partner burst into her friend's house and assaulted her, had a similar experience of emotional freedom:

I did feel a sense of being set free. When I finally saw Adam again after I had forgiven, there was no fear and no uneasiness. This was a liberating feeling for me. I am now in a new relationship, and I am more receptive and attuned to the two of us now. Not being obsessed with anger toward Adam was a great release to both me and my new partner.

Carol's experience was similar in her new relationship with her second husband. Forgiving her first husband Elliot allowed her to focus on the new relationship.

I did experience a release from my first marriage bond. This has given me the energy to concentrate on the man I am now married to. I'm learning to appreciate him for whom he is, instead of reacting and controlling him! I'm learning to trust again because even though Aaron [the new husband] does not share with me a spiritual understanding, he is incredibly respectful of me as a woman, and he has been a blessing with raising the boys.

When Jerrod forgave his mother he, too, reported a greater sense of energy and focus:

By giving up the resentment I had toward my mother, I feel I have been able to take a more mature view of life and use that energy to focus on moving ahead.

When Chad forgave his father, he described it this way:

It was very liberating after I forgave my dad. It was such a relief to go from so much anger to sympathy and understanding. It was refreshing not to think about it on a daily basis. I was losing sleep because of it. It had definitely affected me both emotionally and physically. I was able to concentrate more on my work because my mind stopped drifting and replaying things over and over. My dad never asked for forgiveness, but once I did, we became closer somehow. The biggest benefit of forgiveness is the stronger relationship with my dad.

Anthony also reports a release from negative and an increase in positive emotions:

My overall outlook in life is better. I consider myself to be deliberately more forgiving. I'd say that I have more of a love for life now. My family is stronger.

Maria talks in terms of being liberated after forgiving her partner:

Well, I felt more like my old self—more peaceful that I had resolved the issue . . . I felt liberation.

Regardless of the presenting problem and regardless of whom the offender is, each person here, upon forgiving, sensed an emotional release. The release was not instantaneous or automatic but seemed to unfold. The profiles are typical of those we see who experience deep hurt and then forgive.

Mary Ann believes that her life has been totally transformed.

I am no longer tired all the time, my house is clean, my life is in order. My relationship with my children is terrific. I can remember a time when I was so depressed I could not imagine ever being happy, but it's as though it happened to someone else. I am not that person any more. During the difficult forgiveness process, I held onto a line of scripture from the book of Joel: "I have restored the years the locusts have eaten." I felt that my life was like a field eaten clean by locusts and that God remade me, so that people don't see the victim I was, but the person I would have been.

I can almost see some of you shaking your head in agreement with these people. "Yes, I see myself in their writing," you say. Some of you may be thinking that you are nowhere near this level of release and freedom. Take heart, because all of the writers, without exception, suffered much before the experience of release. They had to wait, sometimes long, frustrating months, before they saw any change. Yet, that change did happen, as you read. Let their experiences be a source of hope for you.

✎ Journal Entry

It may be helpful to review your progress in forgiving to this point. Are you feeling less angry? Are you less tired? Are you less depressed? Are you more able to deal with small problems?

Without looking back at your previous answers, please rate the following questions on a scale of 1 to 10:

- *Question 1—How angry are you now at the one who hurt you?* A 1 means "not angry at all"; a 10 means "as angry as you possibly can be."

- *Question 2—Do you have shame about what happened to you?* A 1 means "no shame at all"; a 10 means "an extreme amount of shame."

- *Question 3—How much energy do you expend each day thinking about the person and dealing with what happened to you?* A 1 means "expending very little energy each day on the person and the event"; a 10 means "expending almost all of your energy on the person and the event."

- *Question 4—Relative to other solutions that you've tried in the past, how effective is forgiveness for you right now?* A 1 means "forgiveness is not very effective relative to other solutions you have tried"; a 10 means "forgiveness is much more effective than previous solutions you have tried."

- *Question 5—How much compassion do you have for the person?* A 1 means "absolutely no compassion for him or her"; a 10 means "tremendous compassion for him or her."

- *Question 6—How difficult or easy is it for you to accept the pain of what happened to you?* A 1 means "finding it very difficult to accept the pain"; a 10 means "finding it extremely easy to accept the pain."

- *Question 7—Have you forgiven the person?* A 1 means "not

at all forgiven him or her"; a 10 means "thoroughly and deeply forgiven him or her."

Now go back in your journal to find your initial ratings for each of the first six questions (there is no initial rating for the last question). Where have you improved? Where have you stayed unchanged? Where have you taken what may appear to be a step backward? For questions 1, 2, and 3, if your new score is *lower* than previously, then you are improving. For questions 4, 5, and 6, if your new score is *higher* than previously, then you also are improving. On the whole, have you become more forgiving, stayed the same, or become less forgiving?

Few people improve to such an extent that they are scoring at the extreme ends of the scale on the questions. I have found that the amount of change is very important. If your ratings, for example, on questions 4, 5, and 6 are in the range of 6 or 7, but these went up from 3 or 4, consider this to be progress. People who improve their emotional health when they forgive do not necessarily score exceptionally high; instead, they have better scores.

Many of you will be able to see measurable progress. Others will not. Let me address the next comments to those who do not. Change takes time. Please be gentle with yourself about your journey into forgiveness. With this in mind, go back to Chapter 4 to the box listing the guideposts involved in forgiving. In your journal, please rate each guidepost on a scale of 1 to 10 of how difficult you have found or are finding that guidepost, with 1 signifying "not at all difficult to deal with" and 10 implying "very great difficulty in dealing with it." After completing the task, see which guideposts were or are the most difficult for you and then ask, Have I truly dealt with or moved through this issue, or should I go back to it for more exploring or work? I urge you to visit again those chapters that discuss each of the guideposts you rated as particularly difficult, especially if you realize that you have unfinished business with them.

Next, rate each guidepost on a scale of 1 to 10 of importance, not difficulty. Which issues are so vital to your own forgiveness process that they are crucial for you to forgive? A rating of 1 means that you found it "very unimportant for your forgiveness" and 10 means that you found it "exceptionally important for your forgiveness." Again, after making the ratings, see which are of the most importance to you, the ones you rated the highest. Are there any that you rated as very important (that you gave a score of 7 to 10) and that you also rated as particularly difficult (again a score of 7 to 10)? If so, these issues may be slowing your forgiveness progress, and you should carefully examine them again.

Because these issues may be painful, you may have a tendency to hurry through them. Take your time. You may need to discuss these issues with your forgiveness companion, which is the very reason you brought him or her along on your journey in the first place.

Some of you will discover that there are more people to forgive or more incidents that need attention, and you will have to start the forgiveness process all over again. The second time through should be easier, although if the new person has hurt you even deeper than did the first or persists in being unfair, the process could be a greater struggle. Yet, consider this: Had you chosen to forgive this second person first, the struggle would have been longer and more grueling, because the first try at forgiveness often is the most difficult.

Sometimes it takes a while to clean out a lifetime of accumulated resentments. Years after a person has gone through the forgiveness process, a new hurt may be uncovered. If you have been harmed by many people and if this pattern of injury began in childhood, the forgiveness process will involve a gradual uncovering of old wounds. Mary Ann found that after the initial forgiveness, she occasionally remembered an old hurt. She applied the forgiveness process, and then a year or so later she discovered yet another old wound. This went on for several years, and each time the forgiveness process was easier. Each time she grew stronger and freer:

> Looking back, I realize that I could not have faced everything at once. I wasn't strong enough. The first time was the toughest. After that it was just applying what I had learned.

Knowing how to forgive is also preparation for the injuries and pain that will come in the future. No one is immune to suffering. Those who have gone through the forgiveness process can face the future with the knowledge that, no matter what happens, you can survive. Even if the unthinkable happens, you can say to yourself, "This is unjust, and I am angry, but I know that I can make a decision to forgive and eventually be free."

ENDNOTES

1. V. Frankl, *Man's Search for Meaning: An Introduction to Logotherapy* (New York: Washington Square Press, 1969).
2. Ibid, p. 70.
3. A. I. Solzhenitsyn, *The First Circle* (New York: Harper & Row, 1968), p. 196.
4. B. B. Cunningham, "The Will to Forgive: A Pastoral Theological View of Forgiving," *Journal of Pastoral Care* 39 (1985), 141–149.
5. S. R. Freedman and R. D. Enright, "Forgiveness as an Intervention Goal With Incest Survivors," *Journal of Consulting and Clinical Psychology* 64 (1996), 983–992.

CHAPTER II

SAYING "I FORGIVE YOU"

It is time now to take a deep breath and realize how much you have already accomplished. You made the courageous decision to admit that you were hurt by someone. You decided to explore what forgiveness is and then to try forgiving. You've done the work of forgiveness and perhaps discovered some insights about yourself, the one who hurt you, and life in general. Take some time to let the learning you've done sink in, and then we can go a little deeper, examining some of the questions people tend to raise after they've tried forgiveness.

One of the first questions people usually ask is whether they should tell the offender "I forgive you." Offering forgiveness can be an important part of the process, but it should be done with care. Actually saying out loud to the offender the words "I forgive you" is not always appropriate or necessary.

Unfortunately, many people use the words "I forgive you" as a weapon or a means of revenge. They confront the offender and recount in lurid detail all they have suffered in hopes of making the offender suffer. Often the offender reacts defensively, and new injuries are added to the old.

Sometimes a person will rush the process. Debbie, a high school senior, heard a talk on the importance of forgiveness, went home, and confronted her father, telling him in no uncertain terms that she forgave him for all the terrible things he had done to her. He heard how he emotionally neglected her, how he was in his "own little world," and how he missed her childhood. As you can imagine, he sat there in stunned disbelief. He did not expect his daughter to come home and dump a truckload of emotional baggage right on his head. Debbie's father had not been physically abusive or an alcoholic, just a somewhat neglectful and insensitive father overly involved with business concerns. He was devastated by Debbie's accusations. The "forgiveness" offered by Debbie caused a further deterioration in their relationship. Years later, Debbie realized that she had been using forgiveness as a weapon in her continuing struggle against her father's sensible restriction on her activities.

Given the possibility that saying "I forgive you" can be an act of revenge, when is it appropriate to say "I forgive you," and how should this be done? Each case needs to be evaluated on its own merits. Most cases will fall into one of the following categories.

THE OFFENDER HAS APOLOGIZED AND ASKED FOR FORGIVENESS

If the offender has apologized and asked for forgiveness, then the forgiver should formally accept the apology and the request for forgiveness with the words "I forgive you." Don't dismiss the seriousness of the request by saying "It doesn't matter" or "Don't think about it." It does matter. This person needs to hear the words "I forgive you." Of course, you as forgiver now must be careful not to rush to forgiveness just because the offender has asked. *Giving* forgiveness and *receiving* forgiveness can happen on two entirely different schedules. The other person may be more than ready to hear the words, but if you are not ready to say them, it is better to say something like, "Yes, I want to forgive you, but please give me some time, ok?" This is a sincere response, whereas a quick "I forgive you" may be less honest if you truly do not want to forgive at that point.

For some people, writing "I forgive you" will be easier than saying it in person. Rev. Walter Everett heard Mike, his son Scott's murderer, apologize during the sentencing hearing. Should he believe the murderer's apology?

> I went home and pondered what I would do about Mike's statement. I could ignore his words; I could respond in anger, believing he had no right to offer a simple apology to atone for Scott's death; or I could write to him and respond to his words as though they were sincerely meant. I chose the third option. . . . I wrote of the unbearable loss I had felt. But I then added, "Having said all that, I want to thank you for what you said in court on the day you were sentenced, and as hard as these words are to write, I forgive you." I added a few lines about the love and forgiveness of God, and then put the letter in the mail, and as I did so, I felt as though a tremendous burden had been lifted from my shoulders.

The letter had a tremendously positive effect both on Mike and on Rev. Everett.

THE OFFENDER HAS NEITHER APOLOGIZED NOR ASKED FOR FORGIVENESS, BUT GUILT HAS BEEN ESTABLISHED BEYOND A REASONABLE DOUBT

If the offender has been convicted of the offense, if adultery has been uncovered, if a parent has deserted the family or failed to pay child support, or if a friend has failed to repay a debt, guilt can be considered as established. The offender may have failed to ask forgiveness because of shame or the belief that the victim will not forgive. Or the offender may be completely unapologetic or even blame the victim. In either case, it is appropriate to offer forgiveness even without an apology in the hopes that the offender will offer an apology after receiving forgiveness. If the offender refuses to apologize, remains unrepentant, or continues to offend, the forgiver can walk away from the situation confident that he or she did all that was possible.

Forgiveness without an apology can be offered when a family formally confronts a relative who is engaged in self-destructive behavior such as alcoholism or drug addiction. Formal, structured confrontations involving family members, which also involve a clergyman or health care professional, have proven to be highly effective in dealing with a person who denies the effects of compulsive behavior. During the confrontation session, family members recount how the alcoholism or other compulsive behavior has hurt them. The goal is to show, for example, the alcoholic the full effect of the drinking on the family and to encourage entrance into treatment. During this type of confrontation, offering forgiveness can be appropriate and helpful if at the same time the family members make it clear that they will no longer enable self-destructive behavior.

THE RELATIONSHIP BETWEEN THE OFFENDER AND THE FORGIVER HAS BEEN BROKEN, AND BOTH SIDES ARE ANGRY

When relationships break down, both sides may feel that they are the injured party. If this is the case, the people going through the forgiveness process may choose to open the process of reconciliation by offering an apology, even if they believe that they are more the recipient of offense than offender. In fact, in these cases, it is often easier for the more innocent of the parties to begin the reconciliation process by saying "I'm sorry." The expression of sorrow can be conditional. For example, if a relationship has broken down and you believe that you are the offended party, you can go to the offender and say "I am sorry for the unpleasantness between us." This can open the door for the other person to say "I am sorry," as you, then, offer forgiveness.

Working together with another person on giving and receiving forgiveness is not easy. Receiving forgiveness, like its counterpart of offering forgiveness, is a process similar to the giving forgiveness process discussed in Chapter 4, as we will see in Chapter 14. Those wanting to be forgiven go through an uncovering phase in which they feel guilt and remorse, along with a genuine desire to change the offending behavior. They then commit to receiving forgiveness by apologizing or some other expression of sorrow. They are willing to wait for the other person to develop a sense of forgiveness without forcing the issue. This is followed by rethinking whom the other is and how much hurt was caused, which tends to induce empathy and compassion for the offended one, usually leading to more respectful behavior in the future toward the offended. The one who is asking for forgiveness usually then enters into a discovery phase, finding greater maturity from seeking and waiting for forgiveness from the other person.[1]

THE OFFENSE HAPPENED A LONG TIME AGO, AND THE OFFENDER IS NO LONGER A PART OF THE FORGIVER'S LIFE

The forgiveness process often brings to light resentments against people who hurt us years ago and whom we haven't seen since. The offender may be a childhood friend, a neighbor, a teacher, or stranger who passed through our lives and left a scar but with whom we have no current relationship. We may not even know how to get in touch with the offender.

Even if we can't track down every teacher who subjected us to ridicule before the entire class, we can still forgive. We don't have to find the children who teased us on the playground or the business man who cheated us, but we need to be free of our anger. Of course, if the opportunity arises to offer forgiveness, we should take advantage of it.

This does not include family members. If you have cut off your relationship with a family member because of your resentment and unwillingness to forgive, some effort should be taken to restore the relationship, unless there is a danger of injury. For example, a son, deserted by his father, might send him a letter and try to restore communication, but a woman who fled from a violent husband should not reveal her present location if she sincerely believes he still presents a threat to her safety.

When communication is established, try to be aware that your need to resolve old issues may not be the same for the other person. We are all on different parts of the forgiveness process and the process of wanting to be forgiven. Try to get some sense of where the other person is in the process by using the guideposts in Chapters 4 and 14.

THE OFFENDER HAS NO IDEA THAT THE FORGIVER IS OFFENDED

We can be offended or deeply hurt by people who have no idea that they have injured us. Would telling the person first that you were deeply hurt and second that you forgive help the offender, or would it be the cause of pain without any benefit? Has the relationship been strained because of your lack of forgiveness?

In some cases, bringing up an old resentment can be beneficial. Sally and Elizabeth, cousins who grew up in the same small town, were each other's best friends and so spent summers together swimming, playing softball, and most importantly, visiting their grandmother, whom they loved and admired. Sally usually visited in jeans and worn-out sports shoes, whereas Elizabeth came in fashionable, stylish clothes; Sally was more reserved, Elizabeth more outgoing. Unfortunately, their grandmother strongly and overtly favored Sally, who was more quiet and shy, and continually criticized Elizabeth, who was more spontaneous and spoke her mind.

Although she did not realize it at the time, Elizabeth began to develop resentment toward Sally. The resentment followed them into adulthood. When both women were in their 30s, Elizabeth brought up the situation and was surprised to learn that Sally felt guilty because she had been favored. Sally explained that their grandmother in later years said that she favored Sally because of her timidity and being from a poor family, whereas Elizabeth had an air of privilege, coming from a rich family. Elizabeth then began to forgive Sally and her grandmother.

FALSE FORMS OF "I FORGIVE YOU" AND "PLEASE FORGIVE ME"

Forgiving and reconciling can lead to healing, but sometimes a family may be caught in a pattern of pseudo-forgiveness, saying "I forgive you" and "please forgive me" without meaning either one, which is counterproductive. Family therapist Virginia Satir, who has analyzed typical communication patterns within families,[2] found that in some families one of the members continually blames and the other continually placates, giving in to unreasonable demands and unjustified criticism. The one who continually blames can end the accusations with "But, I forgive you" when there is nothing to forgive. The one who placates may accept the blame and the offer of forgiveness by saying "Yes, you are right . . . I am at fault . . . I am the one to blame."[3] The apologizer does so not because of real guilt, but to keep the peace.

193

In other words, wanting to be forgiven also can have its false forms, rewarding the blamer for false accusation and perpetuating a negative pattern of communication. In this case, the pseudo-apologizer may need to forgive the false accuser, who needs to stop the pattern of false-forgiving.

There are other false forms as well. An offender's insincere apology can mask a desire to keep things as they are, to manipulate an interaction as a way to perpetuate his or her own unfairness. The compulsive gambler who apologizes, knowing that the offended will forgive and forget, may keep doing this as a way to keep borrowing money and gambling.

Try to be aware of any offender's degree of sincerity when he or she asks for forgiveness. Someone who truly wants to be forgiven needs to realize that he or she is not *deserving* of forgiveness. Forgiveness is a *gift*, something given out of a sense of generosity; the gift-giver is not obligated to give it. At the same time, the guilty party is *worthy* of receiving this present if and when it comes.[4] To be worthy is quite different from being deserving. All people have the capacity for good will and therefore are worthy to receive respect.[5]

Saying "I forgive you" in some cases actually may be a way of excusing, condoning, enabling, or tolerating destructive behavior. As with the compulsive gambler, the other family members who say they forgive may be letting the gambler off the hook. Rather than proclaiming forgiveness while ignoring consequences, the forgiver might add "I forgive you, but because I love you, I will no longer be party to your destructive behavior." Those who have been victimized for years, who have been told that they are wrong for objecting to their victimization, need to remember that forgiveness is compatible with asking someone to stop doing bad things to us, to others, or to themselves.

✎ Journal Entry

In considering your own situation, which of the five descriptions best depicts what you are going through? Have you said "I forgive you," or are you contemplating it? What are the advantages, considering the unique aspects of your situation, in going to the person directly? What are the disadvantages?

Is the person you are trying to forgive working on receiving forgiveness? Does he or she want to be forgiven? What evidence do you have for this opinion? Is the person trying to discern what went wrong and his or her level of guilt and remorse?

Might the person be exploring the possibility of asking for forgiveness? Does the person know what forgiveness is and is not? Does he or she realize that forgiveness is a gift and that you are free to give it whenever you wish?

Is the person doing the active work of receiving forgiveness, seeing what you've been through, feeling empathy and compassion toward you? Is he or she willing to make amends and truly change? Has he or she learned anything from this experience? Is he or she growing as a person?

Where are you in your process of forgiving relative to where he or she is in the process of receiving forgiveness? Are you at somewhat similar places, or are you farther ahead or behind?

It sometimes takes patience and perseverance when you are far apart in your respective forgiveness journeys. How will you handle any discrepancy that exists between how far along you are and how far along the other person is?

ENDNOTES

1. More detail on how to receive forgiveness can be found in R. D. Enright and the Human Development Study Group, "Counseling within

the Forgiveness Triad," *Counseling and Values* 40 (1996), 107–126.

2. V. Satir, *The New Peoplemaking* (Mountain View, CA: Science and Behavior Books, 1988).

3. Ibid.

4. See R. D. Enright and the Human Development Study Group, "Piaget on the Moral Development of Forgiveness," *Human Development* 37 (1994), 63–80, for further discussion. Please keep in mind that one person is not necessarily the only one who has acted unfairly in a relationship.

5. See M. R. Holmgren, "Forgiveness and the Intrinsic Value of Persons," *American Philosophical Quarterly* 30 (1993), 341–352, on this idea.

Part III

GOING DEEPER

CHAPTER 12

MORE QUESTIONS TO HELP YOU FORGIVE

The last chapter covered one of the more frequently asked questions about forgiveness. There are more questions to consider if you want a more subtle understanding of the process. These questions and answers have emerged out of the interactions I've had over the years with audiences when I speak on the topic of forgiveness. I've learned much from the people who ask the questions and from those who work with me on the answers. For some cases, I am still forming those answers. Perhaps you can use the answers as a springboard to your own views as you continue to explore forgiveness. Let's begin with a question that is on many people's minds.

HOW DO I KNOW WHEN I HAVE GENUINELY FORGIVEN?

Many people seek some concrete sign that forgiveness is complete. They are uneasy until they know that they have completed the journey. Some reason, "If I have not yet completely forgiven the one who hurt me, then I am not a very good person." Yet, if we see forgiveness as a process, one that can take time, then perhaps the quest for an end, a complete termination of resentment and a complete embrace of forgiving, is not so vital. Being open to further developments in forgiving might become the goal.

Forgiveness takes time in most cases, with various markers appearing along the path to show that forgiving is, in fact, taking place. An initial marker is the decision to enter into forgiving. Have you decided to try forgiveness? Have you committed to avoiding subtle revenge against the person? If so, you are forgiving and should give yourself credit for this.

Have you begun to see the other person in a different light, seeing him or her as a member of the human community, without harsh, condemning thoughts entering the picture? If so, you can have confidence that forgiveness is occurring. Over time, as the negative thoughts and feelings wane, you may find yourself with a glimmer of positive thoughts and feelings toward the one who hurt you. In his book *Forgive and Forget,* Lewis Smedes's insightful question is, Are you beginning to wish the person well?[1] Do you hope that, for example, he or she gets the promotion at work, or instead do you hope that he or she gets a dismissal letter? You do not have to sacrifice yourself for the other to wish him or her well. You simply hope that his or her life is going all right, whether or not you are a part of that life.

Other tests for deeper levels of forgiving include the expression of kindness, generosity, and moral love toward the one who hurt you, but these are more analogous to final exams, not pop quizzes, and are difficult to achieve and sometimes not reached by the forgiver.

You need not wait until you've reached such distant markers along the path to credit yourself with the act of forgiving. Forgiving is hard work. Trying it is itself a significant step. You should avoid condemning yourself for not moving fast enough or going deep enough.

As we forgive, we sometimes find ourselves angry all over again. This can be frustrating, because we already forgave the person once. These cycles of churning emotion, quieting, followed once again by stirred-up emotions, are not uncommon. In the periods of disruption you will have more work to do. This is not a reflection of some moral weakness or an inability to get it right; it is not a reflection on forgiveness itself. Instead, it is a reflection of your humanity, of your ambivalence toward someone who hurt you. It is in times like this, when the uncomfortable emotions come back to visit, that you need a certain gentleness with yourself. The fact that such anger has ended once should indicate to you that forgiving again can control that emotion.

✎ Journal Entry

Write down those instances in which you have wished the offender well. Be specific. In what contexts have you done so? What is the essence for you of this wishing the person well?

Have you had an opportunity to express kindness toward him or her? As we know, this is not always possible. If this has been possible, what have you done, or what might you do?

Have you experienced the cycles of anger and quiet regarding what happened? Are the angry times less intense or less frequent?

IS IT SELFISH TO FORGIVE FOR MY OWN BENEFIT?

In his book *Is Human Forgiveness Possible?* the pastoral counselor John Patton insists that forgiving is not something we do to improve our own health.[2] Speaking from a Protestant Christian perspective, he sees forgiving as fitting into the divine plan that we all begin to see one another as equals. The motive in forgiving, therefore, is to better understand God's will for us—it is not a self-serving activity. In my opinion, even the most spiritually attuned person did not start out as holy and near-perfect. Because we all develop in our level of maturity, self-condemnation need not befall those who are nearer the starting line than to the finish line.

Motivations change as we gain more insight and experience. If a person is so hurting because of another's cruelty, isn't it reasonable to seek a cure? If you have a chaffing sore on your foot, is it so easy to focus on such values as serving others while your foot hurts? Many will try to cure the foot and then serve. Surely, some will do both at the same time, but the foot still is and should be a focus because the pain is a clear indication that you need to heal your foot.

The emotional pain from another's injustice is like the foot pain. The emotional pain is a signal that you are now to attend to that pain, not in any obsessive, all-consuming way, but in a reasonable, mature way. Your acknowledging that you must confront the pain is not dishonorable. As you deal with the pain by forgiving, you probably will find that your motivations change from a focus on your own pain exclusively to the person who hurt you. I am calling on those who see yourself as selfish to be more patient and gentle with yourself as you courageously acknowledge that you are hurting.

On the other hand, if you begin and end your journey without a glance toward the one who hurt you, then I would question whether you have truly entered the forgiveness arena. Perhaps this is what Dr. Patton had in mind when he insisted that we do not forgive for our own benefit. In my experience, however, most who begin forgiving with the motivation to aid in their own healing are not acting selfishly, are open to exploring whom the injurer is, and in many cases, are willing to reach out to him or her. Selfishness rarely enters into the forgiveness process, because forgiving and selfishness are incompatible approaches to life.

✎ Journal Entry

Have you been focusing on your own pain to the exclusion of focusing on the one who hurt you? Take some time to write about the times you've focused on yourself and the times you've focused on the other person. Can you draw any conclusions about changes you should make?

WILL FORGIVENESS *MAKE* ME FORGET?

Those who have experienced great trauma over another's or others' actions have the legitimate fear that the injustice will continue if they offer forgiveness. As an example, a wife who has been physically abused by her husband feels that she might so dismiss the blows upon forgiving that those blows will surely come again. Those who have experienced political oppression are usually concerned that forgiveness means further exploitation.

This is among the most important questions ever asked about forgiveness because the answer has consequences for people's very survival. My response is that we must first realize that forgiving is a *choice,* one freely entered by the one who was hurt. Never should there be such a pressure to forgive that the injured one feels compelled to dive into it without careful exploration. Blind forgiving, without understanding the serious nature of the offense, without understanding what forgiveness is and is not, without struggling with some of the philosophical questions of forgiveness, is wrong.

Only after careful examination of forgiving, in which a person's confusions, doubts, and reservations are addressed, should he or she embark on forgiving. If forgiving is entered with clarity and conviction, then the forgiver is likely to avoid the issues of forgetting.

I am assuming that by using the word *forgetting* the person is really saying "If I forgive, I am opening the door for continued abuse. As I accept the person (or people) into my life, I become vulnerable if the one who hurt me is still acting immorally." In other words, the one who is questioning forgiving actually is confusing it with reconciling. If one reconciles, comes together again with one who insists on acting unjustly, then, yes, the "forgiver" is risking further injury.

Yet, as we saw in chapter 2, forgiving and reconciling are not always linked. One can forgive but not reconcile. One who has taken the time to understand the subtleties of forgiving should realize and remember this distinction, which is particularly important when faced with people whom you cannot trust. It is possible to forgive and not reconcile. Again, whether a person forgives is his or her own choice. A person should not be reasoning this way: "Ok, I see the distinction between forgiving and reconciling. I *must* forgive, even if I don't reconcile." One may choose to do neither, but in leaving both behind you might ask, What do I have as a response to the injustice that may heal me and others affected by the offense?

If we now have established that forgiving need not bring about an irrational, even rash reconciliation, we still have a lingering question: Will forgiveness make you forget what happened? I do not think that anyone has developed a moral amnesia from forgiving.

✎ Journal Entry

Think back to at least 10 incidences of your childhood that you vividly remember. Write each down in your journal.

Examine what you wrote. How many memories involve difficult, painful experiences, perhaps a broken arm, a lost dog, an insecure first day at school? I suspect that you listed several painful events. We do remember significant, painful events in our lives. Depending on the circumstance, we often do not feel the pain again, but the memory lingers. Why should it be any different when the pain involves another's cruelty toward us? Forgiveness does not blot out memory.

WILL FORGIVING *HELP* ME FORGET?

This is a substantially different question than the previous one. I am presuming that this question is centered on putting the painful past behind the person. A person asking this question usually is not menaced by an unjust person or group who is threatening his or her survival. Instead, the questioner usually has a certain distance from the difficulty and wishes to accept what happened and move forward in his or her life. An example involves Carl, a middle-aged man who did not get along with his mother while he was growing up. The mother was cloying and critical. He could never get grades in school that were high enough for her. She never approved of his dates, and even now he is single. He feels that she never allowed him the independence he needed to grow as a person. She now is deceased, and he wishes a measure of peace.

As Carl forgives, he probably will not remember in the same way he now does. Instead of seeing an overbearing ogre of a mother, he may see a woman who did not know how to control her own insecurities. He may see her as someone offering love, even if that love was expressed in stultifying ways. Will he forget? Certainly he will not forget his mother as he forgives. He probably will remember some of the good times more and de-emphasize some of the bad. Yet in a certain sense, Carl will be forgetting because he will recall happier incidences and not let the memory of decades-old interactions dominate. Will forgiving help him forget? It should as he remembers in new ways.

How, then, is it possible for Carl to forget but not for the abused spouse to forget? Carl is asking a very different question than the person who contemplates entering once again into a relationship that was formerly abusive. Carl's elderly mother is no threat to him now. With some forgiveness effort, he can choose to focus on the memories of childhood that are more pleasant while not distorting those that were bad. If he de-emphasizes the bad experiences, if he puts them aside to "forget" them, he will not lose his life. An abused spouse needs to keep before her the dangers that exist now in life. This does not mean that the one who was abused must continually relive vivid memories of horror—it does mean remembering where the dangers lie.

✎ Journal Entry

What does it mean to you to "forget" as you forgive? What does it mean to you to "remember in new ways"? Have you found yourself remembering like this? Take some time to reflect on how you are remembering the past now that you have begun to forgive.

MIGHT I REPRESS MY ANGRY FEELINGS?

Some people are afraid that their forgiveness will result in an unhealthy repression of the anger they should be feeling toward the one who was unfair. The fear seems based, at least in part, on certain books receiving notoriety for their warnings against the dangers of forgiveness. For example, consider the caution sounded by therapist Susan Forward in her book *Toxic Parents*.[3]

The theme of *Toxic Parents* takes one far from forgiveness and into the realm of adults severing emotional and relational ties with their parents, but the critical examination of forgiveness is also included. Dr. Forward's main point about forgiveness is that it becomes a "trap" as the forgiver "overlooks" offenses.[4] As the forgiver so overlooks, he or she begins to mask all of the hurt and pent-up anger that should be released but is not. As you might expect, the author concludes that forgiving one's hurtful parents not only is unnecessary, but is indisputably unhealthy.

A key to understanding Dr. Forward's approach is in her definition of forgiving, which she sees as overlooking offenses.[5] If overlooking an offense is dangerous to one's health, and if forgiveness is this kind of overlooking, then it follows that forgiveness also is unhealthy. The major problem with this logic is that forgiving and overlooking are two different moral animals. One is emotionally friendly; the other is a beast.

To complicate matters further, Dr. Forward cites case studies of people who seem to misunderstand forgiveness in the same way as the author. For example, Stephanie quickly "forgives" her stepfather for his insidious incestuous advances. She represses rage, and all kinds of psychological complications occur. When we carefully examine what happened here, we must conclude that forgiving did not make Stephanie miserable, but distorting exactly what forgiveness is.[6] Nowhere in the ancient literature or in the modern philosophical or psychological writings is there the slightest hint that one should repress feelings upon forgiving. On the contrary, ample time is allotted to expressing anger, to understanding the nature of the offense, and only then to forgiving.

Should one fear repression of anger upon forgiving? If the person has a clear definition of forgiveness and avoids equating it with overlooking, reconciliation, and the abandonment of justice, then the fear should vanish. It is imperative, however, that anyone starting to forgive first understand precisely what forgiveness is and is not. Dr. Forward's concerns should act as cautions for us. A too-ready stance to jump into forgiveness is dangerous. Let's not only look, but also study before we leap. In fact, rather than leaping, let's walk slowly through the pathway of forgiveness.

✎ Journal Entry

Have you read other books on forgiveness that contradict what you are learning here? If so, discern what the contradictions are. Do the writers differ in how they define forgiveness? You now have enough knowledge to begin making the hard judgment about writers' views. I certainly have no monopoly on the truth, and so I may need to revisit a few details on forgiveness, but so, too, may other writers.

If some idea disturbs you, write in your journal about the confusions, contradictions, and your solutions so that forgiveness becomes more clear to you.

SHOULD I FORGIVE IMMEDIATELY AFTER BEING HURT, OR SHOULD I WAIT?

Circumstances are an important ingredient in the answer to this difficult question. Some offenses are so dreadful that they take much time, whereas others require only a bit of work with much reward. To set a prescribed time for starting forgiveness is to ignore that forgiving is a choice. To suggest that someone must begin forgiving immediately upon suffering a moral injury is to ignore the necessary period of anger that precedes the forgiveness work. Yet, if we realize that anger, appropriately expressed, is a part of the forgiveness process, then it seems reasonable for someone to begin forgiving soon after the injury if the person so chooses.

Rabbi Charles Klein, in his book *How to Forgive When You Can't Forget,* offers an interesting perspective on the answer here.[7] Throughout his work Rabbi Klein refers to the idea of a *trans-*

forming moment, which is akin to the "change of heart" to which both the philosopher Joanna North and I refer when a person decides to alter one's angry course in favor of mercy and kindness.[8] At some point, the person, who may not have even considered forgiveness as an option, now sees it as good and reasonable.

To solidify the point of the transforming moment, Rabbi Klein relates a true story of airline passengers who, upon suddenly realizing that their plane must crash land, quickly converted to merciful, giving people. For 41 minutes they faced their existential selves. Upon escaping death, some survivors told of changed perspectives. The grudges they had for years somehow seemed less important. Angers were cast aside in favor of reconciliation. These transformations did not appear to be fleeting but were more ingrained because of the terror experienced 35,000 feet in the air. The passengers transformed because they realized, perhaps for the first time, that life offers no guarantees. Tomorrow may be too late to forgive and reconcile. Such a perspective can motivate a person to begin forgiving sooner rather than later.

✎ Journal Entry

How have you handled the issue of time? If you've waited to forgive, what circumstances led you to wait? Are there any barriers in your way to forgiving? What are those barriers, and what do you have to do to set them aside?

HOW DO I FORGIVE AN INSTITUTION?

People commonly ask this question when they believe an institution, such as a place of employment, was unfair to them. A person who is fired, must accept a low wage, or tolerate what is seen as unjust rules within an organization all struggle with forgiveness issues. My opinion is that the person wishing to forgive should try to identify those people who are at the center of the discontent. Are there leaders of the institution who could be making life fairer but who choose not to do so? Perhaps the person is long deceased but was responsible for current practice. Finding a specific person or group may make the forgiveness task easier and philosophically more accurate. After all, an institution without the human workers is only a set of lifeless buildings, documents, and machines. Try to find those who could be doing better and forgive them.

It is important to distinguish genuine injustice and a difference of opinion. Suppose that a place of employment bans smoking, annoying those who light up. Should the smokers forgive? It seems that the smokers may need to assess whether there is a true breach of justice or whether one's annoyance at the inconvenience is clouding interpretation of exactly what is and is not fair. In situations in which two sides are both seeking fairness, one side cannot be too quick to point the finger of judgment. Banning smoking, although depriving someone of a perceived individual right, is safeguarding a group's rights to better health in the workplace.

Here we greet the issue of disappointment versus injustice. In your quest to forgive an institution, are you absolutely sure that someone or a group is acting unfairly? If you saw the issue from the other's perspective, would you conclude that unfairness exists, whether intended or unintended? Forgiving within this context requires great scrutiny of the issues on all sides before concluding that injustice happened. Being disappointed does not always mean that others treated you unfairly.

CAN I FORGIVE THE ASPECTS OF SELF THAT ARE IMPERFECT?

I would not even bring up this question if it were not circulating in the literature as an issue. Others' books on the topic of forgiveness have advocated forgiving portly thighs or arthritic hands.⁹ The aim of those who suggest that we forgive body parts is to help those dissatisfied with bodily appearance, degree of sickness, or physical pain to transcend judgment of self and to conclude that he or she is better and more whole than appearance suggests. The writers try to bring a person to an inner peace, an acceptance of sorts.

Is such an exercise as forgiving one's trick knee actually forgiveness? In my opinion, this goes well beyond forgiveness, because the focus is not centered on *people*. If one is upset with one's knee and can forgive it, doesn't it follow that one could conceivably forgive even inanimate objects with which one is dissatisfied? It seems that by this kind of a definition, one actually could be "forgiving" when one accepts an old, fading, peeling house facade as it is. The "forgiveness" of a house is compatible with the idea of forgiving a knee or thighs under the conditions of replacing one's former anxieties about the house (over labor and cost) with well-being, seeing beyond the peeling facade to a warm home filled with decorative potential, and letting go of the need to transform the house's present state. One certainly may be "letting go," one may be quieting, but is one forgiving? If so, then what does the "forgiving" mean?

Can one forgive a body wreaked with pain? I do not think so, precisely because one's body is not acting unfairly. You may be disappointed, you may need to accept the situation, but you are not forgiving as you accept. Can one forgive a dilapidated house? No, because a house is incapable of acting immorally. As we clarify the definition of forgiving, the answers to many of our questions become clearer. When we unwittingly equate the meaning of forgiving with forgetting, disappointment, and acceptance, the precise meaning of forgiveness becomes lost.

CAN I FORGIVE A NATURAL DISASTER?

I regularly receive questions along this line. When Hurricane Andrew swept through Miami, or the devastating tornadoes through Oklahoma, many children became frightened of future storms. I was asked on several occasions if it seems appropriate for the children to "forgive" the hurricane or the tornado. The children tended to ascribe living qualities to the storms, treating them as sentient beings. If the children could forgive the storm, so the arguments went, they may find a greater peace in place of their posttraumatic stress.

The arguments are alluring, because children humanize storms. Hurricanes even have names. If children could forgive and let the trauma go, they would be better off. Forgiveness may help reduce the considerable anger over a destroyed home. A friendlier attitude toward Andrew may generalize to future hurricanes, reducing the fear of another. Should children be taught to forgive particularly destructive storms?

I don't think that children should be taught to forgive a storm because of the distortions engendered in the "forgiving." The hurricane was not immoral. The children never will be able to respond with the principle of moral love toward the hurricane or tornado. When we examine just what a child offers when forgiving, we must conclude that the children simply cannot offer this to a tornado.

Yet, what of the notion of reduced resentment? Couldn't a child, by forgiving a storm, reduce resentment? But can't we help reduce resentment by means other than forgiveness? Can't we work on issues of grief at the loss of a home? Can't grief reduction eliminate some negative emotions associated with a destructive storm? Can't we work on the issue of acceptance, as we might with our trick knees, portly thighs, and arthritic hands? If we can reduce angers by other means than forgiveness when they call for other means, let's do so.

Should we help children who are the victims of natural disasters to forgive? We should help the children by preserving the definition of forgiveness while at the same time working to reduce grief and increase acceptance when disasters outside of our control do happen.

HOW OFTEN SHOULD I DO THE WORK OF FORGIVING?

Forgiving is hard but rewarding work. A person must put effort into understanding what forgiveness is and is not. He or she must strive to know the various points of forgiving, including the sifting and winnowing necessary to answer the critics of the process. He or she must distinguish forgiveness from its many false forms.

Should a prospective forgiver, then, expect to devote most waking hours to the process? Of course not, because forgiving is not meant to be an exhausting exercise, but a refreshing one. One needs to be aware of the value of resting from the difficulties, stepping away from the work. Each of us has certain times for reflection. For some, it occurs on the long ride home from work, for others it is the early morning, when rested from the night. Forgiving is a part of an overall life, not life itself. Just as physical exercise is beneficial, it can lead to knee surgery if one pushes beyond one's capacity.

Do not be in a hurry to run through the forgiveness processes. Recall that accepting the pain for now is a part of the process. If you do not realize this, you may push too hard, with ineffective results. Take time to rest from the labors of forgiving.

Perhaps finding a place for forgiving within the routines of the day is best so that you will always have the time for it. In your journal writing you may already have set aside a time and place for you to work on forgiveness. And you are able to put the journal writing aside when it is time to move to another task.

✎ Journal Entry

How often should you do the work of forgiveness? Are there others you are considering forgiving? Who are they, and why are you considering forgiving them? You may wish to prioritize the people on the list and forgive one at a time in a steady, paced way so that you are not overwhelmed.

HOW LONG UNTIL I EXPERIENCE SOME EMOTIONAL RELIEF?

Many people try forgiveness when they are emotionally uncomfortable. At first, the bottom line for many is emotional relief. I cannot say definitively when anyone will feel less anxious and more settled inside. There is some indication that emotional relief can happen in a matter of weeks, not months or years, as we saw in the study with men hurt by the abortion decision of their partners.

The more entrenched the emotional turmoil, the more time may be necessary. For example, the incest survivors with whom Suzanne Freedman worked required about 14 months on the average before their anxiety and depression levels were within the normal range. This may seem like a long time, but try to put this in perspective. Many participants in that research had sought help other than forgiveness for years, without experiencing a deep, long-lasting change. Most certainly, some received help before they tried forgiveness with us, but they all initially volunteered because the distressing psychological symptoms persisted. After 14 months, all showed substantial improvement in their psychological health. When we compare the years of emotional distress with this wait, it suddenly seems reasonable.

How long must you wait before you feel better? Although I cannot give a specific answer, I can say that our research results are encouraging. Research done elsewhere may not apply directly to any one case, but there is cause for hope. The processes outlined in this book have helped people overcome nagging emotional unrest. Without forgiveness, I wonder what else may be as effective in dealing with considerable resentment from unfair treatment.

✎ Journal Entry

Which of the questions posed in this chapter are important to you? Do you agree or disagree with my answers? Write down each question that is significant to you. Then, respond to my answers by countering, adding to, or agreeing with me. If you are countering or adding to what I wrote, be sure to address why this is so. Was I simply not detailed enough? Was I inaccurate? How do you and I differ in our responses to the question?

Which questions did I leave out? Write down the questions to which you still seek answers. Can an answer be found elsewhere in the book, or did I overlook it? If an answer is nowhere to be found in this book, I challenge you to write your own answer based on the knowledge you've now acquired on forgiveness. Having come this far, you probably have solid knowledge that can form the basis of your answer. I suggest that you visit again the definition of forgiveness, from which everything else flows. Get to know that definition better and then try to answer the questions you wrote in your journal.

ENDNOTES

1. L. B. Smedes, *Forgive and Forget: Healing the Hurts We Don't Deserve* (San Francisco, CA: Harper & Row, 1984).
2. J. Patton, *Is Human Forgiveness Possible?* (Nashville, TN: 1985), p. 175.
3. S. Forward, *Toxic Parents* (New York: Bantam Books, 1989).

4. See Ibid, p. 189.
5. Ibid, p. 189.
6. Further details on Forward's work on forgiveness are in R. D. Enright and colleagues, "Interpersonal Forgiveness Within the Helping Professions: An Attempt to Resolve Differences of Opinion," *Counseling and Values* 36 (1992), 84–103. Critiques of others who discourage forgiveness are presented in this article. For those who want a deeper discussion of what forgiveness is, see R. D. Enright and the Human Development Study Group, "The Moral Development of Forgiveness," in *Handbook of Moral Behavior and Development* (Vol. 1), eds. W. Kurtines and J. Gewirtz (Hillsdale, NJ, Erlbaum, 1991), 123–152.
7. C. Klein, *How to Forgive When You Can't Forget* (Bellmore, NY: Liebling, 1995).
8. See J. North, "Wrongdoing and Forgiveness," *Philosophy* 62 (1987), 499–508, and Chapter 6.
9. See, for example, R. Casarjian's book, *Forgiveness: A Bold Choice for a Peaceful Heart* (New York: Bantam, 1992), especially Chapter 10.

CHAPTER 13

HELPING CHILDREN FORGIVE

Let's now take a short break from the work you've been doing in forgiving a particular person for a specific offense. Once people begin to understand, appreciate, and practice forgiveness, they are interested in giving it away to others, especially to their children and those under their care. This chapter offers that opportunity.

How can you teach your children to forgive? The answer has important implications for the health of the next generation. I am convinced that children not only can but should be taught to forgive.

As we begin the process of forgiveness, we learn that harboring and nurturing resentment is self-destructive. Many of the most harmful resentments begin when we were injured as children, became angry, and did not forgive. I have found that once people forgive, they can't help looking at their children, wanting to protect them from unnecessary suffering borne of long-held resentment. We can rightly think "If only I forgave when I was a child, when I was first injured, all these years of suffering would be prevented." We would, of course, be right. In many cases, harboring resentment makes us suffer even more than did the original injury. The good news is that children can forgive.

HOW CHILDREN THINK ABOUT FORGIVENESS

My colleagues and I did two studies in the United States in which we asked children and adults about their understanding of forgiveness. We then extended the work to Korea and Taiwan.[1]

We used a well-known moral dilemma by professor Lawrence Kohlberg at Harvard University in which a greedy druggist refused to give medicine to Heinz, a poor man.[2] In Dr. Kohlberg's original dilemma, Heinz must decide whether or not to steal the drug to save his wife's life. In our research on forgiveness, we created an unjust situation at the story's end so that there was something for Heinz to forgive. In our story the druggist hid the drug, preventing Heinz from stealing it. As a result, his wife died. Now Heinz has to decide whether or not to forgive the druggist for his unreasonable stance.

When we asked the research participants what forgiveness is and the conditions under which they might forgive, we saw that younger children thought about forgiveness quite differently than did older children, who in turn, had different views than did teenagers and adults. We categorized these differences into six styles that seemed to be connected with different age groups.

Style I—Harboring Revengeful Forgiveness

Some of the youngest children, about ages 9 to 10, equated forgiving with getting revenge. They said that they would not forgive until they were able to punish the person who was unfair. The children were seeing forgiveness as an "eye for an eye" ordeal. If John hit Steven on the arm, then Steven can forgive if he gets the opportunity to hit John back. A sock on the arm does wonders for a relationship gone bad.

A 9-year-old girl who reflected on the Heinz dilemma had this to say:

Interviewer: If Heinz got even with the druggist by causing him to lose his business, would it help Heinz to forgive the druggist?

Child: Yes . . . because he would cause the druggist pain. [It would help Heinz] forget what happened.

Notice how forgiving is equated with forgetting here.
Another 9-year-old girl said this:

> Maybe [it would help Heinz to forgive]. Sometimes [getting even] will make him feel better about it. But, sometimes he'll still realize it [the revenge] didn't do anything.

This child is beginning to realize that such "forgiving" in the disguise of revenge will not bring back Heinz's wife, and so it amounts to nothing.[3]

Style 2—Getting an Apology Before Forgiving

Some children needed an apology to be able to forgive. It wasn't that an apology would be nice, but it *had* to happen. Of course, this is a conditional form of forgiving. Adults also appreciate apologies, but we do not always insist that they occur.

A 10-year-old boy shows both the need for recompense and apology:

Interviewer: Suppose the druggist tries to make it up to Heinz as best he can. Suppose the druggist gives Heinz lots of money. Will it help him to forgive?

Child: It would help . . . but not completely. It doesn't bring his wife back.

Interviewer: If the druggist apologizes for what he did, would it help Heinz to forgive him?

Child: Yes, because now he [Heinz] knows the druggist didn't mean for it to happen.

Notice that the apology indicates for this child a lack of original intent to do wrong by the druggist.

Interviewer: What if the druggist never apologizes. Could Heinz ever forgive him?

Child: No, because he's not willing to ask for forgiveness. It's pretty hard to give it [forgiveness] [when there is no apology].

For this child, an apology is a nonnegotiable must.

Style 3—Listening to Family and Friends

Some children in middle school, and a rare few in high school, were heavily influenced by what their family and friends told them about forgiveness. If the loved ones didn't like forgiveness or did not encourage it, then the teenager frowned on the idea of forgiving. On the other hand, if the loved ones raved about forgiveness, so did the child. In other words, the child was not his or her own boss regarding forgiving. Having good role models at this age is important if the child is to grow in appreciation and understanding of forgiveness.

Consider two examples from the Heinz and the drug interviews. The first is with a 12-year-old girl who is in the seventh grade:

Interviewer: Suppose all of Heinz's friends come to see him and say "Please be more mature about this. We want you to be friends with the druggist." Would it help him to forgive the druggist? Why or why not?

Student: Probably, because Heinz would think they wanted him to. They would influence him.

Another girl, a 15-year-old high school student, said "Yes, it would be his friends showing him the outside view. They would help him."

By the way, we found no gender differences in how people responded to the Heinz dilemma.

The crux for the teenagers was that friends were making the suggestion to forgive. The teenagers seemed to have a refreshing open-mindedness to listen to and learn from peers. On the other hand, I wonder how much learning would take place if these adolescents were surrounded by single-minded friends who wished to close the book on forgiving.

Style 4—Listening to Authorities

Still later in adolescence, some young people listened intently to authorities on the matter of forgiveness. If the authority, a teacher for example, likes and encourages forgiveness, the teenager is likely to listen. The adolescent does not blindly obey what an authority says but instead is beginning to understand the importance of being part of a larger social system than just friends and family. Those who represent that larger system carry weight in the person's moral decisions.

An example of a girl in the 10th grade shows that at first she does not listen to the authority, but then she does. The interviewer stated that Heinz is religious, and his leader suggested to Heinz that it is not good to stay angry at the druggist. Would this help Heinz forgive?

Student: It might not. But it will make him think about it. Because of his beliefs, he would have to [forgive].

At first, the student rejected the idea of listening to the leader. She then seemed to change her mind to imply that the leader's ideas would get Heinz to think in new ways and not blindly follow. Her ending statement, however, seemed more resigned to blind conformity.

This next example, also from a 10th-grade girl, is more consistent with this type of reasoning.

Student: Yes [it would help Heinz forgive] because he trusts his religious leader in guiding him to make the right decision.

There is no blind conformity here. Listening to the leader is based on an ongoing trust. If the leader has made sense in the past, it is good to consider the advice now.

For those of you who are working with a young person who reasons in this way, I recommend that you try to avoid what I call *grim obligation* when forgiving. If a teenager holds certain beliefs that include the importance of forgiving, then try to help him or her see beyond the command to forgive to the deeper reasons. If a command to forgive is part of a system you see as rational and helpful, then what is the rational and helpful basis behind offering forgiveness? Try to help the adolescent see forgiveness as it fulfills the spirit of the belief system rather than as one more mechanical reaction that he or she must perform without understanding why.

Style 5—Focusing on the Consequences of Forgiving

Some older adolescents and some adults, instead of focusing on what must happen before forgiveness is offered (such as an apology or encouragement from friends, family, or authorities), concentrated on what happens after one forgives. If forgiveness leads to restored relations, then it is a good thing. In other words, some people begin to think of the positive effects of forgiveness. These effects become a rationale for trying and staying with forgiveness as a good thing to do.

Consider the ideas of a 34-year-old man:

I'm presuming Heinz is in a small town. Many know him, and many will suffer with him. I think it is a lot easier to get caught up in another's anger when you, too, feel the unfairness. The townspeople may carry a burden of anger for a long time.

The person sees how Heinz's anger may infect many in the town. He then goes on:

If Heinz forgives, it will give others permission to move on as well. Sure, he may benefit from forgiving, but those who care about him will also benefit. The town may be able to get back to normal.

The man has the idea that forgiveness allows many to stop dwelling on the past. He sees it as a moral good that pervades the community.

Style 6—Unconditionally Loving the Offender

Finally, some of the adults took a loving, unconditional view of forgiveness, thinking of the offender as worthy of respect, not because of what he or she did, but in spite of it. This is similar to what we called the *global* and *cosmic* perspectives in Chapter 8. This reasoning is not so concerned about showing positive effects of forgiving. As we all know, sometimes when you offer forgiveness to someone, the person reacts with a righteous indignation: "Why are you forgiving me? I did nothing to you!" Those reasoning in this way, knowing that the offer of forgiveness is a moral, loving thing to do, go ahead gently anyway, even if forgiveness may create a bit of tension at first. Of course, we should remember that how we go about forgiving is important.

This style of reasoning emerged least often in our research, perhaps because moral love is a difficult rule to live by. It also asks the forgiver, at times, to endure suffering for the greater good of the offender.

As an example of this style, consider a 19-year-old college student's answer to the question of whether Heinz could love the druggist, even if he continued unrepentant and devious:

> Yes [Heinz could forgive]. Despite his anger toward the druggist, he'd still love him because he's a human being worthy of respect and love. Heinz would be angry at the druggist's actions, but not at the druggist himself.

We see the person separating the offending one and his actions, just as Martin Luther King, Jr., did when forgiving those who were firebombing his home. This helps put the offender in a certain perspective, making forgiving easier. If the one offending and the offense are fused, then an evil offense equals an evil offender, making both loving and forgiving less likely.

✎ Journal Entry

Not everyone sees forgiveness in the same way. Take the time to ascertain how your child sees forgiveness before you proceed. Even if a child has some growing to do in understanding forgiveness, I suggest that you concentrate on the idea that forgiveness is a loving response to someone who hurt him or her. Even though the child may only dimly understand, you are presenting the essence of forgiveness that may continue to grow in the child. In addition, be very clear that people do not enter back into a relationship with someone who has been and continues to be hurtful. In other words, let the child see the distinction between forgiveness and reconciliation.

You may want to discuss with your child what forgiveness is and the conditions under which he or she is likely to offer it. You can use the ideas discussed earlier as a guide in your interview. For example, you could ask your child to describe a recent situation in which someone was unfair to him or her. You then might ask, Have you considered forgiving the person? Why or why not? What does it mean to forgive someone? If he or she does not apologize, can you still forgive? What if your friends tell you not to forgive? Try to generate other questions from the styles I described.

Record the child's answers in your journal and then compare his or her ideas with yours on the definition of forgiveness. This is only a suggestion, and you should not push your child into this exercise. Let him or her decide whether or not to do this.

FOSTERING YOUNG CHILDREN'S UNDERSTANDING THROUGH TALES

From the beginning of human history, the story has been used to teach values to children. Recently, Former Secretary of Education William Bennett returned to this time-tested technique. He collected stories that taught various virtues in his best-selling *Book of Virtues*, which has been adapted into a children's television show. Stories can teach virtue in three ways, by showing what a virtue is, how virtue is rewarded, and how the lack of virtue is punished.

As a foundation for understanding the breadth of forgiveness, you can introduce children to a number of themes that are the foundation of forgiveness. Consider introducing the child to the ideas of inherent equality, generosity, moral love, and learning from opposites, especially learning from lessons of evil.

Inherent Equality

Inherent equality centers on the insight that even if one person is taller or smarter or richer than another, both inside are equally worthy of respect because they are human beings, part of the human community. The concrete, observable differences should not be an excuse to avoid seeing how the two people are alike.[4]

Parents need to assist the child to "see" inside other people, to see their intentions, their feelings, their humanity. Because younger children are concrete thinkers, they may only see a facial expression or another child's clenched fist. They might ignore the person's inner fear or vulnerability. It takes time for children to understand that people can outwardly show one thing (like bravado) and inwardly feel another (like weakness or confusion).[5] Introducing the concept of inherent equality to a child helps him or her see that, regardless of what someone does, he or she is still a human being.

A note of caution: Forgiveness is a balancing act. One can distort the meaning of inherent equality by the false assumption that all people are equally trustworthy. A child needs to know that all people are not trustworthy. Trustworthiness usually is dependent on the person's behavior or intended behavior. A child must not lose this perspective as he or she explores the person's worth underneath the behavior's surface. A child should know that some people will not have his or her best interests at heart.

Because the idea of inherent equality is hard to grasp, do not wait too long to start working with it. In my opinion, a young child can begin to appreciate the inherent equality of all persons. Dr. Seuss's *Horton Hears a Who* teaches this idea in a story that is appealing to young children. In the tale, the elephant Horton understands long before anyone else that the tiny Whos in Whoville have as much right to exist safely as anyone else. The others surrounding Horton were ready to fry the Whos in a pot of steaming oil. The resounding theme is that "a person is a person no matter how small." The child is challenged to see the equality of the diminutive Whos in contrast to the gargantuan Horton. One's physical size should not be the marker for shared resources, love, or respect.

The educational intent here is not necessarily to engage the child directly in forgiveness, but to begin appreciating the themes that underlie forgiving. Eventually the child will apply this understanding of inherent equality to an offender. You already applied this when you thought about your offender in new ways.

Generosity

Many children's books teach generosity, or the giving of gifts without any strings attached. At this point it is sufficient to introduce the theme of generosity on its own and then eventually apply it to forgiveness.

A classic that illustrates at least four instances of generosity is Chris Van Allsburg's *The Polar Express*. In the story, a boy who absorbs the mystery of Christmas is surprised to hear a hissing steam train outside his home. Not only is generosity illustrated in the free and swift ride to the North Pole, but also in the first-class service when candy and hot chocolate are served on board. A third depiction occurs when the small boy finds himself in the town square, surrounded by the swirling cheers of the elves, the pacing and excited reindeer, the packed sleigh that seems to rise like a mountain, and the giant train as backdrop. Santa gently creates a place of peace as he takes the boy on his knee and asks him to say whatever he would like for Christmas. The humble child had asked for only a single sleigh bell when on Santa's knee, but somehow loses it on the train ride home. To the boy's delight, he finds the treasure underneath his own Christmas tree with a note from the generous Santa.

Moral Love

Many excellent children's books illustrate the theme of moral love. Hirosuke Hamada's *The Tears of the Dragon* tells of a dragon banished to the hills because of the villagers' fears. Living with others' fears, the dragon learns a roaring, repulsive anger. Only little Akito sees beneath the dragon's bellowing to his softer side. Akito approaches the dragon with an unconditional love that transforms the monster to a soft-hearted, gentle creature, who befriends Akito.

Of course, a child must avoid the mistaken belief that unconditional love is always transforming. Sometimes this may occur, and sometimes it may not. The point of *The Tears of the Dragon* is to show that love can be a powerful ally in uniting those previously living apart and in fear.

Learning From Opposites

Linda and Richard Eyre, in their book *Teaching Your Children Values,* make the compelling case that the examination of themes opposite to our targeted theme enhances and deepens understanding. For example, if a child is to appreciate forgiving, he or she should be introduced to themes of revenge and their consequences.[6] Questions that you might pose are these: Think of a story or a situation in which a person took revenge on others. What happened in the short run to the victims? To the revenge-seeker? What happened in the long run to the victims? To the revenge-seeker? *The Three Little Pigs, The Wizard of Oz, The Little Mermaid,* and many other stories illustrate short-term gains and long-term tragedy for the vengeful.

An excellent book for illustrating the pains of revenge is Dr. Seuss's *The Butter Battle Book.* Two villages become embroiled in conflict that escalates into the threat of nuclear war. Throughout the book the quest for revenge leads to the building of larger and more destructive weaponry. A child might first see the inevitable destruction of an unending revenge and then explore forgiveness as its opposite.

FOSTERING TEENAGERS' UNDERSTANDING THROUGH STORIES

Although young children can be directly taught to forgive, teenagers may be resistant to direct instruction. Parents, however, can use literature, movies, and even television dramas as openings for a discussion of forgiveness and related issues. To have a shared story, the parent might have to take the initiative. One way is to check teenagers' assigned readings, read the same books or short stories, and then initiate a discussion of the moral questions raised by the text. Watching television together or going to the movies together can also open up family discussions.

A parent who enters into discussion with a teenager should always treat him or her as a mature person by offering opinions and presenting arguments and not using parental authority to win a point. The parent who says "well, I am right because I am your father" has lost the argument and probably has laid the foundation for some resentment and bitterness.

Dramatic tension is created when a person faces a true moral dilemma. Drama differs from adventure in which the characters are placed in physical jeopardy. When forgiveness is the theme in a real drama, the protagonist is challenged to forgive a serious wrong. Forgiveness is usually a victory and failure to forgive a tragedy.

In *Great Expectations,* Charles Dickens created the terrifying image of Miss Haversham, a woman who allows anger to completely control her life. Having been left at the altar, Miss

Haversham locks herself up in her crumbling mansion, leaving the wedding banquet to mold on the table. Decades after the event, she continues to wear her rotting wedding gown, and worst of all, she plots revenge against all men by raising her beautiful ward to break men's hearts, thus destroying this young woman's hope of happiness. Discussing the opposites of revenge and forgiveness, as the Eyres suggested, is possible with this novel.

Shylock in Shakespeare's *Merchant of Venice* is another character whose refusal to forgive has terrible consequences. Offered double payment for a debt, he demands instead the exact terms of the forfeiture—a pound of flesh. Portia, the heroine who is masquerading as a young lawyer, begs Shylock to be merciful in her oft-quoted speech:

> The quality of mercy is not strain'd
> It droppeth, as the gentle rain from heaven
> Upon the place beneath; it is twice blessed;
> It blesseth him that gives, and him that takes;
> 'T is mightiest in the mightiest; it becomes
> The throned monarch better than his crown.[7]

If the refusal to forgive has terrible consequences, the choice of forgiveness can be beautiful as illustrated in Victor Hugo's novel *Les Miserables*. Near the beginning of the novel, Jean Valjean, after spending 19 years in prison for stealing a loaf of bread, continues his felonious ways when he steals from Monseigneur Myriel, the only one to offer him shelter. When Valjean is arrested and brought back by police, Myriel has mercy on him, claiming that what appeared to be a theft was actually a gift to Valjean. Undaunted by the merciful act, Valjean steals once again from Myriel, who continues to practice mercy. Eventually, Valjean repents and leads an honorable life, including acts of mercy toward others, despite many twists and turns and complications throughout the novel.

Louisa May Allcott's *Little Women,* which appeals to some in middle childhood and early adolescence, illustrates the concept of generosity when the March girls, in spite of their poverty, gave up their Christmas presents for their mother and their Christmas breakfast for the poor. Parents can encourage small acts of generosity in children. Children often want to practice small acts of generosity, and they should be encouraged, but not forced, to do so. Parents can set an example by their own generosity. Although it is true that one should not parade one's generosity in public, a parent can as instruction let a child participate in charity. For example, many organizations collect money for the poor; sometimes such collections are made in public places. The parent could give the child some money to give to the poor when they pass a particular collection point. Examples of generosity are numerous. Make a list in your journal of the ways in which you can practice generosity in your family.

The award-winning movie *Dead Man Walking* is a fact-based film that deals with the relationship between a condemned murderer, Matt Poncelet, and Sister Helen Prejean, a Catholic nun, whom he asked to be his spiritual advisor. The film shows how the families of his victims are consumed with anger and revenge. However, at the end the father of one of the victims considers the possibility of forgiveness. (The unedited video is rated R because of graphic violence and strong language. The film, in edited form, has appeared on television.)

Films with less-obvious forgiveness themes include *Field of Dreams,* a baseball saga about Ray, who builds a baseball field so that the ghost of Shoeless Joe Jackson can return to play ball. The essence of the film, as it turns out, is that the field is built as a forum for Ray and his father John to forgive each other and reconcile. As Ray relates about his father to a passenger as they travel through the countryside,

He never made it as a ballplayer, so he tried to get his son to make it for him. By the time I was 10, playing baseball got to be like eating vegetables or taking out the garbage. So, when I was 14, I started to refuse. Can you believe that, an American boy refusing to have a catch with his father? . . . Anyway, when I was 17, I packed my things, said something awful, and left. After a while I wanted to come home, but I didn't know how.

At the film's end Ray and John are playing catch, reunited. Ray overcame the resentment of being pressed into baseball service. John overcame the insults and abandonment. Both learned to forgive.

Another film worth watching is *October Sky*, about Homer Hickam, Jr., and his attempts to build rockets in Coalwood, West Virginia, in 1957. His goal is to win a scholarship to college. Homer's father, a tough coal miner, has no interest throughout most of the film in the rockets or in his son attending college. The tension between them slowly mounts and culminates in a shouting match. The argument is so devastating that Homer's mother threatens to leave if her husband is not kinder to their son. At the movie's end, Homer's father shows up, for the first time, at the final rocket launch, after Homer wins first prize at the National Science Fair in Indianapolis, securing a college scholarship. The son meekly approaches his father, requesting that he do the honors of igniting the final rocket, which he graciously accepts.

Made-for-television movies, particularly those with a Christmas theme, frequently focus on themes of forgiveness and reconciliation. One example is *The Christmas Wish*. After her husband's death, the character portrayed by Debbie Reynolds discovers the name "Lillian" in her husband's diaries. She asks her grandson to find out who Lillian is and why her husband visited her every Christmas Eve for more than 20 years. The grandson discovers that Lillian is the drunk driver who killed his parents 24 years before and that his grandfather had not only forgiven her, but had paid for her care in a nursing home, visited her at least once a month and supplied a Christmas tree to the nursing home. Following his example, his widow and grandson are also able finally to forgive.

As you become more aware of forgiveness themes, you will find them in the classics, particularly in the novels and works of William Blake, Charles Dickens, William Thackeray, and William Shakespeare.[8] You will find them in television series, including *Touched by an Angel* and *Babylon 5.* Even "classic" television series contained the theme, as seen consistently in *The Love Boat,* although this series was more of a light romantic fare than a drama and may be too syrupy for today's adolescents.

FOSTERING THE MORAL EMOTIONS IN CHILDREN AND ADOLESCENTS

Courage is a virtue that is not only understood or practiced, but also felt. Aristotle believed that one could foster such an emotion as courage by playing music with bold, resounding themes that suggest fortitude. Seeing a play in which an actor demonstrates a fearless bravery is another medium for feeling the virtue of courage. Thus, the child has a chance, upon hearing the music or seeing the play, to experience what it is like to express such an emotion. Just as one can feel what it is like to be courageous, can one feel what it is like to be forgiving and merciful?

If a child does not experience love from a parent, won't it be more difficult for that child to feel and offer such love when he or she is grown? Isn't it the case that as a parent offers genuine moral love to the child that the parent is sowing the seeds of deeper understanding and expression of forgiveness in that child at a later time? A parent's sincere expression of love toward the child may be as effective as, or even more effective than, the vicarious experiencing of love through music or a play.

As you read or discuss any of the books or see any of the films already described, try not only to foster understanding but also a feeling of compassion and love. Children are touched by tender scenes of reconciliation and renewal. Allow them time to be aware of their feelings.

At the same time, parents need to respect their children's feelings and emotions without insisting on certain ways of feeling. For example, anger almost always has a real and legitimate cause, yet some parents act as though anger in a child is an unacceptable emotion. This can lead to the habit of denying angry feelings and other unhealthy defense mechanisms.

Of course, parents have a duty to control how anger is expressed. Violence, vulgarity, or the destruction of objects is not acceptable, but everyone, including a child, has a right to feel angry when they have been unjustly injured.

✎ Journal Entry

Reflect in your journal on your own expressions of love toward your child. How often do you show love? How do you show it? Think about one recent incident in which there was unfairness within the family. Who was unfair? What was the circumstance surrounding the unfairness? How did you deal with the situation? Was forgiveness a part of the solution? If not, how might you have incorporated forgiveness by talking with the children about or even demonstrating forgiveness? What might you try in the future?

WORKING TOWARD FORGIVING AND MERCIFUL BEHAVIORS

If parents want their children to engage in merciful acts, they should praise them for such acts. This can be done casually and naturally. Of course, the ultimate goal is that the child chooses to be merciful because it is the right thing to do, but to reach that higher level of moral reasoning the child needs to pass through the lower levels first. If you reward your child with praise, with a smile, or a hug, when he or she performs an act of true mercy—even a very small one—the child will associate such behavior with a warm feeling. If, on the other hand, you show displeasure when a child is self-centered, the child will learn to feel uncomfortable about selfish behaviors. The goal, of course, is for the child to realize that mercy has its own rewards.

Children can be taught to forgive one another. For the average parent of young children, hardly a day will go by without at least one child crying that he or she has been injured by another. Parents are forced to become judge and jury. Forgiveness should be part of the parental justice system. After blame is determined and suitable punishment meted out, the perpetrator could be encouraged (not required) to apologize and the injured party encouraged (not required) to forgive when both parties are ready.

As a note of caution, some parents insist that their young children forgive. When Timmy hits his little sister Susie, the parents insist that Timmy apologize and that Susie give Timmy a kiss and forgive him. Although the parents' motives in conducting this reconciliation are noble, the process carries some risks. If the children are forced by threats to say something that they don't really feel, rather than encouraged to apologize and forgive, the parents may be encouraging lying and hypocrisy.

If the children are still in the vengeance stage of forgiveness reasoning, they may feel that they have been denied justice. Some parents may go so far as to punish a child for not extending forgiveness. This could leave the child with the impression that forgiveness is punishment for being the victim and that his or her feelings have not been respected. Parents need to be sensitive to the victim's feeling and allow time to work out the anger. On the other hand, children often truly want to reconcile and only need a gentle, kind push to willingly apologize and forgive.

For teenagers, be careful that you do not unwittingly foster a sense of grim obligation about forgiveness. If the adolescent begins to admire certain authorities, be sure you are attuned to what these authorities are saying about forgiveness. Are they indifferent to it? If so, your child may become indifferent. Are they so enthusiastic about forgiveness that they treat it as an unbending command? If so, your child may blindly go ahead and be ambivalent about forgiveness for years to come.

Keeping the lines of communication open with teenagers will allow them to bring up frustrations from school or work that need discussion and solution. Be very careful that you do not preach forgiveness or that you bring up the subject so often that your child dreads talking with you. Try to let forgiveness come out almost naturally when appropriate. Posing questions like "What do you think about trying to forgive . . .?" may be better than suggesting forgiveness outright.

Expect the unexpected when dealing with young people. Dan, a 42-year-old father of three boys, was watching television with his sophomore son Ben one Sunday evening. Ben suddenly got a bit irritated. "Dad, I think that the idea of 'turning the other cheek' is unfair." The TV program had nothing to do with this. Dan then realized that at church that day the pastor gave a sermon on not returning violence with violence.

"Why do you say that?" Dan asked.

"You know Marty [a classmate who tended to annoy others by his teasing]. Well, I had it with him on Friday at the lunch table. I reached over and socked him on the head," Ben explained.

"You did what!" Dan blurted out.

"Oh, it's ok. No teacher saw or anything."

"I don't care if a teacher saw or not. What's this about hitting Marty?"

"Dad, you know I've completely had it with him. Every single lunch period he gets on me. I had to teach him a lesson. I've been turning the other cheek so much that I'm beginning to get a stiff neck," Ben explained.

Ben was truly upset about the sermon in relation to his own behavior on Friday. In fact, rather than feeling guilty about popping Marty, Ben was upset with the pastor for suggesting that he, Ben, continue being abused. Dan explained, as calmly as possible, that having mercy on someone does not at all mean that you have to throw justice out the window. You can refrain from hitting Marty and also seek fairness.

They then discussed the various things that Ben could do, all within the rules of the school, to get Marty off of his back. Ben came to realize that "turning the other cheek" is not a general, unalterable rule to be followed under all circumstances but instead is a challenge under particular circumstances. He also stopped thinking in "either–or" ways about forgiveness and justice.

Teaching a child to conquer injustice and abuse with forgiveness can prepare him or her for the realities of adult life. Ben, in fact, was able to get Marty to stop his verbal abuse without resorting to similar abuse by helping Marty on several occasions with his math. Marty began to see that Ben was a "good guy," and Ben saw Marty as someone who could be grateful for the tutoring help.

Sometimes a parent has to decide that the level of abuse is not acceptable, particularly if sexual or physical abuse is involved. Protecting the children from real harm should be the first priority. In any case, children may still need to learn to forgive under these circumstances.

✎ Journal Entry

Have you been spending enough time with your child, listening to his or her heartaches? To what extent have you discussed forgiveness? What might you do now to prepare for the next time he or she wishes to talk with you about an injustice?

WHAT YOUR BEHAVIOR CAN TEACH A CHILD

Parents can teach a child how to forgive by asking for forgiveness when they as parents have hurt the child. Of course, parents are not required to reveal all of their own hurts and failings.

Parents can help along their children's forgiving by asking for a general forgiveness. A parent might say "I know we had some difficult times while you were growing up, and if I ever did anything to hurt you, I am really sorry. Please forgive me." Or the parent might mention a specific situation. If a child brings up an old injury or mentions old anger, the parent should use that moment to immediately ask for forgiveness.

Of course, parents don't have to wait until their children are grown to ask for forgiveness. Parents can get in the habit of apologizing and asking for forgiveness. Sometimes parents forget that they owe their children an apology when they offend them. For example, almost every parent loses his or her temper now and then. A parent has a hard day at the office and yells at the children who greet him or her at the door with a request. Another parent has just discovered that the washing machine hose has ruptured and flooded the basement and screams at the children for playing in the water. Yet another parent forgets to pick a child up on time. In all these cases and many more, it is necessary for the parent to say to the child "I am sorry. Please forgive me." By practicing the giving and receiving of apologies and forgiveness within the family for both small and large offenses, the parents teach their children a pattern of behavior that will help them deal with serious injustices that may occur later in life.

When the Parents' and Children's Perceptions Differ

Childhood anger is often not proportional to the actual offense, and those things about which the parents feel guilty may not correspond to the things that the children are angry about. For example, Gloria apologized to her children for neglecting them during a period in her life when she was suffering from psychological depression. The children instead remembered the time as very pleasant, because their father spent so much time with them, and they enjoyed taking charge of family activities. On the other hand, Gloria's children were extremely resentful at their mother for not doing more to encourage them as they took music lessons. Yes, they should have taken most of the initiative, but the mother's cavalier attitude was one reason why they let the lessons slide, missing an opportunity that they now wish they had seized. It took time for them to forgive her for this failure.

Karl was deeply offended because his father, after having given Karl his grandfather's trophy when Karl was 8, forgot that he had made the gift and gave the same trophy to Karl's younger brother a few years later. Karl saw the transfer of the trophy as depriving him of his birthright as the older son. His father hadn't considered the original gift as significant, and the transfer occurred casually when he was redecorating. The younger brother had empty shelf space on which the trophy could be advantageously displayed. The father completely forgot the incident and was shocked when Karl brought it up. Rather than defending himself or denying the importance of the incident, Karl's father was able to offer a sincere apology for not recognizing the importance of Karl's feelings.

In another example, a mother promised her 5-year-old son a trip to the beach and then was forced to cancel the trip because she had to take his grandmother to the doctor. The child was furious. He felt betrayed. Rather than punishing the child for his anger, the mother said "I am sorry that you are disappointed. Please forgive me."

You may say, "But the mother did nothing wrong." True, but her son cannot make that distinction. To him, a promise was made, a promise was broken. Once a child's anger is recognized and the child forgives, very often the child will be able to calm down and then understand the true nature of the situation.

By starting with the little annoyances that occur everyday, the child can learn that one way to deal with anger is to forgive. Some parents deal with childish anger by punishing their children for having angry feelings or saying something like "You are a bad child for being angry." If this pattern of interaction between the child and the parent is repeated, the child may grow into an adult who is afraid to express anger. Denial prevents forgiveness, and as we have seen, the anger that is not openly expressed doesn't go away. It comes out in other forms.

On the other hand, parents should not allow temper tantrums to continue unchecked, or worse, to give in to a temper tantrum. The mother who had to change plans should certainly not feel so guilty at disappointing the child that she gives in to the temper tantrum and neglects the immediate need of a sick relative. This would teach the child that temper tantrums are a good way to get what you want and can lead to antisocial behavior.

DO YOUR CHILDREN KNOW THAT YOU LOVE THEM?

I am not asking if you love your children but instead whether you have communicated that love to your children. Tragically many children (and adults who still feel like children) don't believe that their parents love them.

Children and teenagers need to hear the words "I love you," and they need to feel loved. One way to make your children feel loved is to tell them "I forgive you" when they have done something wrong. Another way is to ask for forgiveness when you as a parent have done something wrong. These words shouldn't be restricted to the big things.

Anger and bitterness can not only block love from going out toward others, but also they can block love from coming in. When parents ask for forgiveness, they allow their children to deal with the built-up anger and bitterness.

Donna had become seriously ill with a lung infection when her daughter Lisa was 8 and remained ill for two years. Many days she was so ill that she neglected her daughter's basic needs. Lisa was particularly humiliated when she had to go to school with unpressed clothes. She blamed her humiliation on her mother and became bitter and angry because no one was recognizing how she was suffering. In time, Donna recovered and resumed her household duties, but when she tried to reach out to her daughter, her love could not penetrate the wall of anger that Lisa had built between them.

During her own recovery process, Donna learned about forgiveness. Going through the forgiveness process herself, she saw clearly that her daughter was already trapped by bitterness and anger. Desperate to protect her daughter from the suffering that unforgiveness causes, she begged her daughter to forgive her for the previous neglect. At first, Lisa, who was by this time a teenager, answered with a defiant "No, I will never forgive you." But her mother was persistent, and finally, more worn down than willing, Lisa agreed to say the words "I forgive you, Mother." Slowly, the relationship changed. Lisa was able to experience her mother's love, her defiance and rebellion melted away, and they developed a deeply loving and supportive relationship.

You might ask, "But why should Donna ask forgiveness, after all it wasn't her fault she was sick." And, of course, this is true, as Lisa came to understand once she had forgiven. As an 8 year old,

Lisa was not able to accept that her needs were not being met. Explaining the situation later did not penetrate the accumulated anger. The slightest failure on the part of the mother brought back memories of earlier, horrible humiliations. Once Lisa had forgiven, she was able to see the situation more clearly. Donna's persistent demonstration of love aided Lisa's forgiveness.

FORGIVENESS AS A WAY OF LIFE IN THE FAMILY

I am not suggesting by this title that families lose their balance and make forgiveness the center of attention in the home. Instead, I am suggesting that partners consider forgiving each other, that they ask the children for forgiveness when this is appropriate, that they openly forgive the children when it is appropriate, and that they encourage each child to forgive the others when the inevitable arguments of childhood break out.

Be careful not to use forgiveness as a weapon. Proclaiming your unending forgiveness to all in the family who fail you creates a sense of your superiority and their inferiority. Because forgiveness levels the moral playing field, you as forgiver will have to lower yourself in humility so that the ones who offend you can take their rightful place at the family table.

ENDNOTES

1. The research is described in R. D. Enright and colleagues, "The Adolescent as Forgiver," *Journal of Adolescence* 12 (1989), 95–110; S. T. Huang, "Cross-cultural and Real-life Validations of the Theory of Forgiveness in Taiwan, The Republic of China" (University of Wisconsin–Madison, 1990); and Y. O. Park and R. D. Enright, "The Development of Forgiveness in the Context of Adolescent Friendship Conflict in Korea," *Journal of Adolescence* 20 (1997), 393–402.

2. See L. Kohlberg, "Stage and Sequence: The Cognitive–Developmental Approach to Socialization, in *Handbook of Socialization Theory and Research*, ed. D. Goslin (Chicago: Rand, 1969), pp. 347–480.
3. All of the research participants receive this and all other questions that you read below.
4. More information on this idea can be found in R. D. Enright and the Human Development Study Group, "Piaget on the Moral Development of Forgiveness: Reciprocity or Identity?" *Human Development* 37 (1994), 63–80.
5. R. L. Selman, *The Growth of Interpersonal Understanding* (New York: Academic Press, 1980).
6. L. Eyre and R. Eyre, *Teaching Your Children Values* (New York: Simon & Schuster, 1993).
7. The quotation here is only a portion of Portia's speech.
8. See, for example, J. Moskal, *Blake, Ethics, and Forgiveness* (Tuscaloosa: University of Alabama Press, 1994) and J. R. Reed, *Dickens and Thackeray: Punishment and Forgiveness* (Athens: Ohio University Press, 1995).

CHAPTER 14

WANTING TO BE FORGIVEN

It is time to turn our attention back to you. This time, however, we won't be focusing on your forgiving, but instead on your wanting to be forgiven. When we are in a close relationship with someone, it is rare that one person forgives and the other seeks forgiveness, and that is the end of it. Instead, both people can be unfair at times, necessitating that each person forgive and each seek forgiveness for what he or she did.

Tim "blew up" at his wife Jennifer when he came home and she was not ready for the dinner party at his supervisor's house. Feeling pressured and fighting the flu, she, in turn, verbally lashed out at Tim, telling him how insensitive, uncaring, and self-centered he was. They never made it to the party. The next day, Tim felt awful about how he put his job above Jennifer by placing so much importance on the dinner party. Jennifer, too, felt guilty because she knew how Tim had looked forward to the evening. Both harbored these feelings within, waiting for the other to make the first move. Both were confused by anger left over and not knowing what the other would do when approached. Both wanted to be forgiven.

Is it more blessed to give than to receive? When the question comes to forgiveness, I think it is not only more blessed to give forgiveness, it even may be easier. Being forgiven means admitting that we have wronged someone else and need their forgiveness. Sometimes even though we know we are guilty, acknowledging that guilt to the person we have hurt by accepting the gift of forgiveness can be very painful. On the other hand, sometimes it happens that a person comes to us offering forgiveness for an offense that we didn't think was all that offensive.

Such occasions provide an opportunity for great generosity. We have to measure our offense not by our intention, but by the actual effect. We have hurt another person and that person, having struggled with pain and anger, now offers us the unmerited gift of forgiveness. In such a case, be as generous and apologetic as you can, even if you feel that you are innocent. You might say "I am so sorry. I had no idea that I had hurt you. Please forgive me" or "I had no intention of hurting you. Thank you for forgiving me" or "Please forgive me. Is there anything I can do to make this up to you?"

Be careful about offering too much of an explanation of your actions. It may sound to the forgiver like justification or as though you are evading your responsibility. Focus on their injury and their hurt.

If you were wrong, confess as clearly and openly as possible the full extent of your guilt: "I know that I was guilty. I have no excuse. Please forgive me."

If there were extenuating circumstances, and you think that the forgiver might benefit from knowing why the injury happened, you may add "I know that this isn't an excuse for what I did and it doesn't lessen the pain you have experienced, but I would like you to know that . . . ," and then say as simply as possible anything that might in some way explain your actions.

In some cases, particularly those in which a person was abused as a child and forgives as an adult, the person receiving forgiveness may add "I want you to know that none of this was your fault. You were a child and I was the adult, and in spite of all the circumstances, I should have protected you."

If you can't say anything positive, say as little as possible. If you feel that the forgiveness is a false accusation or delivered as a form of vengeance, you can reply "I am sorry. I don't know what to say. Will you let me have time to think about this?" Whatever you do, don't react with anger. The offer of forgiveness may be a very important first step for the forgiver. The forgiver may not have worked through all the feelings surrounding the injury. Your response can be crucial to a more complete healing. If the charge seems totally unjustified, you might offer the gift of listening: "Please tell me your memory of what happened and how this affected your life." If the forgiver's memory of the situation is entirely different than your own, don't force your view, just listen. You might reply "I had no idea that was what you were feeling."

Although we may not always have to tell people that we forgive them, we should almost always ask for forgiveness when we have wronged another person. Asking forgiveness requires that we confess our faults, which can be difficult. Most of us don't enjoy admitting that we are wrong. Therefore, it may be helpful to admit your wrongdoing to someone other than the injured party and discuss the issue before you take the step of formally confessing to the injured party and asking forgiveness. As you had a companion or support person when forgiving, consider such a confidant when you desire to be forgiven. This intermediary step can give you the confidence that you are accepted and loved no matter what you have done and put your offense into perspective. Of course, you must choose wisely the person to whom you are going to make your confession. Members of the clergy or mental health professionals are specially trained to receive confessions; however a true friend might be trusted with this knowledge. Your own religious tradition probably has some guidelines for this.

Forgiveness is a gift, something given out of a sense of generosity. You don't deserve it. The injured party is not obligated to provide you with it. You can't demand forgiveness. At the same time, as a human being you are worthy of receiving forgiveness.[1] To be worthy is quite different from being deserving. All people have the capacity for good will and therefore are worthy to receive respect.[2] Everyone is forgivable, including you.

GUIDEPOSTS FOR WANTING TO BE FORGIVEN

Just as we have guideposts to forgive, we have similar ones for wanting to be forgiven. Before we explore these guideposts, ask yourself this question: In considering the person whom you offended, have you hurt him or her unfairly? Do you need to seek forgiveness from this person? Do you want to be forgiven? I think that it is best to keep this particular person in mind here, if you have indeed offended him or her at some time.

GUIDEPOSTS FOR WANTING TO BE FORGIVEN

PHASE I—UNCOVERING GUILT AND SHAME

- Have you denied your guilt or pretended that what you did wasn't all that harmful?
- Have you allowed yourself to feel guilt, remorse, or sadness for what you have done?
- Are you ashamed of what you have done?
- Have you lied to cover up what you have done because of shame?
- Has your guilt or shame led to physical or mental exhaustion?
- Do you go over and over the event in your mind?
- Do you constantly compare yourself to the person you hurt or to others whom you consider innocent?
- Has your life been permanently changed by what you did?
- Is your sense of who you are altered by what you did?

continues next page

---

continued

PHASE 2—DECIDING TO SEEK FORGIVENESS

- Recognize that when you wrong another person, you should ask for forgiveness.
- Recognize that when another person offers forgiveness, you should be willing to accept that gift.
- Decide to humbly accept forgiveness when it is offered.

PHASE 3—WORKING ON RECEIVING FORGIVENESS

- Work toward understanding what the other has gone through.
- Work toward gratitude.
- Work toward reconciliation.
- Accept the humiliation.

PHASE 4—DISCOVERING

- Find meaning in your personal failure.
- Recognize that you are stronger because of what you experienced.
- Realize that you are not alone.
- Make a decision to change.
- Experience the freedom from guilt and remorse.

✎ Journal Entry

Consider the possibility of wanting to be forgiven. Try to reconstruct some of the details of one incident, and describe it here. What did you do that was unfair? Why do you say it was unfair?

Phase I—Uncovering Guilt and Shame

The first set of guideposts represents an inventory that will help you face the fact that you need to be forgiven, something we sometimes want to deny. The first question—whether you are denying guilt—is less of an issue if you have already admitted to offending someone. The second question deals with guilt and the third with shame. They are different feelings.

Guilt is that inner voice convicting you of wrong. Shame is usually connected with others peering in, seeing what you did, and judging you. You might feel guilt without shame, or you may feel that others are judging you, but you have no guilt.

As you did when you forgave, you ask yourself certain questions about how these negative emotions have compromised your life, depleted your energy, preoccupied you. If you live too long with excessive guilt, you might find, as you did when living with excessive anger, that your worldview becomes pessimistic.

Samantha, a 20-year-old college student, began seeing another man when her boyfriend Mark took a job in a city four hours away. She recalls her guilt and grief:

> I felt very guilty and often cried after seeing this other man. It was not a sexual relationship, but just allowing myself to become so close to someone besides my boyfriend made me feel very negative about myself. I felt there was something wrong with me if I couldn't wait a few more weeks to be with the one I was in love with. I felt too needy and selfish, and this made me feel ashamed of who I was. I also sometimes felt it was my boyfriend's fault for not being there with me. I blamed him for my loneliness. At times I denied I was doing anything terribly wrong, but that feeling was very brief.

When Tim saw how sick Jennifer was with the flu, he felt much remorse for yelling and insisting that she attend the dinner party. He hardly slept that night because of a mixture of guilt and anger. He realized that he wanted to be forgiven so they could put the whole incident behind them.

✎ Journal Entry

Gauging the amount of guilt that you may have is important. On a scale from 1 to 10, rate how much guilt you have. Let 1 mean "no guilt at all" and 10 mean "tremendous guilt." If you are at a 1 or a 2, perhaps you are already forgiven. If not, are you only going through the motions here, wanting to be forgiven a tiny bit, but not taking this too seriously?

To assess the extent of the damage done, ask yourself if you are ashamed of something surrounding the incident. Has shame or guilt depleted your energy? Have you replayed the situation over and over? When? How often? How much shame do you have on the 1 to 10 scale of shame (1 is "no shame" and 10 is "great shame")?

Are you mentally and physically tired from what you did? To what extent are you replaying in your mind what happened?

When you compare yourself with the one you hurt, what conclusions do you draw? Do you see him or her as more deeply hurt because of your actions? This sometimes increases guilt and shame.

How has your life and your worldview changed as a result of living with the guilt?

Try to get an overall sense of the seriousness of the problem and write down your impressions.

Phase 2—Deciding to Seek Forgiveness

The first guidepost calls on us to recognize that when we wrong another person we should ask for forgiveness. We shouldn't wait for the other person to offer forgiveness. If we know we are in the wrong, we should ask. Asking for forgiveness can be a gift to those we have hurt. This is especially important, because some people believe that forgiveness is possible only when the offender repents and asks for forgiveness. Although we know this isn't true, if we offend people who hold this belief, it is harder for them to forgive and therefore we shouldn't wait for the injured party to make the first move.

The second guidepost calls on us to be willing to accept forgiveness whenever it is offered. Although forgiveness is a gift, it is not always a welcome one. We may not have realized that we injured someone, and therefore the forgiveness, no matter how sweetly it is delivered, carries with it the accusation that we did something wrong. We may know that we hurt another person but almost pretend that they didn't notice or weren't really hurt. The offer of forgiveness means that the pretending is over, and we must face what we have done.

The third guidepost involves the actual accepting of forgiveness when it is offered. When we accept forgiveness, we should apologize if we have not already done so. How much explanation of our actions should be added depends on the situation. Sometimes explanations sound like excuses; other times they can be really helpful. The question we need to ask ourselves is, Will an explanation be helpful to the person giving us forgiveness, or will it sound more like self-justification or even denial of guilt?

You will notice, in contrast to the forgiving process, that there is no step on giving a gift because such gift-giving is the prerogative of the forgiver, not the forgiven. The latter's task is to graciously take the gift when offered. Of course, asking for forgiveness is in a certain sense a gift, particularly if the person offended is unable to forgive without being asked and is burdened by resentment and bitterness.

Samantha, in deciding that she wanted to be forgiven for dating another man, recalls,

> I had the desire to be forgiven, but I knew it was my boyfriend's choice to continue the relationship and forgive me. We had a very long, somber discussion relating to my feelings and actions. I always felt hurt by myself for hurting him. I wanted him to understand I,

too, was hurt by what I did. I realized that his forgiveness was a gift to me.

✎ Journal Entry

Write down your reactions to the guideposts for deciding to seek forgiveness. Are you convinced that you should ask for forgiveness? If so, try to create a dialogue that you might initiate when you approach the person.

Are you willing to accept the person's forgiveness? If so, how will you accept it? If you have to wait a long time as he or she fumes over what happened, are you willing to do so? What will you do as you wait? Finally, what does it mean to "humbly accept" the other's forgiveness?

Phase 3—Working on Receiving Forgiveness

The next set of guideposts are the work of being forgiven. First, you need to understand the feelings of the person offended, in particular understanding how difficult it may have been for him or her to deal with the hurt and to forgive.

The next guidepost requires us to cultivate an attitude of gratitude. We have received a gift we did not merit. We should be grateful. Sometimes having to admit we are wrong may make us so uncomfortable that the exchange may cause us to avoid the person who has forgiven us. This, of course, would be counterproductive for both of you.

Samantha's work in wanting to be forgiven included this:

> I saw my boyfriend as more caring and loving after that. I am more thankful for having him in my life. I stepped in his shoes and real-

ized that I would be hurt if I were him. I decided never to see the other man again, even in a large group of friends.

The succeeding guidepost calls on us to work toward reconciliation, our topic for the next chapter. Reconciliation is not automatic. A person can decide to forgive us and at the same time decide that a continued relationship is not desirable. We may have to accept that decision, but we should not allow our embarrassment to be a barrier to reconciliation.

The final guidepost involves accepting the pain of humiliation. This is no small thing. Ask yourself, would you rather endure an hour of physical pain or five minutes of public humiliation? Most of us would pick the physical pain. Humiliation hurts, which is why we avoid it. Asking for forgiveness or accepting forgiveness means admitting to another person that we were in the wrong. If we want to be free, we must accept the pain associated with this humiliation.

Tim, who wanted deeply to be forgiven by Jennifer, had to wait until the afternoon of the next day before broaching the subject of forgiveness. Jennifer, still feeling quite ill from the flu, stayed in bed all morning. When he thought she was physically stronger, he humbly apologized, saying he was wrong and not thinking of her feelings and needs at the time. She was not quite ready to hear all of this, and so Tim patiently waited until Jennifer felt better later that day.

If humble confession of your faults has been a rare event in your life, this guidepost may be particularly difficult. If you find the very idea terrifying, you may need to look into your past. You may need to forgive someone in your past who treated a mistake you made so harshly and unforgivingly that you have been afraid ever since of making a mistake or at least of admitting one. Ask yourself, How did your parents treat your failures? Were you publicly humiliated by a teacher? When you made a mistake were you forgiven and accepted, or was your error considered as a permanent mark against you that was not erased?

Mary Ann's mother never forgot the slightest mistake Mary Ann made and frequently brought up Mary Ann's childhood mistakes in the presence of company and in conversation. As a result, Mary Ann developed an irrational fear of being wrong. Because she couldn't be perfect, she often resorted to lying to cover up mistakes. She was terrified of having to admit she was wrong. Once she had forgiven her mother, she found it easier to admit that she was wrong and ask for forgiveness when this was appropriate.

✎ Journal Entry

As you put yourself into the other person's shoes, speculate in writing about their thoughts and feelings about the injustice they experienced. Go into some detail about their suffering.

Your feeling grateful may have to await the person's actual forgiveness. Has he or she offered it yet? Is there anything you still should do to aid in their forgiving? Be careful not to press for forgiveness. After all, it is the other person's choice when and how to forgive.

Is there anything from your end of the relationship that is a barrier to reconciliation? What is it, and what can you do to remove it?

Have you accepted the pain associated with all of this? Write down your feelings and reactions associated with the sense of humiliation. How are you coping with this? Again, a confidant can be quite helpful here.

Finally, do you have any situations from your past, as Mary Ann did, in which you have a hard time admitting that you are wrong? If so, was anyone so unfair to you in fostering this attitude that you need to forgive him or her? Take some time to reflect on these past issues.

Phase 4—Discovering

The first guidepost calls on us to look for meaning in our failures and mistakes. Our successes rarely teach us as much as our failures. When we admit to ourselves that through our own negligence or malicious intent we harmed another person, we discover a painful truth about ourselves. We aren't perfect. When we face that truth, we grow. Through that growth we uncover what it means to be human, to be fallible, to be weak. By finding out the truth that we are not perfect, we are better able to accept the faults and weaknesses of others. The success of support groups and 12-step programs in helping people change their lives is based on this principle. Those who have been there, made the mistakes, and changed are often better able to encourage those with a similar problem than those who have never failed in that area.

The guidepost for recognizing that you are stronger involves considering the ways in which the experience of asking for and receiving forgiveness can benefit us. Some people have cultivated the false idea that strong people never admit that they are wrong, when in fact, it is the cowards who are afraid of facing their mistakes. It takes courage to admit that you were wrong. It takes courage to face the person you have harmed and ask for forgiveness or receive forgiveness. If you have successfully asked for or accepted forgiveness, you will be stronger and more able to face future failures without fear. Successful people are not those who never fail, but those who know how to start again after they fail.

The next guidepost involves realizing that you are not alone, in two senses. First, we may need support to go through this process. Second, we realize that we are like other people, not superior to them. Before you asked for or accepted forgiveness from another person, you may have had a very high opinion of yourself. You may have looked down on people who made mistakes or harmed others, and now you realize that you are really part of humanity with all its faults. Most people find this realization liberating. They realize that they have been living a lie—an illusion of superiority—and now they no longer have to pretend. A healthy sense of self-esteem and a false sense of superiority are very different. A person with strong self-esteem does not have to put others down to feel good about themselves.

The succeeding guidepost requires us to at least make a decision that we will try to change. Having to ask for or receive forgiveness can be a painful process, and most of us don't want to have to go through it repeatedly. Therefore, we are motivated to change our behavior.

Finally, asking for and receiving forgiveness, if done properly, produces tremendous freedom. Guilt, remorse, and shame are terrible burdens. If you take the time to traverse the guideposts, you should experience the freedom from guilt and remorse, even if the person from whom you asked forgiveness refused to forgive.

In Samantha's words, once she received forgiveness from Mark,

> I felt a sense of release. I realized how egocentric I had been not thinking of others. I feel *much* better now. Mark never stopped loving me or tried to get revenge to hurt me. I know we are going to deepen our relationship.

Once Jennifer forgave Tim, she asked for forgiveness because of her tirade of the night before. She realized that she had a legitimate point about not going to the party, but how she expressed this, with a considerable display of anger, was inappropriate. Both felt exonerated, their guilt faded, and they became a little more sensitive to the others' needs upon receiving and granting forgiveness.

✎ Journal Entry

Reflect on the learning you have experienced as a result of this process. What new meaning for your life do you have in admitting personal failures and asking for forgiveness?

In what sense are you stronger as a result of this experience? You may want to make a list of positive changes you have experienced as a result of wanting to be forgiven and pursuing it.

Have you sought support in this journey? From whom? Evaluate how the support is aiding your process of being forgiven.

Finally, reflect on your attempts to actually become a better person. How is this developing? Describe your sense of relief as this emerges.

ARE THERE FALSE FORMS OF WANTING TO BE FORGIVEN?

Just as there are false forms of giving forgiveness, there are false forms of receiving forgiveness. The therapist Paul Coleman makes the important point that one's desire to be forgiven must be done with a genuine sense of "confessing." Sometimes a person engages in a behavior that Dr. Coleman calls "confessing innocence" in which the person sees absolutely no wrong in what was done but says "I'm sorry" to appease someone who is angry. In some families this false confession is the expected pattern of behavior. The genuine receiving of forgiveness is accompanied by real remorse for the offense, respect for the one offended, and a willingness to change the behaviors that caused hardship or destruction.

Sometimes, according to Dr. Coleman, people confess to attract sympathy. The false confessor in this case loudly proclaims sorrow or guilt, when in fact neither is felt. It is all a performance designed to make others feel sorry for the confessor. This power play should be viewed as a calculated means to manipulate others. Mary Ann's mother would end many arguments with loud protestation that it was all her fault, that everything was always her fault, that everything she did was wrong. Although she said the words "forgive me," she meant just the opposite. She wasn't asking for forgiveness, but expecting her family to reply "No Mother, it's not your fault, it's our fault." Whenever a family member accepted her apology, she was furious.

In other cases, the person confesses to appear virtuous—a kind of moral one-upsmanship by which the confessor communicates to others "I'm more virtuous than you because I admit I'm wrong and you don't." Still others confess superficially without any recognition of the seriousness of the injury they have caused, with no purpose of amendment or change. The confessor may simply want to avoid criticism and cut off discussion of the offense.[3]

There are times, however, where the innocent can ask for forgiveness. Sometimes we unintentionally hurt another person. Sometimes we make a decision that we know will make someone uncomfortable but that we believe is nevertheless the right decision. Sometimes people irrationally believe that we hurt them intentionally. In these cases, it is proper and helpful to say "I am truly sorry that my actions hurt you. Please forgive me." As we saw in the previous chapter, parents can use this kind of apology with their children.

CAN IT BE WRONG TO ACCEPT FORGIVENESS?

Some people feel that it is irrational to receive forgiveness.[4] They argue that an offensive act cannot be wiped away—it occurred and now is part of the historical record. Those who use this argument may insist that accepting forgiveness is an attempt to rewrite that and pretend that the problem never happened and is therefore both impossible and morally wrong. Those who refuse to receive forgiveness may be coming from two different places. On the one hand, the refusal to accept forgiveness may be based on the false belief that what has been done is so terrible that it can never be forgiven and so the offender must continually suffer for the injustice. This is often a cover for a deeper refusal to change the behavior that caused the problem in the first place. For example, an alcoholic may choose to stay on skid row because his alcoholism caused him to desert his family and that is "unforgivable" and therefore he is no good and might as well keep on drinking.

On the other hand, some people may refuse to accept forgiveness because they believe that the past is past and should be forgotten. They insist that everybody should just move on, because nothing can change the past. This is a not-so-subtle way to avoid facing real guilt, the real harm done by offenses and the duty to try to remedy past wrongs. The fact is, without forgiveness, the past can be very present, and past wrongs can continue to do great harm. What do you think would have happened to the people and the relationships if Anthony had not forgiven the principal, who might have rejected the gift? Or to Rose and her alcoholic father? Or to Mary Ann and her mother? Or Jerrod and his mother? Forgiveness, the giving *and* receiving, has allowed each to alter their todays and their tomorrows. It has altered their view of the past, so they are not dominated by it.

Both arguments against being forgiven reveal a failure to understand forgiveness. Forgiveness requires admitting that the offense occurred and admitting that real injury was done. The past cannot be changed, but the future can.

ENDNOTES

1. See R. D. Enright and the Human Development Study Group, "Counseling Within the Forgiveness Triad: On Forgiving, Receiving Forgiveness, and Self-Forgiveness," *Counseling and Values* 40 (1996), 107–126, for further discussion. Please keep in mind that one person is not necessarily the only one who has acted unfairly in a relationship.
2. See M. R. Holmgren, "Forgiveness and the Intrinsic Value of Persons," *American Philosophical Quarterly* 30 (1993), 341–352, on this idea.
3. P. W. Coleman, *The Forgiving Marriage* (Chicago: Contemporary Books, 1989), pp. 190–192.
4. As one example, see A. C. Minas, "God and Forgiveness," *Philosophical Quarterly* 25 (1976), 138–150.

CHAPTER 15

RECONCILING

We have come near the end of the forgiveness journey. Forgiveness is such a powerful experience that it can, under the right circumstances, heal you emotionally, help the one forgiven, and even heal your relationship. Forgiveness makes possible the reuniting of people torn apart by unfairness and hurt. Of course, forgiving someone does not guarantee that you will be reunited, if such union is your goal. You can offer only so much. The other has to do his or her part also. Let's look at some of the elements of reconciliation as you contemplate the possibilities of reconciling.

In Charles Dickens's classic *A Christmas Carol,* Ebeneezer Scrooge's road to reconciliation must have been slow in light of his biting ways with so many people. He had a life-changing experience, but no one except the Spirits knew this at first. He was ready for change, but everyone else expected him to behave as usual—an acerbic, pompous, money-mad churl. Because his path was cluttered with others' mistrust, how was he to demonstrate sincerity after all those years?

When people reconcile, they come together again in mutual trust following a division caused by at least one person's unfairness. In my view, giving and receiving forgiveness precede genuine reconciliation, otherwise remnants of resentment can make people stand a bit to one side and not enter into a relationship as before.

Those who actively work together on the processes of giving and receiving forgiveness are far along the journey toward reconciliation. Nevertheless, there are several issues involved in rebuilding the relationship beyond forgiveness: trust, open communication while rewriting the contract, and restored justice.

TRUST

Because trust is part of reconciliation following significant betrayal or wrongdoing, coming together again can be difficult. Of course, the injured one has no guarantee that the problem will not resurface.

Yet, can't the injured person take some steps to avoid recurring cycles of betrayal? As psychiatrist R. C. Hunter reminds us, those who say they forgive but who have not truly forgiven retain a certain "smug" quality to their interactions.[1] If the one forgiven can uncover false forgiving, then can't the one who forgives detect false forms of forgiveness received? Might not the smugness that unmasks the false forgiving be a primary way to unmask an insincere receiving of forgiveness?

Scrooge's joyous pronouncement "I am as light as a feather, I am as happy as an angel, I am as merry as a schoolboy" showed more relief and humility than smugness.[2] His was a genuine change. In your own case, let us suppose that you are currently working on forgiving, and the other person with whom you seek reconciliation is also working on receiving forgiveness. Indicators that he or she is receiving forgiveness are showing some guilt and shame, making amends, showing empathy and concern for you, and being willing to wait until you are ready to offer forgiveness. If many of these are absent or seem to be expressed in a smug, insincere, or uncaring way, then your trusting the other person will be difficult and perhaps even unwise.

You may need to determine in what areas the person should not be trusted. The compulsive gambler should not be trusted with even just a small loan if gambling remains a problem. To presume that he or she will be free forever from certain scars is unrealistic. To presume that he or she will never change may be equally unrealistic if the person seems to be working through the forgiveness processes.

Psychologist Terry Hargrave, in his book *Families and Forgiveness,* suggests that the injured party carefully observe those small instances in which the offending one is now actively compensating for the injuries inflicted.[3] Scrooge's spontaneous generosity to Bob Cratchit's family on Christmas Day is one step in this direction. As another example, Alice was married to the hot-tempered Derek for 11 years. He always seemed so tired as he took off his sport coat and tie and slumped in the sofa in his nightly ritual of watching television and ignoring all in the household. Yet, he was never too tired to tell Alice what she failed to accomplish that day. He was never too tired to yell at one of the children, Beth and Brian, for not doing their homework well or for not picking up their toys. He has so many worries, Alice would reassure herself, but she was growing increasingly angry at Derek's inattention and explosive anger. They separated but did not divorce.

Because Derek has, at least temporarily, left the family, Alice now has custody of the children. The partners decided that she would drive the two children to his apartment every week. As she does this, Alice might observe how he interacts with the children as she drops them off and picks them up after a visit. Is his anger still explosive? If Derek shows concern and a genuine caring, Dr. Hargrave believes that this is a small beginning of his showing a capacity to be trusted. With more and more lengthy observations, Alice may see a gradual change in Derek that strengthens her trust in him. The trust, in other words, is earned in small increments. Without some indication of his willingness to truly receive forgiveness, however, those brief observations could lead to false conclusions about Derek's level of maturity and his readiness for reconciliation. If Alice knows he is ready to receive forgiveness and sees him demonstrate his capacity and willingness to love, then she might proceed further.

✎ Journal Entry

On a scale of 1 to 10, rate your degree of trust in the person on whom you have focused in this book. Let 1 stand for "no trust at all" and 10 for "complete trust." How far away is the rating from the 7 to 9 range? Please keep in mind that we are all imperfect, and so a rating of less than 10 is not a condemning judgment against the person as a moral being or you as a rater.

If the trust is low, what must the person do to re-establish it? Was the trust ever there in the first place? How would you rate your level of trust before the hurtful event occurred? If the rating is low, what was the person doing to lower your trust? What must the person do in addition to making amends for the hurtful event to win your trust?

OPEN COMMUNICATION AND REWRITING THE CONTRACT

When a written or an unwritten contract is broken, the two parties must take steps to rewrite it, presuming that each is interested. If Alice now has enough trust and Derek the willingness to change, both together may try rewriting the informal marriage contract. I am not suggesting a formal, written contract here, but an agreement between equals. Forgiveness, being centered in mercy, is not enough for this task. The two need to explore issues of justice, or how fairness will be restored. A first step is to begin talking to one another about the existing problem or problems.

Dozens of books offer advice on resolving conflicts or re-establishing fairness with others.[4] Unfortunately, most do not discuss forgiveness as part of the message. The books on conflict resolution represent diverse approaches and differing kinds of counsel to re-working the broken contract. I offer three themes common to many. In my opinion, forgiving and receiving forgiveness should precede these methods, otherwise the participants may come together with a cold indifference toward one another.

Listening and Understanding

On Christmas Day, when Scrooge offered a considerable sum to the portly gentleman raising money for the poor, that man's first comment was "My dear Scrooge, are you serious?"[5] The man had heard Scrooge but had expected something quite different. Scrooge's words contradicted what the gentleman had come to believe about him.

When reconciling, both parties willingly must begin listening to one another toward the initial goal of genuinely understanding each other in regard to the unjust event.[6] This can be difficult because of one's prior expectations, as in Scrooge's case. The authors Rusk and Miller recommend that each person try to discern the other's feelings and reasoning regarding the broken contract. This should be done in a spirit of open-mindedness, without quick judgments or condemnations. In other words, Alice will be given a chance to vent her frustrations and why she feels this way; she, too, must be willing to listen as Derek talks of his disappointments, no matter how much Alice may disagree with his view. If the processes of forgiving and receiving forgiveness have begun, perhaps defensiveness will be reduced. The goal is to identify and define the various sources of conflict, as psychologist Thomas Gordon, who has written extensively for hurting people, clarifies.[7]

Dr. Rusk and Dr. Miller make the helpful suggestion that each party figuratively step inside the other's shoes to see the conflict from the other's viewpoint. Alice must see Derek's anger, and he must see her exasperation. If both have begun working on forgiving or receiving forgiveness, some of this perspective-taking will already be accomplished.[8]

Generating Solutions

The next area involves proposing many varied solutions to the conflict.[9] Writers suggest that both parties generate several solutions so that each may examine the offerings and look for other ideas to consider if the first few are found inappropriate. Through active perspective-taking and careful listening, the parties eventually should settle on the best way to begin solving the problem. Perhaps Alice and Derek will agree to spend some time together while Beth and Brian are visiting Derek.[10]

An initial solution such as this must be seen as fair and willingly entered by both spouses. Both adults might come up with ways to implement the plan.[11] Of course, such a preliminary solution of spending more time together in Derek's and Alice's case is not yet complete reconciliation, but it is a start.

Evaluating How the Solutions Are Working

The third suggestion for effective communication is to evaluate how the plan of action actually worked.[12] If Bob Cratchit still is impoverished, Scrooge's plan is bankrupt. If Alice and Derek are beginning slowly to trust each other, they might decide to lengthen his visits with the family. If the couple remains in conflict, they may decide to shorten them. The point is to work on understanding each other and, from such a position, begin solving the problem together while monitoring the progress. The informal contract that is being rebuilt may require a series of gradual changes and improvements before it is entirely rewritten by both parties. Again, I am not suggesting a formal, written agreement.

✎ Journal Entry

Do you communicate well with the person? What level of confidence do you have that you can sit down with him or her and discuss your implicit contract?

Is he or she a good listener? Are you? If you answered no to either question, perhaps you will need to work this out and set a few ground rules before discussing the contract.

When you consider possible solutions, you may wish to jot them down in your journal first and evaluate how the other person is likely to respond when you present each one.

RESTORING JUSTICE

Some injustices can never be adequately repaired. The wounds are so deep that compensation cannot be found that is equal to the original offense. What was taken from an incest survivor or a parent whose child was murdered cannot be replaced. Thus, when psychologist Paul Coleman, in his book *The Forgiving Marriage*, recommends that the injurer engage in reparation, he is not literally expecting a perfect repair of the original damage.[13] The wrongdoer's intentions are important. Is the trespasser now truly concerned about the injured party to such an extent that there is a loving outpouring for the injured person's sake? An angrily withdrawn spouse, like Derek, may attempt more amiable interactions.

A person prone to excessive criticizing may try praising. A person prone to selfish acts may try good will. Recall that it was said of Scrooge "that he knew how to keep Christmas well, if any man alive possessed the knowledge."[14]

The key to genuine acts of reparation is the hurtful one's intent now to aid the recovery of the one hurt. False reparation is done for the self's benefit. As an example of false reparation, Dr. Coleman relates the story of an abusive father who would not change his behavior but instead would buy his child a gift every time the father was abusive. Once, upon receiving a teddy bear as a "peace offering," the child angrily threw the bear into the fireplace. The father then showed his typical anger, demanding that the child reach into the fire to rescue the burning bear. The child was singed in the process. The father was not trying to repair the relationship for the child's sake, but was instead trying to reduce guilt for the father's own sake. His was false reparation.

Genuine reparation is not a necessary part of forgiving. Otherwise, the forgiver is bound in unforgiveness whenever the offender refuses to repair. At the same time, one must not feel compelled to forgive just because someone is ready to receive forgiveness and makes reparation. Finally, one who demands the other's reparation before forgiving is not approaching it with the proper attitude. Even though it may not be necessary, reparation has its place within both forgiveness and reconciliation.

✎ Journal Entry

What is the quality of the injustice you and the offender are dealing with? Is it so bad that amends cannot be made? Why do you say this?

Is the injustice easily amended, and if so, why has there been a rift in the relationship over an easily restored injustice? Perhaps you or the other person or both were overreacting.

Are you both satisfied with any attempts at reparation? Why do you say this? If you are dissatisfied, what must change so that you are both satisfied?

DIANE AND ELLEN: AN EXAMPLE OF COORDINATING FORGIVING, RECEIVING FORGIVENESS, AND RECONCILING

This example involves a 37-year-old daughter and her mother. Ten years ago, at age 27, Diane was mourning her father's death from lung cancer when she called her mother Ellen for support. Theirs had been a turbulent relationship ever since her mother and father's divorce more than 20 years ago. In those child-rearing years, Ellen heaped verbal abuse on the children to such a degree that Diane, in her own words, felt "unloved, worthless, and . . . if someone does care about me it is because they don't know how awful I am."

Three years after her father's death, Diane called her mother in the hope of building a stronger relationship with her. Diane, in other words, was ready to give the gift of forgiveness. Ellen's caustic response was reminiscent of earlier days. She chastised Diane for feeling a warmth toward her father. Ellen lashed out at her deceased husband, saying she wished she had never married the man. "Then we never would have been born," Diane suggested. Diane, in describing her mother's biting words recalls, "She said that we [the four children] weren't happy, so if she never married him, but instead married someone else, we'd all be different people and supposedly better, happier people."

In her grief, Diane took her mother's words to mean that she did not want the children: "I told my mother that she was wishing our lives away and that hurt my feelings. My mother said, 'I can't help it. That's the way I feel.'" Diane slammed down the telephone. From that point on, in disgust she began to distance herself from Ellen. Diane was ready to extend the peace of forgiving, but Ellen was far from receiving it, not only rejecting the offer, but also pouring more insults onto the hot coals of hurt and mistrust that burned over the years.

For eight years, Diane and Ellen were estranged. A major change in the relationship occurred when Diane divorced two years ago. Her situation was now similar to Ellen's. Diane was left with two small children and abandoned by her husband. Diane recalls,

> I suddenly realized I had no true marriage, and I began trying to imagine how my mom felt—being divorced, thrown away after 14 years of marriage with four kids under 13 years old, no marketable skills, no money, and no feelings of self-worth.

Her insight into her mother's circumstance sparked an empathy and compassion that allowed her to try the path of forgiveness once again with Ellen. This time, both were far along the path, ready to give and receive the gift. In Diane's words,

> One New Year's Eve, I wrote a story for my mother. It was about her, written in a way that described how I thought she was treated so badly as a child and as an adult. I wrote how she probably felt about this. . . . When I gave it to her, I thought she'd be mad because she doesn't like to reflect on her life. But she made me feel special that day because she told me she'd cried over the story and would always keep it.

Over time, Diane slowly is realizing how difficult her mother's life has been since childhood. Ellen now understands that she is loved by Diane, despite the years of difficulty. The relationship is solidifying, especially when the two can converse about Diane's painful divorce. Ellen took Diane's children to the zoo last week and is hoping to spend even more time with them, helping the family adjust to the absence of a husband for Diane and father for the children. Because both were ready for forgiveness on that New Year's Eve, emotional burdens are lifting from both of them. All, including the children, are better off for the forgiving and reconciling.

Forgiveness and receiving forgiveness, understood as a moral exchange between or among equals, offers some the hope of reconciliation. As understood in this chapter, such reconciliation is not the domain of the naive or the weak, but of the patient and courageous who are willing to work toward healthy change. Forgiveness in some cases breaks a cycle of anger and revenge that recurs across generations. Reconciliation is the restoration of the relationship after the anger quells.

Families like Derek's and Alice's need at least to hear the ideas about giving and receiving forgiveness before decisions that may reunite or separate them. If forgiveness is a choice, which I believe to be true, and if families are not given the knowledge even to consider forgiveness as a choice, then our future generations are the ones who must bear the consequences of this silence.[15] Those modern choices excluding forgiveness that are currently available to warring couples have not shown themselves worthy to dominate the discourse on "what next?" Doesn't forgiveness deserve a place at the bargaining table?

YOUR OWN SITUATION

If you have practiced forgiveness to any extent, you may now realize that the process can be wonderfully transforming. You also may be realizing that forgiveness is more than a skill that you practice, or a series of thoughts that you consider, or even a new way of feeling or behaving. Forgiveness actually can alter your sense of identity, your sense of who you are. You are no longer a victim of others or of your past. You are no longer defined by certain events that may have occurred years ago. As you change how you think, feel, and behave, your very sense of yourself may change for the better.

✎ Journal Entry

Who are you? Take some time to carefully reflect on this question in your journal. Who are you relative to who you were before doing the work of forgiveness?

As I have been emphasizing throughout the book, forgiving one person seems to lead to your forgiving another, especially if your identity begins to change and makes room for the idea that you are a forgiving person, not just someone who has forgiven a few people. Are you a forgiving person? Are there others you must forgive? Do you still need my guidance to forgive? If so, I'll see you at the front of the book.

ENDNOTES

1. R. C. A. Hunter, "Forgiveness, Retaliation, and Paranoid Reactions," *Canadian Psychiatric Association Journal* 23 (1978), 167–173.
2. P. Haining ed., *The Complete Ghost Stories of Charles Dickens* (New York: Franklin Watts, 1983), p. 147.
3. T. D. Hargrave, *Families and Forgiveness* (New York: Brunner/Mazel, 1994).
4. See, for example, R. E. Alberti and M. L. Emmons, *Your Perfect Right: A Guide to Assertive Living* (San Luis Obispo, CA: Impact, 1990); G. T. Beck, *Love Is Never Enough* (New York: Harper & Row, 1988); C. J. Bohler, *When You Need to Take a Stand* (Louisville, KY: Westminster/John Knox Press, 1990); J. L. Creighton, *Don't Go Away Mad: How to Make Peace With Your Partner* (New York: Doubleday,

1990); A. S. Hough, *Let's Have It Out: The Bare-Bones Manual of Fair Fighting* (Minneapolis, MN: CompCare, 1991); P. Jakubowski and A. Lange, *The Assertive Option: Your Rights and Responsibilities* (Champaign, IL: Research Press, 1978); S. R. Lloyd, *Developing Positive Assertiveness* (Menlo Park, CA: Crisp Publications, 1995); R. McFarland, *Coping Through Assertiveness* (New York: Rosen, 1992); J. Paul and M. Paul, *From Conflict to Caring* (Minneapolis, MN: CompCare, 1989); B. Perkins, *Lion Taming* (Sacramento, CA: Tzedakah Publications, 1995); B. Phillips, *The Delicate Art of Dancing With Porcupines* (Venice, CA: Regal Books, 1989); T. Rusk and D. P. Miller, *The Power of Ethical Persuasion* (New York: Viking, 1993); and A. Schwebel and colleagues, *A Guide to a Happier Family* (Los Angeles: Jeremy P. Tarcher, 1989).

5. P. Haining, *The Complete Ghost Stories of Charles Dickens*, p. 149.

6. See C. J. Bohler, *When You Need to Take a Stand*; R. Casarjian, *Forgiveness: A Bold Choice for a Peaceful Heart* (New York: Bantam Books, 1992); J. L. Creighton, *Don't Go Away Mad*; and T. Rusk and D. P. Miller, *The Power of Ethical Persuasion*.

7. T. Gordon, *PET, Parent Effectiveness Training* (New York: Wyden, 1970) and *TET, Teacher Effectiveness Training* (New York, Wyden, 1974).

8. T. Rusk and D. P. Miller, *The Power of Ethical Persuasion*.

9. Some authors proposing solutions are C. J. Bohler, *When You Need to Take a Stand*; T. Gordon, *PET, Parent Effectiveness Training*; P. Jakubowski and A. Lange, *The Assertive Option*; T. Rusk and D. P. Miller, *The Power of Ethical Persuasion*; and A. Schwebel and colleagues, *A Guide to a Happier Family*.

10. This is different from Hargrave's suggestion for increasing trust in which Alice observes from a distance his new behavior toward the children.

11. T. Gordon, *TET, Teacher Effectiveness Training*.

12. Authors discussing this strategy are T. Gordon, *PET, Parent Effectiveness Training*; P. Jakubowski and A. Lange, *The Assertiveness Option*; and A. Schwebel and colleagues, *A Guide to a Happier Family*.

13. P. W. Coleman, *The Forgiving Marriage* (Chicago: Contemporary Books, 1989).

14. P. Haining, *The Complete Ghost Stories of Charles Dickens*, p. 151.

15. In fact, K. A. Ashleman's, "Forgiveness as a Resiliency Factor in Divorced or Permanently Separated Families" (Madison: University of Wisconsin, 1996), showed that when divorced women do not forgive their ex-spouses, there is a greater tendency for those mothers to show some hostility and neglect while parenting their children. The anger, in other words, is being passed through the generations. Ashleman did not find this kind of parenting for the women who forgave their ex-husbands.

REFERENCES

Adams, K. 1998. *The way of the journal: A journal therapy workbook for healing.* Lutherville, MD: Sidran Press.

Alberti, R. E., and Emmons, M. L. 1990. *Your perfect right: A guide to assertive living.* San Luis Obispo, CA: Impact.

Aldrich, A. H. 1998. *Notes from myself: A guide to creative journal writing.* New York: Carroll & Graf.

Alexander, F. 1939. Emotional factors in essential hypertension: Presentation of a tentative hypothesis. *Psychosomatic Medicine* 1:173–179.

Al-Mabuk, R., Enright, R. D., and Cardis, P. 1995. Forgiveness education with parentally love-deprived college students. *Journal of Moral Education* 24:427–444.

Ashleman, K. A. 1996. Forgiveness as a resiliency factor in divorced or permanently separated families. Master's thesis, University of Wisconsin–Madison.

Baldwin, C. 1991. *One to one: Self-understanding through journal writing.* New York: Evans.

Barefoot, J. C., Dahlstrom, W. G., and Williams, R. B. 1983. Hostility, CHD incidence, and total mortality: A 25-year follow-up study of 225 physicians. *Psychosomatic Medicine* 45:59–63.

Beck, G. T. 1988. *Love is never enough.* New York: Harper & Row.

Bergin, A. E. 1988. Three contributions of a spiritual perspective to counseling, psychotherapy, and behavioral change. *Counseling and Values* 33:21–31.

Bohler, C. J. 1990. *When you need to take a stand.* Louisville, KY: Westminster/John Knox Press.

Casarjian, R. 1992. *Forgiveness: A bold choice for a peaceful heart.* New York: Bantam Books.

Cheney, L. V. 1995. *Telling the truth.* New York: Touchstone Books.

Close, H. T. 1970. Forgiveness and responsibility: A case study. *Pastoral Psychology* 21:19–25.

Coleman, P. W. 1989. *The forgiving marriage.* Chicago: Contemporary Books.

Coyle, C. T., and Enright, R. D. 1997. Forgiveness intervention with postabortion men. *Journal of Consulting and Clinical Psychology* 65: 1042–1046.

Creighton, J. L. 1990. *Don't go away mad: How to make peace with your partner.* New York: Doubleday.

Cunningham, B. B. 1985. The will to forgive: A pastoral theological view of forgiving. *Journal of Pastoral Care* 39:141–149.

DeCharms, R., and Wilkins, E. J. 1964. Some effects of verbal expression of hostility. *Journal of Abnormal and Social Psychology* 66:462–470.

Diamond, E. L. 1982. The role of anger and hostility in essential hypertension and coronary heart disease. *Psychology Bulletin* 92:410–433.

Downie, R. S. 1965. Forgiveness. *Philosophical Quarterly* 15:128–134.

Eastin, D. L. 1989. The treatment of female incest survivors by psychological forgiveness processes. Doctoral dissertation, University of Wisconsin–Madison.

Ellis, A. 1977. *Anger: How to live with and without it.* New York: Citadel Press.

Ellis, A., and Dryden, W. 1987. *The practice of rational–emotive therapy.* New York: Springer.

Enright, R. D., Eastin, D. L., Golden, S., Sarinopoulos, I., and Freedman, S. 1992. Interpersonal forgiveness within the helping professions: An attempt to resolve differences of opinion. *Counseling and Values* 36: 84–103.

Enright, R. D., Freedman, S., and Rique, J. 1998. The psychology of interpersonal forgiveness. In *Exploring forgiveness,* edited by R. Enright and J. North. Madison: University of Wisconsin Press.

Enright, R. D., and the Human Development Study Group. 1991. The moral development of forgiveness. In *Handbook of moral behavior and development* (Vol. 1), edited by W. Kurtines and J. Gewirtz. Hillsdale, NJ: Erlbaum.

———. 1994. Piaget on the moral development of forgiveness: Reciprocity or identity? *Human Development* 37:63–80.

———. 1996. Counseling within the forgiveness triad: On forgiving, receiving forgiveness, and self-forgiveness. *Counseling and Values* 40: 107–126.

Enright, R. D., Santos, M., and Al-Mabuk, R. 1989. The adolescent as forgiver. *Journal of Adolescence* 12:95–110.

Erikson, E. 1968. *Identity: Youth and crisis.* New York: Norton.

Eyre, L., and Eyre, R. 1993. *Teaching your children values.* New York: Simon & Schuster.

Fitzgibbons, R. P. 1986. The cognitive and emotional uses of forgiveness in the treatment of anger. *Psychotherapy* 23:629–633.

Flanigan, B. 1992. *Forgiving the unforgivable.* New York: Macmillan.

Forward, S. 1989. *Toxic parents.* New York: Bantam Books.

Frankl, V. 1969. *Man's search for meaning: An introduction to logotherapy.* New York: Washington Square Press.

Freedman, S. R. 1991. Anger and the value of catharsis: A developmental analysis of differences in expression, intensity, causes, and duration. Doctoral preliminary examination paper, University of Wisconsin–Madison.

———. 1994. Forgiveness as an educational goal with incest survivors. Doctoral dissertation, University of Wisconsin–Madison.

Freedman, S. R., and Enright, R. D. 1995. Forgiveness as a therapeutic goal with incest survivors. Paper presented at the meeting of the American Psychological Association, New York.

———. 1996. Forgiveness as an intervention goal with incest survivors. *Journal of Consulting and Clinical Psychology* 64:983–992.

Friedman, M., and Rosenman, R. H. 1974. *Type A behavior and your heart.* New York: Knopf.

Gardner, G. E. 1971. Aggression and violence: The enemies of precision learning in children. *American Journal of Psychiatry* 128:77–82.

Glick, B., and Goldstein, A. P. 1987. Aggression replacement training. *Journal of Counseling and Development* 65:356–362.

Goldstein, H. S., Edelberg, R., Meier, C. F., and Davis, L. 1988. Relationship of resting blood pressure and heart rate to experienced anger and expressed anger. *Psychosomatic Medicine* 50:321–329.

Gordon, T. 1970. *PET, parent effectiveness training.* New York: Wyden.

———. 1974. *TET, teacher effectiveness training.* New York: Wyden.

Haber, J. 1991. *Forgiveness.* Lanham, MD: Rowman & Littlefield.

Haining, P., Ed. 1983. *The complete ghost stories of Charles Dickens.* New York: Franklin Watts.

Harburg, E., Blakelock, E. H., and Roeper, P. J. 1979. Resentful and reflective coping with arbitrary authority and blood pressure: Detroit. *Psychosomatic Medicine* 41:189–202.

Hargrave, T. D. 1994. *Families and forgiveness.* New York: Brunner/Mazel.

Harris, R. E., Sokolow, M., Carpenter, L. G., Freedman, M., and Hunt, S. P. 1953. Response to psychologic stress in persons who are potentially hypertensive. *Circulation* 7:874–879.

Hebl, J. H., and Enright, R. D. 1993. Forgiveness as a psychotherapeutic goal with elderly females. *Psychotherapy* 30:658–667.

Hepp-Dax, S. 1995. Forgiveness education with inner-city fifth grade children. Doctoral dissertation, Fordham University.

Hoffman, M. L. 1991. Empathy, social cognition, and moral action. In *Handbook of moral behavior and development* (Vol. 1), edited by W. M. Kurtines and J. L. Gewirtz. Hillsdale, NJ: Erlbaum.

———. 1993. The contribution of empathy to justice and moral judgment. In *Readings in philosophy and cognitive science,* edited by A. I. Goldman. Cambridge, MA: MIT Press.

Hokanson, J. E. 1970. Psychophysiological evaluation of the catharsis hypotheses. In *The dynamics of aggression,* edited by E. I. Megaree and J. E. Hokanson. New York: Harper & Row.

Holmgren, M. R. 1993. Forgiveness and the intrinsic value of persons. *American Philosophical Quarterly* 30:341–352.

Horsbrugh, H. J. N. 1974. Forgiveness. *Canadian Journal of Philosophy* 4:269–282.

Hough, A. S. 1991. *Let's have it out: The bare-bones manual of fair fighting*. Minneapolis, MN: CompCare.

Huang, S. T. 1990. Cross-cultural and real-life validations of the theory of forgiveness in Taiwan, the Republic of China. Doctoral dissertation, University of Wisconsin–Madison.

Hughes, M. 1975. Forgiveness. *Analysis* 35:113–117.

Humphrey, C. W. 1999. A stress management intervention with forgiveness as the goal. Doctoral dissertation, Union Institute, Cincinnati, OH.

Hunter, R. C. A. 1978. Forgiveness, retaliation, and paranoid reactions. *Canadian Psychiatric Association Journal* 23:167–173.

Ironson, G., Taylor, B., Boltwood, M., Bartzokis, T., Dennis, C., Chesney, M., Spitzer, S., and Segall, G. M. 1992. Effects of anger on left ventricular ejection fraction in coronary artery disease. *American Journal of Cardiology* 70:281–285.

Jaeger, M. 1998. The power and reality of forgiveness. In *Exploring forgiveness*, edited by R. D. Enright and J. North. Madison: University of Wisconsin Press.

Jakubowski, P., and Lange, A. 1978. *The assertive option: Your rights and responsibilities*. Champaign, IL: Research Press.

Kahn, H. A., Medalic, J. H., Neufeld, H. N., Riss, E., and Goldbourt, U. 1972. The incidence of hypertension and associated factors: The Israeli ischemic heart disease study. *American Heart Journal,* 84:171–182.

Kalis, B. L., Harris, R. E., Bennett, L. F., and Sokolow, M. 1961. Personality and life history factors in persons who are potentially hypertensive. *Journal of Nervous and Mental Disorders* 132:457–468.

Kaplan, R. M. 1975. The cathartic value of self-expression: Testing catharsis, dissonance, and interference explanations. *Journal of Social Psychology* 97:195–208.

Kaufman, G. 1980. *Shame: The power of caring*. Cambridge MA: Shenkman.

Kaufman, M. E. 1984. The courage to forgive. *Israeli Journal of Psychiatry and Related Sciences* 21:177–187.

Kiel, D. V. 1986. I'm learning how to forgive. *Decisions* (February), 12–13.

King, Jr., M. L. 1963. *Strength to love*. Philadelphia: Fortress Press.

Klein, C. 1995. *How to forgive when you can't forget*. Bellmore, NY: Liebling.

Kohlberg, L. 1969. Stage and sequence: The cognitive–developmental approach to socialization. In *Handbook of socialization theory and research*, edited by D. Goslin. Chicago: Rand McNally.

Kolnai, A. 1973–1974. Forgiveness. *Proceedings of the Aristotelian Society* 74:91–106.

Larsen, E. 1992. *From anger to forgiveness*. New York: Hazelden.

Lee, J. 1993. *Facing the fire: Experiencing and expressing anger appropriately*. New York: Bantam Books.

Leon, G. R., Finu, S. E., Murray, D. M., and Bailey, J. M. 1988. Inability to predict cardiovascular disease from hostility scores or MMPI items related to Type A behavior. *Journal of Consulting and Clinical Psychology* 56:596.

Lewis, C. S. 1996. *The great divorce*. New York: Touchstone Books.

Lewis, M. 1980. On forgiveness. *Philosophical Quarterly* 30:236–245.

Lloyd, S. R. 1995. *Developing positive assertiveness*. Menlo Park, CA: Crisp.

Mace, D. R. 1976. Marital intimacy and the deadly love–anger cycle. *Journal of Marriage and Family Counseling* 2:131–137.

McCranie, E., Watkins, L., Brandsma, J., and Sisson, B. 1986. Hostility, coronary heart disease (CHD) incidence and total mortality: Lack of association in a 25-year follow-up study of 478 physicians. *Journal of Behavioral Medicine* 9:119.

McFarland, R. 1992. *Coping through assertiveness*. New York: Rosen.

McGary, H. 1989. Forgiveness. *American Journal of Philosophy* 26:343–351.

McKay, M., Rogers, P. D., and McKay, J. 1989. *When anger hurts*. Oakland, CA: New Harbinger.

Miller, C., & Grimm, C. 1979. Personality and emotional stress measurement on hypertensive patients with essential and secondary hypertension. *International Journal of Nursing Studies* 16:85–93.

Minas, A. C. 1975. God and forgiveness. *Philosophical Quarterly* 25:138–150.

Moskal, J. 1994. *Blake, ethics, and forgiveness.* Tuscaloosa: University of Alabama Press.

Neblett, W. R. 1974. Forgiveness and ideals. *Mind* 83:269–275.

North, J. 1987. Wrongdoing and forgiveness. *Philosophy* 62:499–508.

———. 1998. The "ideal" of forgiveness. In *Exploring forgiveness,* edited by R. D. Enright and J. North. Madison: University of Wisconsin Press.

Novaco, R. 1975. *Anger control.* Lexington, MA: Lexington Books.

Park, Y. O., and Enright, R. D. 1997. The development of forgiveness in the context of adolescent friendship conflict in Korea. *Journal of Adolescence* 20:393–402.

Patton, J. 1985. *Is human forgiveness possible?* Nashville, TN: Abingdon.

Paul, J., and Paul, M. 1989. *From conflict to caring.* Minneapolis, MN: CompCare.

Peck, M. S. 1997. *People of the lie.* New York: Simon & Schuster.

Perkins, B. 1995. *Lion taming.* Sacramento CA: Tzedakah Publications.

Perls, F. C. 1969. *Gestalt therapy verbatim.* Lafayette, CA: Real People Press.

Phillips, B. 1989. *The delicate art of dancing with porcupines.* Venice, CA: Regal Books.

Poloma, M. M., and Gallup, G. H., Jr. 1991. *Varieties of prayer: A survey report.* Philadelphia: Trinity Press.

Potter-Efron, R. 1994. *Angry all the time: An emergency guide to anger control.* Oakland, CA: New Harbinger.

Reed, G. 1998. Forgiveness as a function of moral agency in the context of infidelity and divorce. Master's thesis, University of Wisconsin–Madison.

Reed, J. R. 1995. *Dickens and Thackeray: Punishment and forgiveness.* Athens: Ohio University Press.

Rozanski, A., Krantz, D. S., and Bairey, C. N. 1991. Ventricular responses to mental stress testing in patients with coronary artery disease: Pathophysiological implications. *Circulation* 83(Suppl. II):137–144.

Rubin, T. L. 1970. *The anger book.* New York: Collier.

Rusk, T., and Miller, D. P. 1993. *The power of ethical persuasion.* New York: Viking.

Sarinopoulos, I. 1996. Forgiveness in adolescence and middle adulthood: Comparing the Enright Forgiveness Inventory with the Wade Forgiveness Scale. Master's thesis, University of Wisconsin–Madison.

————. 1998. Forgiveness and physical health. Doctoral dissertation, University of Wisconsin–Madison.

Satir, V. 1988. *The new peoplemaking.* Mountain View, CA: Science & Behavior Books.

Schwebel, A., Schwebel, B., Schwebel, C., Schwebel, M., and Schwebel, R. 1989. *A guide to a happier family.* Los Angeles: Jeremy P. Tarcher.

Selman, R. L. 1980. *The growth of interpersonal understanding.* New York: Academic Press.

Shekelle, R. B., Gale, M., Ostfeld, A. M., and Oglesby, P. 1983. Hostility, risk of coronary disease and mortality. *Psychosomatic Medicine* 45: 219–228.

Smedes, L. B. 1984. *Forgive and forget: Healing the hurts we don't deserve.* San Francisco, CA: Harper & Row.

————. 1996. *Forgive and forget* (2nd ed.). San Francisco, CA: Harper.

Smith, M. A., and Houston, B. K. 1987. Hostility, anger expression, cardiovascular responsibility, and social support. *Biological Psychology* 24:39–48.

Solzhenitsyn, A. I. 1968. *The first circle.* New York: Harper & Row.

Straus, M. A., Gelles, R. J., and Steinmetz, S. K. 1980. *Behind closed doors.* Garden City, NY: Anchor Doubleday.

Subkoviak, M. J., Enright, R. D., Wu, C., Gassin, E., Freedman, S., Olson, L., and Sarinopoulos, I. 1992. Measuring interpersonal forgiveness. Paper presented at the annual meeting of the American Educational Research Association, San Francisco.

————. 1995. Measuring interpersonal forgiveness in late adolescence and middle adulthood. *Journal of Adolescence* 18:641–655.

Tavris, C. 1989. *Anger: The misunderstood emotion* (rev. ed.). New York: Simon & Schuster.

Ten Boom, C. 1971. *The hiding place.* Old Tappan, NJ: Revell.

Tocqueville, A. D. 1835/1980. *Democracy in America* (Vol. 1). New York: Knopf.

Tutu, D. 1998. Foreword. In *Exploring forgiveness,* edited by R. D. Enright and J. North. Madison: University of Wisconsin Press.

Twambley, P. 1976. Mercy and forgiveness. *Analysis* 36:84–90.

Wallerstein, J. S., and Blakeslee, S. 1996. *Second chances: Men, women, and children a decade after divorce.* New York: Tichnor & Fields.

Wallerstein, J. S., Lewis, J., and Blakeslee, S. 2000. *The Unexpected legacy of divorce.* New York: Hyperion.

Williams, R., and Williams, V. 1993. *Anger kills.* New York: Times Books.

Wolff, H. S., and Wolf, S. 1951. A study of experimental evidence relating life stress to the pathogenesis of essential hypertension in man. In *Hypertension: A symposium,* edited by E. T. Bell. Minneapolis: University of Minnesota Press.

Woodward, C. V. Ed. 1981. *Mary Chesnut's civil war.* New Haven, CT: Yale University Press.

Yandell, K. 1998. The metaphysics and morality of forgiveness. In *Exploring forgiveness,* edited by R. D. Enright and J. North. Madison: University of Wisconsin Press.

INDEX

ABOUT THE AUTHOR

Robert D. Enright, PhD, is a licensed psychologist and professor of educational psychology at the University of Wisconsin, Madison. Since 1985, Professor Enright has pioneered the scientific study of how people forgive others who hurt them deeply and how the act of forgiving affects physical, mental, and emotional health. He is the recipient of numerous awards for both his teaching and his forgiveness studies. Professor Enright's work has appeared in such publications as *Time, McCall's,* the *Wall Street Journal,* the *Washington Post,* the *Chicago Tribune,* and the *Los Angeles Times.* He has appeared on ABC's "20/20," NBC's "Nightly News," and many other television and radio shows and he has authored more than 80 publications on the study of forgiveness and related areas.